The Solution Focused Approach with Children and Young People

The Solution Focused Approach with Children and Young People: Current Thinking and Practice brings together leading figures and innovative practitioners from different professions, contexts and countries to provide a unique overview of Solution Focused work with children and young people. Presenting a range of applications in individual, group and community work, it puts the spotlight on diverse fields, exploring how the Solution Focused approach can work in real-world contexts.

This book showcases a powerful, engaging approach which helps children and young people find the resources and strengths to manage difficulties and make the most of their lives. It contains interesting case studies, narrative descriptions of original practice, programmes of work developed using Solution Focused principles, and thought-provoking discussions of key elements of practice. With chapters presenting perspectives from coaching, therapy, consultancy and education, and applications including learning assessments, child protection, bereavement, edge of care and youth offending, the book provides an overview of the current state of practice and provides pointers to potential new developments.

The Solution Focused Approach with Children and Young People will help both experienced practitioners and those new to the approach to develop and update their knowledge and skills, as well as introducing them to creative and cutting-edge tools to inspire fresh ideas and thinking. It will be essential reading for Solution Focused practitioners and students, as well as coaches, social workers, school counsellors and mental health professionals working with children and young people.

Denise Yusuf is a qualified social worker and Solution Focused coach and supervisor who works across a variety of settings. She brings experience, expertise and passion to her work with children and young people, as well as a keen interest in, and admiration for, the work of her Solution Focused colleagues around the world.

"This is a timely and important book for practitioners working with children and young people. Drawing on an international field of experts in Solution Focused practice, Yusuf has gathered together a powerful collection of evidence and narratives to provide a genuine alternative to the deficit models prevalent in many parts of practice with children. With the rise in global challenges, it is increasingly important that our children and young people are supported to develop confidence in their ability to create sustainable solutions, rather than being made to feel they are a problem to be solved. This is essential reading."

— Rayya Ghul, *National Teaching Fellow,*
University of Edinburgh, Scotland

"This book is a Solution Focused treasure! There isn't another book that captures how to use the SF approach with such a wide range of issues that confront children and young people. Yusuf has compiled amazing contributions from across the globe that give practical, cutting-edge tools for working with children, teens and young adults. This book is a valuable resource for all practitioners interested in creating hope and optimism with their young clients."

— Adam Froerer, PhD, LMFT; *Associate Program Director,*
MFT Program Mercer University, USA

"This book is useful not only for Solution Focused practitioners but for anyone wanting to develop their work with children and young people. For practitioners already using the Solution Focused approach with children and young people, it is, in my view, essential reading."

— Harry Korman, MD, *Child Psychiatrist,*
Psychotherapist SIKT Malmö, Sweden

"This is an important book in view of the difficulties experienced by many children around the world. There are 26 chapters, most of which are by well-known authors, who display a wide range of expertise. Ten authors practise in the UK and others write from the USA, Canada, Finland, Denmark, Hungary, Ukraine, South Africa, Belgium, Singapore and New Zealand. As well as 'traditional' Solution Focused themes, there are chapters about its use in paediatrics, speech and language therapy and police work."

— Dr Alasdair J. Macdonald, MB ChB, FRCPsych, DPM, DCH;
retired Consultant Psychiatrist and former Medical Director;
UKCP Registered Family Therapist, UK

The Solution Focused Approach with Children and Young People

Current Thinking and Practice

Edited by Denise Yusuf

LONDON AND NEW YORK

First published 2021
by Routledge
2 Park Square, Milton Park, Abingdon, Oxon OX14 4RN

and by Routledge
52 Vanderbilt Avenue, New York, NY 10017

Routledge is an imprint of the Taylor & Francis Group, an informa business

© 2021 selection and editorial matter, Denise Yusuf; individual chapters, the contributors

The right of Denise Yusuf to be identified as the author of the editorial material, and of the authors for their individual chapters, has been asserted in accordance with sections 77 and 78 of the Copyright, Designs and Patents Act 1988.

All rights reserved. No part of this book may be reprinted or reproduced or utilised in any form or by any electronic, mechanical, or other means, now known or hereafter invented, including photocopying and recording, or in any information storage or retrieval system, without permission in writing from the publishers.

Trademark notice: Product or corporate names may be trademarks or registered trademarks, and are used only for identification and explanation without intent to infringe.

British Library Cataloguing-in-Publication Data
A catalogue record for this book is available from the British Library

Library of Congress Cataloging-in-Publication Data
Names: Yusuf, Denise, editor.
Title: The solution focused approach with children and young people : current thinking and practice / edited by Denise Yusuf.
Description: Abingdon, Oxon ; New York, NY : Routledge, 2020. | Includes bibliographical references and index.
Identifiers: LCCN 2020007935 (print) | LCCN 2020007936 (ebook) | ISBN 9780367187613 (hardback) | ISBN 9780367187620 (paperback) | ISBN 9780429198120 (ebook)
Subjects: LCSH: Solution-focused therapy for children.
Classification: LCC RJ505.S64 S65 2020 (print) | LCC RJ505.S64 (ebook) | DDC 618.9289/147—dc23
LC record available at https://lccn.loc.gov/2020007935
LC ebook record available at https://lccn.loc.gov/2020007936

ISBN: 978-0-367-18761-3 (hbk)
ISBN: 978-0-367-18762-0 (pbk)
ISBN: 978-0-429-19812-0 (ebk)

Typeset in Times
by Apex CoVantage, LLC

To my husband Evan George
our children Hannah, Ieuan and Meirion
and their partners Rollo, Rachel and Rhiannon
Always in my heart

Contents

List of figures	x
About the editor and list of contributors	xi
Foreword	xvii

1 **Introduction**   1
DENISE YUSUF

2 **There's more to children than meets the eye**   8
CHRIS IVESON

3 **Solution Focused play therapy**   15
PAMELA K. KING

4 **Voice and choice: the vulnerable child and the Solution Focused process**   22
RACHEL CARRICK-BIRTWELL

5 **Kids'Skills – a creative Solution Focused method for helping children overcome difficulties and problems**   28
BEN FURMAN

6 **From challenging to outstanding**   35
YASMIN AJMAL

7 **Bridging cultural divides in international schools with Solution Focused approaches**   43
FELINA HEART

8	**The butterfly effect** ELLIOTT E. CONNIE	50
9	**Building co-operation and engagement with adolescents** EVAN GEORGE	55
10	**Solution Focused practices in the assessment of learning problems: panning for gold** JEFF CHANG AND DON BRAUN	61
11	**A Solution Focused team conversation: helping educators create lasting solutions with students** LINDA METCALF	72
12	**Put the numbers in! The value of scale questions** HARVEY RATNER	79
13	**Dream . . . believe . . . achieve: a school in South Africa that has developed a philosophy based on Solution Focused principles** NICK BIRKETT AND MERRITT WATSON	87
14	**Solution Focused practice in a British University** PETER J. ELDRID	95
15	**Coaching for youth offenders in an institutional setting** JOE CHAN	103
16	**Solution Focused "injections": Solution Focused working in acute paediatric settings** HARRIET CONNIFF	108
17	**Using the Solution Focused approach within New Zealand Police to create happy endings for young people and their families** EMMA BURNS	116
18	**Trusting the child: using the Solution Focused approach with children and young people on the edge of care** LUKE GOLDIE-MCSORLEY	123

19 Facing new challenges using a Solution Focused approach: creating a supportive learning process for Roma adolescents in a volunteering project in Hungary 130
ÁRPÁD BÁRNAI AND VIKTÓRIA SŐREGI

20 Figuring Futures: the art of reframing challenges 140
ELKE GYBELS AND RIK PRENEN

21 Solution Focused work in high-risk child protection cases: how the Solution Focused mindset and creativity helped put the children in the centre of the work and create possibility for change 149
MICHAEL PETERSEN AND RIKKE LUDVIGSEN

22 Yes ... and: useful conversations around trauma 156
PAMELA K. KING

23 Incorporating the Solution Focused approach in tackling selective mutism 162
ANITA MCKIERNAN

24 A tiny little piece of hope: accompanying parentally bereaved children and adolescents in their journey through parental terminal illness, grief and healing via a Solution Focused pathway 171
XENIA ANASTASSIOU-HADJICHARALAMBOUS

25 High-conflict divorce and parenting: how Solution Focused presence can help 179
JEFF CHANG

26 Spreading kindness: the alchemy of translation 194
DENISE YUSUF

Index 203

Figures

2.1	Simon's Solution	14
20.1	A Visualisation of a Client's Story and Their Best Hopes	140
20.2	Mary's Sparkling Treasure Chest of Strengths Right in Front of Her	141
20.3	The Treasure Chest of Best Hopes	143
20.4	The Client's Treasure Chest	144
20.5	The Treasure Chest of Significant Others	146

Editor and contributors

The editor

Denise Yusuf is a coach and coach supervisor, working in schools, education settings and charities and in private practice. She worked in mental health and with children and families as a qualified social worker for many years and holds a diploma in life coaching and the Brief Diploma in Solution Focused Practice. One of her passions is working with children and young people; the other is supervision. She has written a number of articles on working with children and young people and is co-author, with Harvey Ratner, of *Brief Coaching with Children and Young People, A Solution Focused Approach*.

The contributors

Yasmin Ajmal, a former teacher and educational psychologist, co-authored the first book on SF Practice in UK schools (Rhodes & Ajmal 1995). Following 10 years working for BRIEF as a trainer and counsellor, she volunteered with VSO (2008–2010) working in Zanzibar alongside the Ministry of Education. Yasmin is currently a self-employed Solution Focused (SF) consultant and trainer working in schools and supporting innovative organisations such as the Young Women's Trust phone coaching service for young women (18–30 years) and the DMD Pathfinders, a charity run by adults with Duchenne muscular dystrophy which began with an initial SF consultation and has continued to grow.

Dr Xenia Anastassiou-Hadjicharalambous, CPsychol, is an associate professor of child psychopathology at the University of Nicosia, Cyprus. She is a chartered psychologist of the British Psychological Society and a member of the Society of Clinical Child and Adolescent Psychology (APA), the European Society for Traumatic Stress and the European Brief Therapy Association. She is an editorial/advisory board member and ad hoc reviewer of several well-established psychology journals and author of over 60 scholarly publications in the area of child psychopathology.

Árpád Bárnai is a Hungarian facilitator, experiential learning trainer, outdoor educator and coach. He started his career in youth work as an educator in a foster home. In the last 15 years, he gained experience in working with youth at risk and in training youth workers and educators. He is a trainer of the NGO Academy of Experience and member of the Hungarian Solution Focused Association. He lives in Budapest.

Nick Birkett completed his honours degree in education in 2011, where he focused on the use of picture books to teach a variety of philosophical issues to high school learners. As Principal of School of Merit Primary School in Johannesburg, he has been one of the driving forces in motivating and guiding the teachers' usage of Solution Focused principles at the school. Nick has presented and assisted in courses and programmes offered by the Solution Focused Institute of South Africa, where he has provided practical examples and ideas of Solution Focused Brief Therapy in a South African school context.

Don Braun has worked in schools for 27 years as a youth support worker, teacher and school administrator. Don is a registered psychologist in the Province of Alberta, Canada. He specializes in providing psychoeducational assessments for children, youth and young adults who experience an array of cognitive, learning and mental health problems. Don became acquainted with Solution Focused thinking through his work with Dr Jeff Chang. He has become a passionate advocate for strengths-based, positive approaches to assessment. Don lives with his wife and young adult children in Calgary, Alberta, Canada.

Emma Burns has spent seven years using the Solution Focused approach working with young offenders and has recently moved into the family harm team within New Zealand Police. Prior to this, Emma worked in mental health, education and suicide bereavement. She has also presented at the Solution Focused World Conference in Frankfurt in 2017 and at the Australasian Association of Solution Focused Brief Therapy Conference in Melbourne in 2018. She is the vice-president of the AASFBT and coordinates the Hawke's Bay Solution Focused practitioners' group. Emma is also the mother of four children and is a competitive swimmer.

Rachel Carrick-Birtwell completed a PGCE after a degree in applied linguistics. She taught in primary schools for 16 years, was a deputy head and SENCO and lectured on the BA(Ed) course at the University of London for nine years. Rachel trained in Solution Focused Brief Therapy at BRIEF from 2003 and completed her Diploma in Solution Focused Practice in 2013. She now works in schools as a Solution Focused practitioner with vulnerable families and as a staff coach. Rachel also coaches with Young Women's Trust, supporting young women towards greater self-efficacy in the workplace. She lives in South East London with her husband and two young children.

Joe Chan is Head of Youth Service at REACH Community Services Society (RCSS) in Singapore and a professional certified coach (PCC) and master Solution Focused practitioner (IASTI). Joe has been at RCSS for the past 15 years, specializing in working with troubled youths and their families. He started as a caseworker and experienced the challenges and thrills of youth work in overseeing individuals, families and youth programmes in the community. Currently, Joe supervises and coaches the staff at the Youth Service of RCSS, providing comprehensive youth programmes through sports, arts and casework, serving different youth clientele groups from voluntary and community to mandatory clients.

Dr Jeff Chang lives and works in Calgary, Alberta, Canada. He was hooked on Solution Focused Brief Therapy in the mid-1980s. Jeff is Associate Professor at Athabasca University in Alberta, Canada. He's been a registered psychologist for more than 30 years and is a clinical fellow and approved supervisor of the American Association for Marriage and Family Therapy. Jeff also works as a therapist and supervisor at Calgary Family Therapy Centre and has a small private practice, mainly with families embroiled in high-conflict divorce. His annual five-day Solution Focused Brief Therapy intensive in Calgary is the highlight of his work life each year.

Elliott E. Connie, MA, LPC, is a psychotherapist practising in Keller, Texas. He has worked with thousands of individuals, couples, and families applying the Solution Focused approach to help them move their lives from the current problems towards their desired futures. He is Founder and Director of The Solution Focused University, an online learning and training community, and a world-wide presenter at national and international conferences and events, training practitioners to use Solution Focused questions and techniques. He has authored or co-authored four books including *The Art of Solution Focused Therapy*, *Solution Building in Couples Therapy*, *The Solution Focused Marriage* and *Solution-Focused Brief Therapy with Clients Managing Trauma*.

Harriet Conniff is a mother, Solution Focused practitioner and clinical psychologist. She first trained at BRIEF in 1999 after hearing about it from her mum, stepdad and sister! She has regularly trained with BRIEF since and been lucky to take part in workshops with Insoo Kim Berg, Steve de Shazer, Yvonne Dolan, Ben Furman and recently Elliott Connie. She went on to train as a clinical psychologist specialising in paediatrics primarily using a Solution Focused approach with children, young people, families and staff teams. She lives in London, her hometown which she loves for its diversity.

Peter J. Eldrid has worked as a counsellor at Brunel University London since 2003. He is Solution Focused in his approach and accredited by the British Association of Counselling and Psychotherapy. He has worked in counselling since 1981 for the Samaritans, ChildLine and Parentline Plus. He has trained trainers and call takers throughout the UK and internationally with Child

Helplines International. At Brunel University, Peter is particularly interested in working with staff to help them support students through individual consultation, tutor training and other workshops. He is also interested in developing peer support schemes to enable students to support each other more effectively.

Ben Furman is a Finnish psychiatrist, cofounder of Helsinki Brief Therapy Institute, and internationally active trainer of Solution Focused Brief Therapy. He is the author of more than 20 books on Solution Focused psychology. Find more information about him on his personal website.

Evan George is a founding partner in BRIEF, the UK's leading Solution Focused teaching, training and clinical organisation. Evan is the author of many articles and chapters and the co-author of three books on the Solution Focused approach. Evan has taught and presented his work throughout the UK, across Europe and further afield, from Singapore, Lebanon and Abu Dhabi to Peru, Texas and New Mexico.

Luke Goldie-McSorley is a passionate social worker from Essex County Council working within the Divisional Based Intervention Team (DBIT) edge of care service. Growing up surrounded by social work values and practice, Luke developed an unwavering belief and a devotion to working with people, gaining a degree in psychology and a master's in social work. Since becoming acquainted with the Solution Focused approach in 2012, his love for this approach and skill has grown, and he completed the BRIEF Diploma and is continuing his progression in his role as practice supervisor in DBIT. A future of possibility continues with constant practice, training delivery (Essex and beyond) and writing.

Elke Gybels is co-founder of "De Content". She is a Solution Focused therapist, coach and trainer in Belgium. Many years of experience in working with families, couples and individuals, mostly in settings where resources were scarce, challenged her to develop Figuring Futures, a creative approach that encourages people to envision their strengths and best hopes. Elke teaches at the University College Leuven-Limburg and is Coordinator of the postgraduate course Solution Focused Therapy (SFT). Previously she worked as a police social worker and also for several youth care offices. Together with Rik Prenen, she wrote the book *Van klacht naar kracht*, a treasure chest for Solution Focused practice.

Felina Heart was born in Chicago but raised in Texas. She holds a bachelor's degree in communications and a master's of education in school counselling. Felina has 20 plus years' experience in education. As a school counsellor, she worked for two years in Texas and five years at Pechersk School International School in Kyiv, Ukraine, and is currently at the American International School in Budapest, Hungary. Felina has one son, Cody, who lives and works in Texas; three sisters; five nephews and one niece. Further, Felina comes from a diverse background, her late father being originally from Greece and her mother's family being originally from Austria.

Chris Iveson was a teacher, social worker and family therapist before setting up, with Evan George and Harvey Ratner, BRIEF, the UK's first Solution Focused Brief Therapy centre. He divides his professional time amongst doing, teaching and writing about Solution Focused practice.

Pamela K. King, LMFT, is an enthusiastic and experienced Solution Focused practitioner, international speaker, author and trainer. Pam has designed and implemented Solution Focused play therapy treatment programmes with children and families; she has specialized training in play therapy, trauma, family violence and child development. Pam earned a bachelor's degree in theatre arts and a master's degree in family and human development from Utah State University. She is author of *Tools for Effective Therapy with Children and Families: A Solution-Focused Approach* and the 2017 recipient of the Steve de Shazer Memorial Award for Innovations in Solution Focused Brief Therapy.

Rikke Ludvigsen is an independent social worker, supervisor and trainer with more than 15 years of experience in working with children at risk and their parents in different contexts, including residential homes, safe houses, child protection investigation work and safety planning. She was trained by Andrew Turnell, Sonja Parker and Susie Essex in safety planning, has a diploma in Solution Focused practice from BRIEF and is also an EMDR trauma therapist. Since 2012, she has trained social workers, family therapists and other professionals in Solution Focused practice and safety planning and is also continuously working to bring knowledge about trauma into the practice field.

Anita McKiernan works as a speech and language therapist (SLT) with children, young people and adults with a range of communication needs, including selective mutism, stammering, and autism. She also works part-time as a clinical tutor and visiting lecturer for City, University of London and as an SLT with City Lit, London. She spent several years working in the NHS in clinical and leadership roles, and when she trained with BRIEF in 2013, she felt inspired to explore ways to use the approach effectively in her work and also in life, and so the journey continues.

Linda Metcalf, PhD, LMFT, is a professor and director of the Graduate Counseling Program at Texas Wesleyan University in Fort Worth, Texas, where she has a private practice specializing in school issues and consults with school districts internationally. She is the author of 11 books including *Counseling Toward Solutions* (1995, 2008, 2019), *Teaching Toward Solutions* (2003, 20120, 2015, Crown House) and *Solution Focused RTI* (2010, Wiley). Since 1993, she has presented hundreds of seminars to trainees and educators in the United States, Australia, Japan, Newfoundland, Germany, Scotland, England, Norway, Amsterdam, Singapore, Thailand, Canada and China.

Michael Petersen has a master's degree in sociology from the University of Copenhagen and a master's in vulnerable children and young people from

Aalborg University. Since 2006, his work life has been concentrated around Solution Focused work with vulnerable children and families, and since 2012 his work has been concentrated around child protection and safety planning in high-risk cases. Working as a consultant since 2014, he has trained child protection workers in Solution Focused practice and safety planning. Since 2017, he has also trained social workers working with war veterans and combat soldiers with severe trauma and PTSD.

Rik Prenen is a supervisor and trainer at "De Content", an independent practice for Solution Focused therapy and coaching in Belgium. He is Senior Guest-Professor at the University of Leuven and at the University College Leuven-Limburg (UCLL). Previously, he served as coordinator of the Flemish Centers for Pupil Guidance. For many years he worked with families, teachers, police officers and officials of the justice department. Halfway through the 1990s, Rik became highly dedicated to the Solution Focused approach. Together with Elke Gybels, he is a key trainer at the postgraduate course on Solution Focused therapy at UCLL.

Harvey Ratner is a founder member of BRIEF. He works with children, young people and families in schools and at BRIEF. He has co-authored several books including *Solution Focused Coaching with Children and Young People* (with Denise Yusuf) and *Solution Focused Practice in Schools* (with Yasmin Ajmal).

Viktória Sőregi is a Hungarian facilitator, experiential learning trainer and outdoor educator. In the last 10 years she has gained extensive experience in working with youth at risk, high school students and young adults, both in Hungary and in the international environment. She has been an Outward Bound instructor since 2013 and lives in Budapest.

Merritt Watson is an educator and educational psychologist. She is the owner of the School of Merit and has served many years as its Principal. She has extensive experience in dealing with children who experience different barriers to learning. She is passionate about children who are differently abled. Merritt has lectured at numerous institutions both locally and internationally, including the University of Texas and institutions in various states in America and throughout Europe. She has co-written a book on Solution Focused teaching strategies as well as contributed a chapter to a book on Solution Focused Brief Therapy across Southern Africa.

Foreword

As I write this, I have just returned from the European Brief Therapy Association (EBTA) conference in Florence, Italy. Nearly 300 Solution Focused practitioners from Europe and beyond met to share ideas, celebrate the Solution Focused approach and learn from one another. There were 49 separate presentations listed in the programme. Some were theoretical, most related to some area of clinical practice. There were presentations about Solution Focused work with the elderly, with refugees, in social action, with grief, in coaching, in supervision and more. Of the 49 presentations, only three titles referred specifically to working with children. That's 6%!

Compare this to the fact that (by my rough estimate) more than 50% of the centres, agencies and organisations using Solution Focused Brief Therapy (at least here in Australia) are either child and family, adolescent or school agencies. In the many training courses that I conduct across Australia and New Zealand, more than 50% of the participants come from child welfare, child protection, child and adolescent mental health, juvenile justice, schools and other children and young people settings.

So, what is it about working with children and young people?

There seems to be a belief that working with children and young people is somehow more difficult or challenging. Indeed, one survey found that trainee clinical psychologists and their supervisors often reported that their children/young people clinical placements were more challenging than their various adult placements (Bristow & Roberts, 2015).

One of the biggest problems we have in working with children and young people is that virtually all of the people who present or write about working with children are adults. Most of us adults (not just Solution Focused people) have a whole lot of ideas about what children "need to do" . . . or what adolescents "ought to do" . . . in order to overcome the various difficulties they might have (or that adults think they have!).

However, if we step back and think about how children think, we might see that Solution Focused work fits absolutely with the way children and young people operate and so offers an approach to therapeutic work with these age groups that need not be daunting.

Children and young people are pragmatic

Most children and young people just want things to be better. They just want to feel better, to get on better with the other kids at school, to not have so many fights with Mummy and Daddy, to have the teachers "off their back" and so on. They naturally warm to an approach that simply aims to help things be better rather than trying to understand all the ways in which the problem has developed.

Children and young people don't come with preconceived ideas about "THE therapeutic process"

Sitting around and talking about your problem, exploring its intricacies, and understanding how it develops are essentially white, middle class, ADULT activities. Adults are encumbered with a myriad of ideas about what NEEDS to happen. "You need to work through the problem"; "You must come to terms with what happened to you"; "You need to re-experience the trauma"; "You must learn new ways of responding"; and so on (almost *ad infinitum*).

Children and young people don't necessarily have these ideas . . . thus they might be less surprised (and, so, less hesitant) when we ask a question that doesn't come from the traditional therapeutic script.

Children and young people are naturally future focused

I am an adult (more or less). In the last 40 years, my life has had some major ups and downs; however, my adult sense of myself has been fairly consistent. While various external things have changed, for most of my adult life I have experienced myself as more or less the same person. It is easy for me to look BACK, so see how events have led to where I am now. Backwards is the natural stance of adulthood.

Children and young people experience constant change. They are looking forward to "being more grown up", "being in high school", "being able to stay up as late as my sister can". Given that their ideas of "reality" and "fantasy" are nowhere near as fixed, they are sometimes looking forward to "becoming prime minister", "being an astronaut" and so on.

If we give some thought to how we phrase them, future-focused questions are actually easier for children.

Children and young people like to have fun

Because the Solution Focused approach doesn't focus much on the problem, it fits with ideas about not taking problems too seriously.

Troy, aged 10, vomited every school holiday as he thought about returning to school. Crippled with what some called "anxiety", every school holiday he was house-bound (or toilet-bowl-bound). I discovered that he had been to the cinema to see the newest superheroes movie. As I gently explored HOW he had been able to do this, I asked, "Did you get Mum to buy a really big tub of popcorn, so you had something to vomit into?" (You can get away with the grossest comments to 10-year-old boys.)

As he laughed at this idea (and his Mum squirmed a bit), I knew that this exception was real to him.

Children and young people like to feel good about themselves

In Solution Focused work, we are likely to find exceptions, successes and strengths and ask, "How did you do that?". We are likely to identify a preferred future that relates to strengths and successes and to feeling better, and we are likely to ask, "How will that make a difference?", "What will your Mum and Dad see you doing when . . .", "What will your teacher notice about you in class when . . ."

Children and young people haven't yet learned that they are not supposed to promote themselves, so they are more likely to respond to gentle questioning about their successes.

In this volume, Denise Yusuf brings together 27 Solution Focused practitioners with real experience working with children. Denise's own commitment to, and excitement about, Solution Focused work with children and young people is evident in the impressive group of authors she has assembled, some already well-known in the Solution Focused world and others becoming well known as word of their cutting-edge work permeates. These people have expertise in school settings, in child psychiatry, with university students, in children's involvement with the police, in child protection, as speech and language therapists, with challenging adolescents, in family conflict and breakdown . . . and more. They also represent work in 12 different countries.

Words such as "challenging", "disadvantaged", "vulnerable", "acute settings", "young offenders" recur frequently. These chapters will demonstrate ways of negotiating the real challenges that can arise.

My personal experience of Denise is that her energy and enthusiasm for her Solution Focused work is infectious. That same energy and enthusiasm radiate from the printed page.

Michael Durrant
Kurrajong, NSW, Australia

Reference

Bristow, F., & Roberts, A. (2015). *Top Tips for Working with Children, Young People and Their Families*. The Division of Clinical Psychology of the British Psychological Society. https://www1.bps.org.uk/system/files/user-files/Division%20of%20Clinical%20 Psychology/public/CYPF%20Top%20tips%20ID711%20web.pdf.

Michael Durrant is a psychologist and is Founder and Director of the Brief Therapy Institute of Sydney in Australia. He has previously taught Solution Focused Brief Therapy at Western Sydney University and at the University of Sydney. His books, *Residential Treatment* and *Creative Strategies for School Problems*, which both relate to working with children and young people in particular contexts, have been published internationally.

Chapter 1

Introduction

Denise Yusuf

A little girl I worked with, called Alice, was afraid of clouds. She had developed a fear of clouds, rain and thunderstorms. She was anxious about being left at school and about being in class. Her attendance was suffering and she would often cry in the mornings when she came to school and worry about what the weather would be like that day. Both her family and her teachers were wonderfully supportive. Her mother read her stories about the sun, the clouds and the rain and played tapes of different weather sounds to help her, as well as having a star chart full of rewards. Her teacher started a fun weather project with the whole class. All this was really helpful. However, if it was cloudy, she didn't want to stay at school or go into the playground.

Alice and I began talking together every week. She enjoyed drawing pictures of her strengths and skills and demonstrating them to me. She loved playing with sand, running, trampolining, making slime and watching TV. She shared lots of stories about all the things she could do. She decided that she wanted to get better at football; at being calm, for example, when her mum left her at school; and at being brave, for example, if it was cloudy or raining. As the sessions progressed, Alice began to enjoy noticing that she was good at some of these things some of the time and that she was getting better at them too. She was improving her football skills all the time. She noticed that she could sometimes say goodbye to her mum even though she was feeling sad. She was really creative and liked to draw pictures of the adults in school, such as her teacher and her class teaching assistant, who looked after her at those difficult times. She remembered what her mum told her, that rain helped flowers to grow and she imagined saying 'yay' when she was in the rain. One day she drew a 'super-caterpillar' who could keep her company in the rain and make her a den in the clouds. She gave herself a coaching card (Ratner & Yusuf, 2015), writing on it: 'well done for being in the clouds!' and drew clouds on it. Sometimes she chose to go out in the rain for a short time, running out and inside again. She began to notice braveness everywhere; for example, she ate potato for the first time and enjoyed asking her family for their stories of being brave.

I never asked Alice why she was afraid of clouds and rain, and she never told me very much about this or any other difficulty. Instead we paid attention to what she was good at, what she wanted to get better at, all the little successes she was already enjoying and the steady signs of more successes. We talked, drew and acted things out. She made a paper magnifying glass to keep an eye on signs of progress, since they can be small and hard to see at times. She loved using coaching cards, 'well done' cards to herself, and 'thank you' cards to people who were helping her. She even helped another child who was upset about being left at school, *'Don't worry,'* she said, *'you will see your mum in the afternoon, she will come back.'*

Solution Focused (SF) practice with children and young people is not so very different from Solution Focused practice with adults. We are inviting people to think about what they want to do differently or have different in their lives, to recognise their skills and strengths, to notice that their past and present are littered with small successes, and to create and enjoy the beginnings of the successful future for which they yearn. Sometimes when we are talking with children we may find ourselves changing the order of this conversation, helping them to share or show us their strengths and resources and their past successes before we come to understand what they might want to be different for themselves. However, practitioners adapt and select from the SF approach aspects of its positioning and stance, and some of its tools and techniques, in different ways. They will choose what works well for them as practitioners and what they see as effective in their practice with a child or young person. They might do something in a session which seems to be useful at the time, even though it might be different from what they have learnt, what they have been taught or what they usually do. SF practice with children and young people is broadly the same as SF with adults, but it is also different. Those similarities and differences are what I hope will interest and inspire you in this book. It is a book about SF practice, about SF practice with children and young people and about the people who practice and what excites and inspires them.

The Solution Focused approach

There are some particular characteristics of SF practice which make it an approach that children and young people find easy to engage with and participate in from the beginning and make it an extremely effective approach to use (Kim, 2008; Kim & Franklin, 2009). Overall SF practice is concerned with the 'how to' of success rather than the 'why' of failure. This is its beating heart, and children skip to this beat too. They often cannot answer the 'why' question and may not yet have developed the skills needed to abstract and theorise, but they can and do try things out. Insoo Kim Berg and Therese Steiner were leaders in showing us how the Solution Focused approach to therapy fitted with children's natural way of being (Berg & Steiner, 2003):

> We believe there is good harmony between solution-focused brief therapy [SFBT] and children because there are so many similarities between how

children think and make sense of the world around them and the assumptions and procedures of SFBT.

For example, children rarely need to know what caused the problem that they are facing.

They certainly do not think deductively or search for explanations of what caused the problem. Close observation of children shows that they experiment with a variety of approaches and solve problems through trial and error. This is all similar to the way solution-focused brief therapy developed: in an inductive manner by finding out what works and what doesn't. Children by and large think 'out of the box,' and are just interested in what will work.

(p 14)

Older children and young people may have a few ideas about the 'why,' but a walk down this rocky path with you would not be attractive to them, as it risks leading only to more of a sense of failure. Starting sessions with problem-free talk (George et al., 1990) about interests, skills and strengths is also particularly useful with children and young people. It not only engenders hope and optimism and identifies transferable skills but also challenges problem labels or negative labels. These can come from the child about themselves, but can also sometimes be found in the far, quiet reaches of the practitioner's head. Children and young people are often prone to label themselves quickly – 'I'm no good at maths,' 'I can't make friends,' 'I can't control my temper once I get mad' – and resource-based conversations from the beginning can start to create a new story for the child about themselves. This story can be embellished throughout the sessions in all sorts of ways, from the simple listening for and naming of resources, to the sharing of an SF activity such as a child's time line of successful or memorable events and the qualities they showed.

The positioning of the practitioner in SF practice is one that I believe fertilises growth and change in children and young people. We place ourselves by the side of the child, rather than leading from the front or pushing from behind. This means that we take what the child says at face value, as much as possible, rather than trying to work out what is 'true.' This acceptance can create a sense of connection and a feeling of being understood for the child, which is likely to lead to more useful conversations and better outcomes. It also means we do not tell children what to do. Telling children what to do, however generously intended, is also telling them they don't know what to do. Conversely, asking them what they want to do starts to build a sense of autonomy and agency in them, which is more likely to help them to deal with any particular challenges facing them, as well dealing with future challenges in their lives. Using a Solution Focused approach can help children and young people to develop and recognise their skills in being able to get through tough times and in being able to do things differently. This can build their resilience and optimism for the present and the future and sometimes help their friends too! I have often had children who have had SF sessions telling me about how they have been helping their friends by asking them questions such as *'What did you do that worked?'* and *'When did it go well?'* or *'Say what you are good at first.'*

Elements of SF practice

Centralising the child or young person by asking about their best hopes (George et al., 1992) is the best way to give children a sense of validation and control. Of course, some children may be too young to answer this question independently, as Chris Iveson points out (www.facebook.com/BRIEF.SolutionFocus). If this is the case, Chris Iveson talks about how to help small children to define an outcome by, for example, asking: *'Would you like to be happier in school?'*. The enquiry about what they want is still embedded in the conversation.

Conversely, if the child seems to be repeating what an adult wants for them without any ownership, a Solution Focused practitioner might follow up their answer with other questions, such as asking the child in what ways they think this outcome might be good for them or why this might be important to them. This is to help the child to establish or remember their own good reasons for wanting such an outcome. With teenagers especially, it is always worth assuming that they have their own good reasons for talking with you, even if they have been referred by someone else, and even more, that they have their own ways of doing things.

The best hopes of children and young people, what they want from the conversation, the outcome or difference that the outcome will make to them, can be one cake on a plate or cakes piled high. A single small cake that belongs to the child is plenty. A pile of cakes can also be useful. I worked with a child who wanted to talk to people more, think about talking to some new people, make her handwriting neater and complete her set targets. Perhaps the jostling together of her hopes, with the different feelings she might have had about them and the different skills they might encompass, made the process of change easier for her. Sometimes, with younger children, we might twin track a hope from the child and a hope from an adult, but even if we included an adult's best hope, we would make sure to focus on what the child might notice if they were putting this into practice *'in the right way for them.'* This would be to ensure that the child experiences their own sense of agency as much as possible. Best hopes are at their best when they belong to the child or young person. Tampering too much with them can drain the life from the conversation and minimise the possibilities for change.

Preferred future questions can often startle children and young people, just as they can do with adults. However, they can also engage children and young people in beginning the process of building an ongoing narrative of possibilities for themselves, reaching back into their pasts, across their present and out into their futures. The concrete, behavioural and positive aspects of these descriptions which practitioners invite in SF conversations seem to appeal to children and young people. It seems easier for them (and perhaps all of us) to visualise and describe small sequences of actions than to identify and describe feelings without their translation into action. It helps to keep children and young people in an expert role on themselves in the conversation. There are many interesting examples in this book of SF practitioners using different ways to help children to talk about what they might see when things are better, inviting descriptions but maintaining faith that the SF process will work even when descriptions are short.

Scales, whether in number or picture form, or using toys or other things as markers are particularly attractive to children and young people, and you will see in the following pages some wonderful examples of such different scales, as well as a practitioner using mostly scales in a conversation with a teenager. Scales make concrete what might be conceptually difficult for children: they are a visual demonstration of starting points, progress and directions. They invite children and young people to evaluate themselves instead of being evaluated by others. They enable practitioners to have conversations with children and young people about anything without having to know everything. They offer a sense of mobility and possibility where there might have been a sense of being caught or stuck. For example, practitioners can ask scale questions about how things are at the current time, how they were yesterday and the day before and last week. Although the question *'Tell me about the times when you were able to do that'* serves the same purpose, scale questions are a magic tool for opening up that treasure chest of exceptions and instances, that is, times when the problem is not happening and times when the wished-for future is happening (Ratner et al., 2012). Once this treasure chest is opened, it can seem to be bottomless, if the practitioner believes it to be so.

The creation of lists of changes (Ratner & Yusuf, 2015) during a session is another SF tool or technique which I think particularly lends itself to working with children and young people. Lists help to generate detail but in a playful, arbitrary and less serious way. When a practitioner asks, *'what has been better?'* it can leave the young person feeling they have to find the 'right' example. Conversely, asking for 10 or 20 things changes the criteria for inclusion, and it is often the 10th or 20th answer which is the most useful to the young person, perhaps because it is the one which did not immediately spring into their mind or perhaps because the 'roll' of the conversation just produces more useful ideas. The SF practitioner has multiple questions at hand, so that creating a list with a child or young person can be fun, interesting, surprising and useful. They might ask the child what they have noticed but also enquire about the perspectives of others, about what has been noticed across the multiple contexts of the child's life such as the classroom, the playground, with family and during other activities, and about the qualities or skills demonstrated.

In the following chapters of this book, I am hopeful that you will find something to interest and inspire you. There are SF practitioners from different countries, professional backgrounds and work contexts. There are examples of SF practice being used in schools, education, higher education and learning environments, in paediatric hospitals and speech clinics, in social work teams and voluntary projects, in child safety, child care, youth offending and police teams, in parental divorce contexts and in progressive private practice settings. Topics such as working with trauma, developing cooperation, building resilience, designing and running effective meetings, the therapist's mindset and many others are explored, and practitioners demonstrate creative ways of using Solution Focused practice and share programmes and approaches that draw on SF practice, such as Future Play, Kids'Skills and the Figuring Futures approach. There are examples of practitioners using an SF approach in short five-minute conversations with children and families, in single sessions, in sequences of sessions, in meetings, and in groups and practitioners who are using all the elements of an SF session or drawing on particular SF techniques. Change for children can occur at multiple levels, from the most personal and individual, through the system around the child, to social and societal systems. Though practice can be aimed at particular levels, change can occur in multiple ways, often small ways which begin a life of their own. For example, a child gives an adult a 'thank you' card for helping them in a particular way that the child appreciates: the child notices more of their own successes, the adult sees more of this and does more of the same kind of helping, the child responds more to this, and a positive change interaction flows. There are many examples of change in the following chapters.

Waiting for certainty in our expertise and practice before we share it is a loss to us all in the field. We may never be certain, or certainty may come from the journey we take as we share and write about SF practice, and not at any starting point or from a point of completion. SF practice is not something to learn and practice alone but something that is created between people, between us and our clients and between us as colleagues and fellow professionals. Communities of SF practitioners hear stories of what has worked for colleagues and build on these by trying aspects of them in their own practice. Then as practitioners we create our own version of the SF model by taking up some aspects of what others do and neglecting other aspects. The Solution Focused model has always been essentially a practice driven model, and we are more likely to notice that something works and do more of it than to try to explain to ourselves exactly why it has worked, although of course practitioners do think about and share ideas on this too! I like to think of ideas as lines drawn in the sand. The expression *'Drawing a line in the sand'* is a metaphor with two meanings; it is seen as a line of permanence, either never crossed or once crossed there is no return. However, in practice, we all know that lines in the sand blow away in time, so it is best to seize and appreciate them now as there may be a different pattern there tomorrow.

It may be that in the chapters that follow, in the different explorations and adaptations of practice, lie the seeds from which the SF model will grow in different directions.

What will remain the same in the model, in my view, as well as in the practice, is the hope and optimism that this way of working engenders in ourselves as practitioners, and most importantly, in the children and young people with whom we have the privilege to work.

The idea for this book, and the reason for creating it, came from my desire to read just such a book as this and not being able to find it! So, with hope and optimism I approached friends, colleagues and fellow professionals and was rewarded with their enthusiasm and generosity in being willing to share their practice and to learn. I am hopeful and optimistic that whatever good reason you may have for taking up and reading this book, somewhere on these pages you will find just what you want, just what you need, or even something that you just didn't expect that will help you to take the next steps in your own practice.

References

Berg, I. K., & Steiner, T. (2003). *Children's Solution Work*. New York: W. W. Norton.

George, E., Iveson, C., & Ratner, H. (1990, 1999). *Problem to Solution*, revised and expanded edition. London: BT Press.

Iveson, C. (2019, March 10). *Ten Ideas About Work with Children*. www.facebook.com/BRIEF.SolutionFocus/. Accessed 10 March 2019.

Kim, J. S. (2008). Examining the Effectiveness of Solution-Focused Brief Therapy: A Meta-Analysis. *Research on Social Work Practice*, 32, 49–64.

Kim, J. S., & Franklin, C. (2009). Solution-Focused Brief Therapy in Schools: A Review of the Outcome Literature. *Children and Youth Services Review*, 31, 464–470.

Ratner, H., George, E., & Iveson, C. (2012). *Solution Focused Brief Therapy: 100 Key Points and Techniques*. London: Routledge.

Ratner, H., & Yusuf, D. (2015). *Brief Coaching with Children and Young People: A Solution Focused Approach*. London: Routledge.

Chapter 2

There's more to children than meets the eye

Chris Iveson

Amir: joining a circle

I had seen Amir and his parents three times with little progress to show for it, so little progress that I was surprised that they wanted to continue. In my mind I had tried to blame the parents for my failure; after all, they had insisted at each of our meetings on cataloguing all of Amir's many failings. However, the failing was actually mine; all they were doing was trying to fill me in on the details of the problem, hoping that this would make the finding of a solution more likely. My failure was not finding a way to invite them into a different sort of conversation. Luckily (or so I thought), the parents were unable to make the fourth meeting but were so keen for it to happen they arranged with Amir's school for me to see him there. I thought that without the parents' helpfulness I might be able to do better with Amir. Not so! It was worse. Amir was clearly irritated at being brought out of class, irritated with my questions and seemingly irritated with everything else. Just more so than when he was with his parents.

Amir was six and was loved to distraction by his parents, but somehow things were not working out for him at school. He had few friends and those friendships he made did not usually last long, sometimes ending in fights. The school had become worried by increasing violence in Amir's behaviour, which would eventually lead to his exclusion. And there I was, totally failing to make a difference.

It is in these moments of failure and frustration, when we tell ourselves to change jobs because we are no good at the job we are doing, when we feel stretched beyond the limits of our knowledge and skills, when we want the ground to open and swallow us up, that we sometimes do our best work, and, sadly, more often than not, we don't even notice. All we remember is we got by – thank heavens!

Sitting in the corner of the school hall with this six-year-old bundle of irritation, I suddenly jumped up and demanded that he take me to his classroom. With this clear instruction backed up by my obvious belief in his ability to perform the allotted task, Amir transformed himself into a confident and sociable guide, pointing to his brother's class and one of his own pictures as he led me round the school. It was when we reached the classroom door that I lost my own confidence and seriously thought of pushing Amir in and running away. But his expectant look restored enough of my courage to knock on the door. Even before my last rap I began to shrink. The door became larger and larger and as I watched Amir's teacher through the glass she grew by several feet, towering above me as she opened the door. I was now six and terrified! I don't remember my primary school being that frightening, nor can I fathom why I should find myself reverting to a six-year-old when faced with a charming young woman half my age simply because she is a teacher. But the experience was real enough for me to be almost surprised that she spoke to me as a responsible adult colleague and asked how she could help me. Yet more panic surfaced since she would surely be outraged at the impertinence of my request. In almost a whimper I asked:

"Please could I borrow six of your children?"

What hard-pressed teacher wouldn't jump at such an offer, and before I could apologise for the foolishness of my request, I had six more children to take back to the hall. I wasn't even sure of what we were all going to do together and what came to mind seemed ridiculously inconsequential. However, it was all I could think of, so we got on with it.

"Could you all sit in a nice round circle and hold hands?" I asked the new six, which they did.
"Amir, I'd like you to join the circle nicely. Can you do that?"
"Yes," said Amir, launching himself at the group and nearly puncturing eardrums with his elbows as he forced his way in.
"Is that joining the group nicely?" I asked my little band.
"No!" they cried in unison.
"Does anyone know how to join the group nicely?"
"Me!" "Me!" "Me!" "Me!" "Me!" "Me!" was the cacophonous response.
"And what's your name?" I asked the nearest. "Emma," she answered.
"Emma, can you show us how to join the circle nicely?"
"Yes," she said, and turning to the group she asked (with a little lisp)
"Please may I join the circle?"

No one responded until I suggested they might let Emma join them, whereupon a chorus of yesses gave her permission. I then suggested that some room may need to be made, and two of the children immediately shuffled apart so Emma could take her place.

"Who else would like to show us how to join the circle nicely?" And five more pleading voices and waving hands. Warren was next with his "Please may I join the circle?" followed by the "Yes you may" chorus and the eager shuffling of bottoms to make room for him.

By the eighth turn, Amir's second go, they were unquestionable experts, Amir included, and they wanted to show me just how good they were so we had seven more "Please may I join the circle?"s and seven more "Yes you may"s with associated shufflings.

What next? Another act of courage on my part – back to the class.

This time I managed to hang on to the remnants of my adulthood as Amir's teacher's face visibly brightened at my reappearance. "The children want to show you a little play we've been performing. Would that be possible?" Still doubtful about my licence to make such a request, once again I was surprised by the teacher's enthusiasm for this interruption to her plans. Immediately she called all the children to sit on the floor in a big semicircle in order to watch the performance. And they did! Seven times each with a different principal. As we finished and took our bows amid tumultuous (albeit teacher-led) applause, a little voice broke through the noise to ask, "Please can I do it?" It was the start of an avalanche, the whole class waving their hands pleading for the chance to show off their own skills. As (my now friend) the teacher began to organise them into small groups, I quietly took my leave and hoped against hope that word of this foolish enterprise did not leak out into my 'high-flying' professional world. Two weeks later, I changed my mind. The parents phoned to say what a transformation they and the school had seen in Amir's behaviour. Suddenly I had turned from fool to hero.

There is a large body of aids for promoting conversations with children, but these are only accessories to the main 'tool' which is yourself, the person inside the professional. A puppet on your hand won't engage with a four-year-old child; the puppet is just a conduit for *you*. So that needs to be the starting point – finding your way to relate to children. If you have children of your own or have regular social contact with the children of friends and family, notice how you are when you are most at ease with them or when they are most interested in you. This will give you the best insight into how to be with children professionally. My grandchildren call me 'silly' and I find this 'silliness' helps me engage with small children. On the other hand, adolescents remind me of my own uncomfortableness as an adolescent, and I often feel inadequate in their presence. I have dealt with this by being the opposite of silly and assuming the mantle of an interested but 'out of touch' older person. This too seems to work, which is just as well since I often see teenagers in their schools. This is not to say that social and professional relationships are the same, but rather we, the professionals, are the same whether at work or not; we do best by being our best and this cannot be faked.

Lucy: "the voice of the child"

Lucy was just four and had been raped by her fifteen-year-old brother six months earlier. The family was in a rehabilitation programme aiming to keep them together while safeguarding Lucy. Significant progress had been made, but one voice was missing – Lucy's. Lucy hadn't spoken since the abuse took place. Otherwise she seemed a well-adjusted happy child. The trouble with relationships in which one person doesn't speak is that they don't get spoken to – so don't speak. This is what had happened to Lucy. For several sessions, no attempt had been made to ask her questions. Eventually becoming wise to this, the therapist realised that Lucy had not been as 'quiet' as was thought. In the file were various drawings, but none that gave a clue about Lucy's feelings. However, there was another clue. One drawing was an outline of Lucy's two hands showing her ten fingers, while another was a jumbled collection of numbers from one to ten. The therapist had been using scales to 'assess' each person's idea of safety but had not thought to ask Lucy. Unfortunately, bringing out the drawings and asking Lucy about them seemed to irritate her, and she withdrew to the toybox corner. The therapist returned to Lucy's mother until he saw that Lucy had placed a number of farm animals in a row. Having, at last, got the message, the therapist sat on the floor with Lucy and counted out the animals; as expected, there were ten. The conversation with the mother had been based on a safety scale, so the therapist asked Lucy how safe she felt – which animal represented her felt level of safety. Lucy slowly pointed at the first, second, third, fourth and fifth before settling on the sixth, a pig. "What makes you this safe?" asked the therapist, whereupon Lucy rummaged through a box to produce a small female doll in 'adult' clothing. "Is this your mummy?" asked the therapist to which Lucy nodded. "And what's your mummy doing?" Another rummage from which came a little girl doll which Lucy placed very close to her mother. "Is that Lucy?" produced another nod, as did the question "Is your mummy keeping you safe?" Moving on, Lucy was asked "If you moved from the pig to the next animal, this cow, what would be different?" More rummaging brought out her 'daddy,' whom she placed a little farther away and her 'brother,' whom she put close to the 'daddy.' "What are your daddy and brother doing?" asked the therapist, forgetting that Lucy "did not speak." Lucy gave the therapist a disdainful look for asking such an obvious question and replied, "Going to football, of course!" Lucy, only having just turned four had, in her own way, articulated the textbook conditions of safety in such cases: her mother to watch out for her and her father to build a closer relationship with her brother.

With experiences like this, it makes no sense to limit our expectations of children or hold strong views about how we might work with them. Each child is going to be different and each will challenge us to discover their 'language' and rise to their level. At the same time, we have to remember that Solution Focused Brief Therapy has a very specific focus: the client's hoped-for future and those aspects of the past and present which may support that future. Working with children does not exempt us from these simple guidelines. However, the guidelines are just that. They give us guidance about the sorts of question to ask, and they provide a coherent framework for our conversations, but they give us no clues about *how* to ask those questions or *how to operate* within the framework. That is the human side of our work, the 'self' that we put into our conversations, and I doubt that this can be taught. Instead, we each must find our own way of being sufficiently 'with' each client, so they remain in the conversation because it is the conversation that does the work, not the 'relationship.' Paradoxically, any reasonably competent Solution Focused conversation will generate a powerful relationship during the conversation because it requires of the therapist an absolute focus on the client's words and the linking of every question to those words. This is very intense listening, and being actively listened to is one of the main ingredients of a successful relationship. However, it is not the relationship that carries the therapeutic message; rather, it is the client's answers, the client's words that make the difference. All we are trying to do is ask questions which the client has never been asked before and which lead them to say things they've never said before in the hope that they hear something in their answers which opens up new possibilities for their future.

Aaron: "silence is golden"

Aaron was five and not doing well at school, and so the school had referred him to me. He seemed unable to follow even the simplest of instructions and had been deemed to be insufficiently emotionally and cognitively developed to manage mainstream school. The head teacher asked me to meet with school staff first and, with a little persuasion, agreed to Aaron and his mother, Doreen, also attending. At first the meeting focused on Aaron's problems, not in an unkind way but still a way likely to lead to his transfer to a 'special' school. When it was my turn to speak, I asked what everyone thought of Aaron's behaviour during the meeting, as he had been sitting quietly for more than ten minutes. Initially this was dismissed as situational – he wouldn't be like this in the classroom! However, I had been told that Aaron was incapable of such self-control, and sitting quietly for that length of time was surely an act of self-control. Talking to Doreen about this, she cited many situations where Aaron was perfectly able to behave well, not that he always did so. In the Solution Focused world, any behaviour which occurs in one situation can be transferred to others. I asked Aaron whether he liked being a good boy at home and when he said yes, I asked if he would like to be a good boy at school. Again he said yes, so I embarked for the first time on a routine which has been hugely effective in helping four-, five- and six-year-olds to settle into school.

"When you are a good boy what's the first thing you do when you come into the classroom in the morning?" is a typical first question, and then perhaps it is adjusted to fit the child's understanding. So far, I have not met a child who doesn't know how to hang up their coat and put their lunch box, homework or whatever else they have in the appropriate places and then sit on the carpet with their arms folded. This knowledge might flow smoothly, or it may be teased out with "what next?" questions, and eventually it will lead to sitting on the carpet. Here the fun starts:

"Do you know how to sit on the carpet?"
"Yes."
"Can you show me?"
"Yes."
"Let me see if I can do it, too."

The child and I are now sitting on the floor.

> "What do you have to do when you are sitting on the carpet?"
> "You have to fold your arms."
> "Like this?"
> "Yes."
> We are now sitting on the floor with arms folded.
> "Wow! You really do know how to sit on the carpet, don't you?"
> "Yes."
> "Shall we see whether everyone else can do it as well as you?"
> "Yes."
> "Come on everyone, let Aaron teach us all how to sit on the carpet!"

Head teacher, class teacher, teaching assistant, educational psychologist and Doreen with varying degrees of enthusiasm joined us on the floor.

> "And what do you have to do while you are sitting on the carpet?"
> "Be quiet."
> "Do you know how to do that?"
> "Yes."
> "Okay! Then show us how quiet you can be and see whether everyone else can be as quiet as you."

Sitting quietly on the carpet might be a challenge for some, but not for Aaron or his mother. The head teacher and psychologist were the first to break, with the class teacher and assistant soon following.

"Wow! Aaron! You really do know how to sit quietly! You are one of the quietest children I've ever met! Didn't he sit quietly, Doreen?"

Carrying on with the morning routine, we learn that standing in line quietly comes next, followed shortly by walking quietly. Aaron is invited to lead both these activities, which he does with confidence and pleasure. He and his mother are repeatedly complimented on his knowledge and performance before he is sent off to his class.

The head teacher was both pleased and doubtful: pleased that Aaron performed so well in an activity only the school could have taught him and doubtful that such exemplary performance would transfer to the less protected reality of the start of the school day. Arrangements were made for Aaron and Doreen to attend the clinic the following week, where they were able to report a major improvement in Aaron's behaviour at school. No further meeting was necessary.

There is a continual debate in the Solution Focused field (and beyond) about whether techniques constrain or free the practitioner. If they do constrain, then it might be because it is an approach which does not fit that practitioner, something to be welcomed if we want a diversity of therapeutic approaches. On the other hand, if the techniques are seen as the 'model,' then they are likely to lead to

Figure 2.1 Simon's Solution

ineffective therapy. The model itself is a set of principles rather than techniques; the techniques are simply ways to implement the principles and we should expect them to evolve over time.

Simon and his "bags of confidence"

Simon was seven and afraid of the monster under his bed. He thought that being more brave would help him, so we talked about all the ways he could remember being brave. He came back for a second session with a plan. He had felt braver and this had made him feel stronger. His plan was to get the monster to sit on a seesaw so that when he (Simon) became strong enough, he could catapult the monster up to the moon. We then thought about what would make him stronger, and he came up with "confidence," so we began filling a bag with past examples of confidence. Good stories also helped him feel calmer and more confident, so we began filling that bag. By the third session, Simon had done the job himself. He had calculated that five bags of confidence and stuff would be enough to send the monster on its way, and this had proven to be the case. This is a copy of the picture he brought to illustrate his victory. He was also pleased not to have to spend so much time lining up his toys exactly: "What's the point?" he said, "I'll only mess them all up tomorrow!"

Chapter 3

Solution Focused play therapy

Pamela K. King

I love kaleidoscopes, filled with colourful beads and bobbles which form the basis of beautiful patterns, and have several in my office. Some are works of art turned from exotic hardwoods, and others are cardboard and plastic. Kaleidoscopes invite people to look through the mirrors at their surroundings, which become kaleidoscopic images. Whatever I look towards, a bouquet of flowers, fireworks, a knit sweater, or pebbles on the ground, becomes the basis of a beautiful radial pattern. I imagine you have looked through a kaleidoscope, if only long ago in your childhood.

Kaleidoscopes and Solution Focused practices share the ability to look at ordinary items and events and realise they are in fact extraordinary. If someone looks through a kaleidoscope at a bright spot, they will see more than if they look in a dark corner. When we look for small indicators of a preferred future, we'll find them. It matters where we look. An individual's seemingly simple thoughts, beliefs, and decisions can be translated to concrete actions, that we can see, hear, and experience and from which we can build client specific solutions. Beautiful!

Play therapy

Early in my life as a therapist I was trained in play therapy. I found it could open up conversations in a useful way. When children, teens, and many adults, for that matter, have something to fiddle with, conversation comes a little more freely. Sometimes the item in their hands or the toy they are playing with leads to an interesting conversation about their own life and future. Kaleidoscopes, building blocks, puppets, pens, and paper are a few of the interesting supports in my office.

Solution Focused play therapy takes a collaborative approach with the child, parent, and therapist co-constructing the conversation (King, 2017). There is a client-centred foundation in the assumption that children and their parents are the experts on their own lives and therefore experts in their own unique solutions. With children, as with adults, therapists select the elements, in verbal and play conversations, which will be highlighted and built upon. De Jong and Berg (2013) call this co-constructive process 'listen, select, and build'.

1   Listen and watch for strengths, competencies, and hints of desired future.
2   Select those areas for continued play and verbal conversations.
3   Build on emerging solutions.

Play as a therapeutic tool

Play, like talk, is transtheoretical. Play is a tool and, like talk, is an important communication tool (King, 2017). 'Solution-Focused play therapy (SFPT) uses play and toys as conversational tools to not only increase client engagement, but to design the ideal future and move towards it' (King, 2017, p. 12). In a first session, I might use a magnet board, blocks, or a building game so children and adults can take turns telling something about themselves. I like to learn a child's age, grade in school, interests, and hobbies. From parents, I ask what they admire about their child, what they see as the child's strengths and skills, as well as what resources are available in the family and community. It matters whether a child is in scouts, loves skiing, or is a champion knitter. I don't need to know everything about them; five minutes of problem-free talk is usually sufficient to give me enough ideas that I can suggest areas of play. 'The therapist's role is to make the child's strengths, competencies, and abilities more evident to the child and to the involved adults' (Berg & Steiner, 2003 p. 5).

'Toys in SFPT are conversational tools, versus symbolic (as in many traditional forms of play therapy). As a therapist, I don't infer meaning about selected toys' (King, 2017, p. 12). Rather than make assumptions about a child's selection, we can simply ask questions when we need to understand a child's meaning.

Play scaling

Scaling is a useful and concrete way for adults and children to discuss their preferred future. I coined the term *play scaling* to describe an integration of Solution Focused scaling and play therapy (King, 2013). Children can usually imagine what they want to be different or better. Placing this desired future on a scale makes the discussion all the more concrete. The experiential component of using toys to represent points along the scale enriches the descriptions and serves as a profound verbal and symbolic conversational tool. The conversation about the toys serves as a client-centred metaphor that can be mined for solutions in the person's life. The therapist focuses on the client's past accomplishments and coping skills rather than pathology or problematic dynamics (King, 2013, pp. 313–314).

An estranged mother-daughter dyad I worked with found play scaling to be a safe way to hear each other's desired future and detail small steps forward. The family had been homeless for many months, and the 10-year-old daughter blamed

Solution Focused play therapy 17

mom and her actions for their predicament. The play scaling intervention proceeded as follows:

Therapist: I'd like you to imagine a scale from 1 to 10, where 10 stands for the best possible outcome for your family and 1 is the opposite: for example, the frustration or difficulty that brought you into therapy. (Both nod.) On the table there are a variety of objects for you to choose from; select one or more items to represent the 10 on your scale and choose something to represent the bottom of your scale.

In the area they decided was the 1, Mom selected a mother pig and laid it on its side. The daughter added a sheep and a person. Together they placed 10 or 12 additional animals laying on their sides and on top of each other and a broken fence. The animals included what one might consider prey and predator type animals. Although I noticed the selection, I did not interpret or infer meaning by their selections. They looked up at me, signalling they were done. I wanted the bulk of our conversation to be about their 10, what they wanted instead, rather than the details of the 1, so I was careful in how I proceeded.

Therapist: So, this is the 1? (Both nod.) And the 10? What do you want instead?

Mom set up a fence and the daughter chose a number of animals in family groups, that is big pigs, rabbits, cows, and horses with little pigs, rabbits, cows, and horses. Some were inside the fence and some were outside the fence. They placed trees and rocks and logs in the setting.

Therapist: Aahh, so this is your 10. Tell me about it.
Girl: Well back here (pointing at 1) there are way too many people and nobody likes it. It's confusing.
Mom: The kids don't know where they are going to sleep, and everyone is sad.
Girl: (Looking at mom) The kids don't trust the adults.
Mom: I suppose not.
Therapist: And here (pointing to the 10) it is different?
Mom: Here they have a home and it's safe. The family is together and listening to each other.
Girl: The people who don't live here stay out but they can visit. It's nice.
Mom: Yeah, safe and orderly.
Girl: Nobody is confused, mom comes home after work.
Mom: The kids help and everybody is more relaxed.
Therapist: When the family is together, and it's nice, what are they doing?
Girl: Eating.
Mom: Eating home cooked meals. (Girl smiles and nods.)
Therapist: What do they like to eat when it's a home cooked meal?

We spent 10 or 15 minutes with the minutia of their 10 diorama. I pointed and asked questions. I didn't call anything by name. For example, I would point at an animal and ask *what does this one do?* rather than saying *the cow*. Mom and daughter described favourite meals they want to eat when they have a kitchen and games they want to play. I asked relational questions including:

- What are the brothers doing? (I said *the brothers* instead of *your brothers* so they could stay within their metaphor.)
- How will these guys know things are good for the family? (Pointing to a group outside the fence.)
- Who else will know things are going well?

My curious questions centred on the 10 diorama. Their answers often focused on the 1 diorama, saying things like: 'I don't like it when. . . ' to which I would say 'what do you like instead?' This redirection keeps the focus on what they want rather than what they don't want.

Therapist: On this same scale, where are you now? Choose one or more figures and place them where they go on the scale.
Girl: (Placed several rocks between the two ends of the scale and moved her person and sheep up a little ways.) A 2.
Mom: (Placed a little bridge in the path and set the mama pig on her feet next to it.) Maybe a 3.
Therapist: Wow, a 2 and a 3. How come there and not lower?
Mom: (Pointing to a rock.) Are these the problems?
Girl: Yeah.
Therapist: It looks like they (pointing to sheep and person on its back) already got over one problem. How did they do that?

Mom and daughter were able to have a conversation about what was working, even though they were currently without a home. I commented on what hard work that must be and wondered how they were able to work together to be as high as a 2 and a 3. After eliciting strengths, capabilities, accomplishments, and coping skills currently in place, we moved on to imagining what will be happening at the next number up the scale.

Play scaling was an effective conversational tool for this family. Starting the conversation through metaphor and letting them lead the way gave them an opportunity to have an important conversation with enough distance to make it feel safe and doable. They spent most of the time looking at the toys and talking through the toys. They followed my invitation to talk about the future and what they wanted. Prior to the appointment, the mom said they were at a stalemate and the daughter wasn't talking to her at all. Their prior conversations had been about the problems and contained a lot of blame. This dyadic session gave them a new way to talk. By the end of the appointment, they were laughing and collaborating on their future home story.

Good targets

I saw Madilyn, a mother of 5, for a handful of individual appointments. She had been referred by the Division of Child and Family Services for neglect and child endangerment. Though her children had individual therapists, she decided it would be useful to have each of her children join her for an appointment with me so I 'could see what a handful they are'. The children were indeed full-spirited and had developmental delays that made parenting each child quite individualised.

Jonathan, age 8, was the first child to attend a session with his mom. I would likely have only one appointment with mother and son. My best hopes for the session were to help them notice what was already going well in their relationship, in his behaviour, and in her parenting skills. I spent my 50 minutes in the following ways:

3–5 minutes: get to know you

Using magnets and a metal board, I asked mom and son to tell me about personal skills and hobbies, what mom admired about son, what son liked to do with mom, what was good in the family, and basic demographics about Jonathan, that is age, grade in school, and pet names. I often do this for the first few minutes of a session. This problem-free talk sets the tone for the session and I believe honours the unique being of the child and the parent–child relationship. I introduce it as a 'get to know you' game.

Therapist: How about if we play a game while I get to know you? I have this magnet board . . . for each thing you tell about yourself you get to choose a magnet and place it on the board. We'll see how many magnets you can get.

I have found this to be a simple, quick way to engage children in conversation. The element of a game increases engagement and sets the tone for the session.

20 minutes: Best hopes

Jonathan really liked the magnets, especially the magnetic darts. He was backing up and throwing them towards the board. Mom told him to 'settle down and listen', and he kept throwing the darts.

Therapist: Hey, you are good at throwing those. How about if we make another game? I have a big magnetic white board; shall we draw a target and you can throw the darts at it? (Boy: Yeah, yeah.) Is that OK with you? (Looking at mom, mom nods and smiles.)

Utilisation is an important part of Solution Focused play therapy. What might have been characterised as misbehaviour (throwing the darts) was turned into a therapeutic path forward. I wanted to seek not only the boy's confirmation but mom's approval as she had asked him to stop that behaviour. Any time you can capitalise on something that happens in the session, do it! It has great power. Jonathan drew a target and threw the magnet darts at it. He handed mom a dart so she could throw as well. They laughed at their varying dart throwing skills, which gave me numerous opportunities to complement their ability to play together, share, try new things, and have fun.

Therapist: So you know how you are aiming for the target on the board? (Boy: Uh-huh.) Let's get some markers and write things in your life and your family that you want, that you are aiming for.
Mom: I want you boys to play nicely and help me.
Therapist: OK, play nicely and help are 'mom ideas'. What colour should we use for mom ideas? (J: Purple.) And what colour should we use for your ideas? (J: Red.) When mom says help, what does she mean? What do you help with?
Mom: He is supposed to do dishes and put his laundry away. And no fighting with your brothers.
Therapist: What do you want instead of fighting? What should he aim for?
Mom: Just play nice.

We continued our conversation and filled in the target with things Jonathan wanted to do, like play with his dad, wrestle, and build things. Mom wanted him to stop breaking things. We had a lively conversation about how much fun it is to break things and take things apart. Jonathan said he liked seeing the wires and everything inside the stuff he broke. Mom said it was unacceptable for him to break her kitchen appliances but that they might have an old radio or something he could take apart. So 'break OK things' was added to the target. I complimented him on his curiosity and her willingness to foster that curiosity.

20 minutes: Scaling current progress and next steps

I drew a 1–10 scale on the board and described 10 as hitting the targets all the time and 1 as the opposite. This scale allowed us to discuss what was already going well for them as a pair and individually. Mom said she was able to get all the kids to school, usually on time, and occasionally make dinner. Jonathan said he helped with his baby brother and fed the dog and that he was already really good at breaking things. I asked them to imagine one step higher and show me what will be happening then. We threw darts, talked about concrete details of target behaviours and what was working, and had fun with prediction tasks.

3–5 minutes: Session summary

I usually ask my clients what they liked about our time together. They both said making the target together and throwing darts was fun. Jonathan was excited to hear he could take apart and break appliances as long as his parents approved them. Mom was happy to have a plan and said she hadn't thought about Jonathan's desire to break things as curiosity. I complimented them on coming up with such good ideas and invited them to take a picture of their creative home life target.

In this single session, we were able to touch on all the elements of a Solution Focused play therapy session. Namely:

- Problem-free talk
- Identify a play activity to facilitate conversation
- Use the play activity to elicit individual and relational best hopes
- Identify elements of their preferred future that are already happening and next steps

Magnetic darts, kaleidoscopes, miniature animal families, or a stack of blocks are the tools of the trade in Solution Focused play therapy conversations. It is not the toy that matters, it's the conversation it facilitates. Solution Focused conversations, whether with words, or toys, or a combination of the two, point toward the future and highlight the useful past. By following a child's interests and using their skills, abilities, and passions, we can define and rehearse their ideal future in a personalised and developmentally rich fashion.

References

Berg, I. K., & Steiner, T. (2003). *Children's Solution Work*. New York: W. W. Norton.
De Jong, P., & Berg, I. K. (2013). *Interviewing for Solutions*, 4th edition. Belmont, CA: Brooks Cole.
King, P. (2013). Solution Focused Brief Therapy and Play Scaling. *Journal of Family Psychotherapy*, 24(4), 312–316.
King, P. K. (2017). *Tools for Effective Therapy with Children and Families: A Solution-Focused Approach*. New York: Routledge.

Chapter 4

Voice and choice
The vulnerable child and the Solution Focused process

Rachel Carrick-Birtwell

I've lived and worked in South East London for nearly 30 years, formerly as a teacher and lecturer and more recently as a Solution Focused practitioner. During this time, the majority of my work has been with vulnerable families in areas where socio-economic deprivation is at its highest. My current practice in a large primary school in South East London is no exception. Occasionally, I have found myself questioning the usefulness of a few brief conversations with a vulnerable child. However, my faith in the Solution Focused process remains firm, as, time and again, I have witnessed children developing the ability to recognise the choices they can make and the voice they can use, leading to change for the better in both the home and school environment. 'Conversation' literally means 'turning things over' and, utilising this approach with a Solution Focused methodology, can demonstrably support vulnerable children in finding their own voice. I aim to show examples of conversations which elicit detailed descriptions of a preferred future and draw out a coherent sense of strengths-identity, revealing the latent choices that a child can discover through articulating, with their own voice, the resources and strengths that they had hitherto been unaware of. This can be powerful in transforming a family dynamic. The stories that follow are mostly described in my own voice, borne from the children's narratives.

Sam

I first started working with Sam in January 2017. He was in Year Four and eight years old and had been referred by a member of staff who had ongoing concerns about his behaviour: nothing the school had put in place to support him had 'worked'. Sam had been described as verbally antagonistic, non-compliant, uncommunicative, difficult to 'handle', and having a general air of aggression. I didn't doubt that those behaviours characterised him at times; however, it was important for me to make no assumptions about this. I was mindful of the fundamental tenets of Solution Focused (SF) practice: that this behaviour didn't happen all the time; that in the instances it didn't, strengths and resources could be identified; and that, in our work together, the solution may not be related to the problem as it initially presented itself.

From Sam's classroom, we walked together to the room I work in. As usual, I took the opportunity to engage in some 'problem-free talk', classically used by SF practitioners to discover areas of clients' lives in which they experience more interest and enjoyment. Sam shared a love of football and told me that he lived with his Mum and big sisters and that Dad had left home but was still in touch. In that first conversation, Sam appeared friendly, thoughtful, articulate, and strikingly mature for his age. He also exhibited an emotional depth and vulnerability that went far beyond the 'angry' boy who'd been described to me, serving as a salutary reminder to approach each new client with an open mind, whilst also maintaining respect for the referrer's concerns. Sam then mentioned that his Mum had been 'ill and moody', and described himself feeling 'stressed' about this. Telling him that my job was to have 'helpful conversations' with people, I asked how he'd know, by the time he went back to class, that our chat had indeed been helpful. This was crucial to our session being truly Solution Focused, as it placed Sam's perspective at the centre of our conversation: from that point we could co-create and define a focus for our work together. Sam's immediate response to my question was that he wanted to feel 'calmer' at school and to 'enjoy life more'. Over the course of the next eighteen months, we had around ten conversations. It transpired that Mum suffered from anxiety and was being treated for both bipolar disorder and fibromyalgia. Sam was her primary carer and a source of constant support, undertaking the caring of his mother quietly and diligently, whilst also feeling the weight of containing her anxieties keenly. Throughout our conversations, he would weigh up how to balance his hopes and needs with those of others 'without being selfish'. As he had described in our first session, it was often 'too much to take': he longed to enjoy life more and not be so burdened. After all, as he reminded me: 'I'm just a kid'.

Staying close to Sam's own voice, I elicited reality-based imaginative self-description by exploring together what 'being calmer' and 'enjoying life more' would look like. He described himself being more chilled out; letting things go a bit; not retaliating at school when provoked; ignoring when his youngest sister wound him up; and generally standing up for himself in a way that showed he was 'more in charge'. He expressed a desire to be his own person, making his own decisions: 'me being me'. Asking him what that would look like led to detailed descriptions of how he hoped to handle Mum's worries and demands in a way that showed love and care, whilst also establishing some boundaries. This would enable him to feel more in control and more 'like myself'. One of his recurring challenges was how to handle Mum greeting him after school with her worries and worst-case scenarios. When asked what he'd notice if he was handling conversations in a way that would show him being 'more in charge', Sam decided that initiating more chats with Mum himself would be worth a try. We role-played this together a few times, so that he could experiment with finding language that would be useful for him.

When we met up next, I asked what had been better for him and Sam described how he had been chatting more about his friends and his school day with his

Mum and seeking her views and opinions. This seemed to have made a significant difference to their conversational pathways, leading to her being more inquisitive about his life. Sam felt that this had balanced their relationship a bit, which Mum had also appeared to enjoy. Sam recognised that in allowing himself to be emotionally open with Mum, she had stepped into a more nurturing role with him. In turn, she had been sharing fewer worries. Vulnerable children can often be viewed as 'trapped' in their circumstances: not having a voice or being able to make choices and ultimately being powerless to change anything, as everything is 'being done to' them. A Solution Focused approach tells a different story: that eliciting strengths, skills, strategies and qualities that demonstrate resourcefulness, in the tiniest detail, at whatever minute level, brings a recognition of the pre-existing ability to make choices and use their individual voice.

Thinking about how the future might look if children made more of those choices and spoke up more for themselves can make for a degree of previously undiscovered liberty and discovery.

In a later session, Sam disclosed that his Mum had become more anxious about the possible surgery on her back, and he again expressed worry about the future and annoyance with her candidness. His sense of stability had been knocked, so I asked whether he'd noticed any times when, in spite of being worried about Mum, his stability had not been knocked as much. He thought about this at length, then replied that this would be when he didn't pay too much attention to Mum's worries, knowing from experience that they may be unfounded or not as serious as first suggested. In my work with vulnerable children, I find that opening up the possibility of incremental shifts is very useful, hence my use of the phrase 'as much'. In this case, it acknowledges a change in his stability, concurrent with the stability still existing: a resource rather than deficit model. I probed for a richer description of this, and Sam went on to describe how choosing to focus on his own happiness was helpful: keeping busy and playing outside more, which led to him feeling more energetic. I was interested in exploring the difference he thought this made to Mum, and he said that she always seemed pleased when he had more energy. He went on to say that at times like that, he noticed Mum being in a 'better mood' and 'making more of an effort' herself, which he liked to compliment her on. In order to maximise this description of stability, I went on to find out what he'd notice about himself that would please him, if he were to see more of that in the future. He said he'd feel 'more in charge' and that he would be on 'more solid ground': he'd be less bothered by what was thrown at him as it wouldn't knock him so much.

Towards the end of my work with Sam, we continued to explore his analogy of being on solid ground, at school as well as at home. The school staff had noticed far fewer altercations and a 'better attitude', which Sam put down to being more sure of himself and not having to fight everything as much. He felt he'd got some respect back from the teachers because he'd been able to discover a new voice, explaining himself calmly and letting things go a bit more. He recognised that he still felt angry at times at school but that he was now able and empowered to weigh situations up more carefully, making better decisions that took account of the consequences. Over the course of our work together, Sam made several key choices that had a significant impact on his enjoyment of life at home. He found a bolder voice with his mother and teachers, enabling him to establish clearer boundaries and to take increased charge of his own happiness.

Molly

Some of my work is far less structured than the regular sessions I had with Sam, one example being my three very brief 'walking conversations' with Molly. At eleven years old, she was the eldest of five children (one with complex needs), living with both birth parents, in a family struggling to keep afloat financially. Molly had been referred to me after refusing to go into her form class for the last couple of months. She was being supported by several members of staff, all of whom were trying very hard to find out where the problem lay and how they could get her back into class. During the school day, Molly was accommodated in various locations and enjoyed looking after the school's pet rabbits. Her isolation made her stand out from the crowd, as did the fact that she didn't wear a school uniform. I was advised that she often refused to engage with the adults attempting to help her, so I decided to try an informal approach.

After we were introduced, I asked Molly whether she'd show me the rabbits and tell me a bit about them. She was very knowledgeable and, being strengths-focused, I was keen to know more. It transpired that she and her family owned many pets and she had ambitions to be a nurse in a vet's practice. At this point, I wanted to encourage her to view herself from another's perspective and asked what she thought this said about her. Molly replied that she was quite caring and thoughtful. I continued to shape the linguistic landscape of our conversation by encouraging more of this strengths-description, and Molly responded by recognising that she was also good at researching facts and applying new knowledge. That I was interested in eliciting this level of self-awareness at a point when she was being considered a problem, was, I imagine, a refreshing change. I then asked whether she'd like to see more of that ambitious self, which got a shrug and another smile, to which I asked what she'd notice that would be different if she did. She then grinned and said: 'I'd probably go back into class – but I don't want to'. My response was that I realised that did seem to be the case – 'at the moment'. My comment was casual, yet the inclusion of this reference to time was deliberate: my intention was to open up the possibility of future change, therefore challenging any assumption that things were stuck.

My next chat with Molly was in the corridor during class-time. She was warming herself by a radiator and I joined her, noticing she had her school uniform on. To my Solution Focused mind, this was indicative of a shift, a possible sign of hope and change which I thought would be useful to explore, so I asked how this had come about. Molly described how, since the start of Year Six, the staff had given her a 'hard time' over not wearing her uniform. It was now three months later and close to the end of the first term. She said that once they had 'backed off' and not mentioned it for a week or so, she had independently chosen to put on her uniform again. I asked what difference that decision had made to her, and she described feeling more 'in charge' of herself, more independent and responsible for her own choices. At this point, our conversation felt energetic and purposeful: focusing on Molly's strengths enabled us to recognise her reclamation of some power and the ability to make decisions that were good for her in helping her move forwards in her life.

My last, brief conversation with Molly was at the start of the second term. I greeted her, then asked what she'd noticed that had been better so far that term. She told me that she had chosen to spend a part of every day in her class, having made the decision to ease herself in, with the help of a teaching assistant, who she'd taken the initiative to approach. Initially, she had helped with paperwork and then had begun to participate in her English classes at a desk on her own. I asked what difference this had made to her, and she described feeling more 'confident' and 'proud' of herself and also very happy that her mother seemed proud of her.

During our work together, I was determined to resist any curiosity about the 'problem' and why Molly had decided not to go into class or wear her uniform in the first place. She was able to recognise that she could speak up for herself and be in charge of her own decisions, which seemed to dislodge the 'problem' and move things forwards. This supports my belief that solution-building conversations are invaluable in eliciting strengths, which can then act as a catalyst for change. I was mindful of conversing at Molly's own pace, the end result being that Molly and the school's worlds had become more closely aligned.

Sofia

Many other examples spring to my mind when considering how vulnerable children can find their voice and be able to make choices through Solution Focused questions. Sofia, the ten-year-old eldest of four half-siblings, felt the weight of responsibility for her two-year-old sister Ivy, when the Local Authority put them into the care of Sofia's father. Sofia had taken the role of 'mother' from Ivy's birth, their own mother being addicted to drugs and alcohol. The home environment had been unsafe and the girls had suffered extreme neglect. Moving in with Sofia's father and his two other children shifted the tenuous balance of Sofia and Ivy's previous life, and although they were now deemed 'safe' by the authorities, she was finding the adjustment challenging. She now acknowledged that she no longer needed to be the protector and, in our work together, expressed hopes of being able to 'let go' of the worries of her past and start 'enjoying life' but that she was at a loss as to how to 'do' this. Rather than focusing on any action she could take, I encouraged Sofia to describe what she'd notice that would be different if she did let go a bit and start to enjoy life more. This included expressing her worries and anger; trusting others with her emotions; acknowledging painful memories; feeling happier and being more creative. Sofia had already begun to find a 'voice' through writing and drawing in a journal, and over the course of our work together, within a persistently Solution Focused conversational framework, she gradually began to voice her hopes for the future, rather than record the pain from her past. Her choice to 'let go' and enjoy herself saw her expressing her creativity through song and dance. The negative effects of Sofia's past were becoming less powerful as she continued to notice her adaptability and inventiveness in shaping her present and future.

I maintain an unshakeable belief that change is possible and that vulnerable children benefit enormously from iterating where they choose to go in life, rather than describing where they've been. Transformation occurs after describing desired possibilities in minute detail, and this remains my motivation to continue asking questions that specifically focus on children's extraordinary capacity and resourcefulness, rather than being distracted by the challenges they are facing. The discovery of their voice and the subsequent hitherto unimagined life choices available to them in their everyday reality can be truly empowering and transformative. And once discovered, the power of the Solution Focused approach to voice and choice is that it can be sustained independently, as a mindset by the vulnerable child.

Chapter 5

Kids'Skills – a creative Solution Focused method for helping children overcome difficulties and problems

Ben Furman

Children don't have problems – they only have skills that they have not acquired yet.

Kids'Skills is a step-by-step method to help children learn skills and overcome emotional and behavioural problems with the help of family, friends and other people close to them. It is designed for children aged three to twelve, but its principles are also applicable to teenagers and even adults.

The method was originally intended as a tool for teachers, therapists, counsellors and other professionals who in their work help children to overcome problems. However, because of its relative simplicity, it was soon discovered that it could also be used by parents with their own children at home with minimal professional coaching.

Adults tend to see problems as symptoms of an underlying disorder that needs be treated, whereas children tend to see problems as a lack of skills that they need to learn. Kids'Skills adheres to the children's skill-focused view of problems. Its objective is to encourage and help children acquire the skills they need in order to overcome their problems. In Kids'Skills, family and friends play an important role: they help and support children in learning skills. This ensures that the method has an impact not only on the child but on the entire ecosystem of the child.

One of advantages of Kids'Skills is that it is child-friendly. Most children dislike having to talk with adults about their problems but do not mind at all talking about skills they might need to learn to be happier. Another advantage is that Kids'Skills automatically fosters cooperation between professionals and parents by regarding parents not as the culprits of the child's problem but as respected partners, useful helpers and important supporters of the child.

Kids'Skills is a transdiagnostic approach that can be used regardless of the child's diagnosis. It can be used with all kinds of behavioural problems, with ADHD, mood disorders, OCD, autism, aggression and so on. In fact, Kids'Skills is suitable whenever there is a problem that can be solved or ameliorated by the child learning some specific skill.

Kids'Skills may at first glance appear simply as one more version of cognitive-behavioural therapy, but with a closer look it becomes evident that the method is not designed to influence only the child but everyone around the child as well.

How Kids'Skills came about

In the 1990s, the author was a supervisor of the teachers of a preschool in Helsinki, Finland, caring for children with special needs. Together with these teachers, we decided to develop a practical step-by-step method for helping the children in close collaboration with their parents. Inspired by the therapeutic ideas of Milton H. Erickson and Solution Focused therapy, we drafted a protocol that we named Kids'Skills, which shifted focus from problems to skills and included several steps to motivate and help children learn skills. The method worked well and attracted attention, first amongst educators and gradually amongst counsellors as well. We produced materials; there was an illustrated workbook for children, a handbook for teachers and a guide for parents. Since those days, two books have been published about Kids'Skills and have been translated into over twenty languages.

Kids'Skills step by step

Kids'Skills is a protocol for talking with children consisting of fifteen steps, or suggestions. These steps can be covered creatively. Some steps can be omitted, additional steps can be added, and the order of the steps can be varied. The steps are as follows:

1. Convert the child's problem into a skill that the child can learn.
2. Make an agreement with the child about the skill for them to learn.
3. Discuss the benefits of learning the skill for the child and for other people.
4. Ask the child to give a name to the skill they will learn.
5. Ask the child to pick an animal, a superhero or some other character to be their imaginary supporter.
6. Have a discussion with the child about why you, the child's parents and their other supporters are convinced that the child will be able to learn the skill.
7. Ask the child to name the people that they want to ask to be their supporters.
8. Ask the child to show the skill in role-play and, if possible, record a video of them showing their skill.
9. Discuss with the child how they want to celebrate, together with their supporters, when they have learned their skill.
10. Agree with the child about how the child will inform their social network about the skill they are going to learn.
11. Figure out, together with the child, how they can practice their skill using role-play as well as using the skill in real situations and make sure there is a way for the child to be praised by their supporters when they practice their skill.
12. Ask the child how they want their supporters to remind them when they forget their skill and need someone to remind them of it.
13. When the child has learned the skill and they celebrate their achievement with their supporters, ensure that the child thanks their supporters for their help and support.

14 Help the child find a way to teach their newly acquired skill to another child or to somehow support other children who need to learn the same skill they have learned.
15 When the child has learned the skill and their achievement has been celebrated, open a discussion with the child about the next skill they might want to learn – or need to learn – with the help of the Kids'Skills method.

Case example

Mark was a nine-year-old boy in Elin's class. He was generally happy and positive, and he had several friends with whom he enjoyed playing. His problem was that when things didn't go his way, or someone objected to what he wanted, he tended to get furious. When this happened, he would shout, hit his friends, throw things around or rip apart books and other school materials. A number of times, Mark had gotten mad at Elin too. For example, once when it was cold outside and Elin told him to get dressed and go out for recess, Mark lost it and started shouting at her in a totally unacceptable manner.

Finding a skill for the child to learn

Having participated in a workshop on Kids'Skills, a Solution Focused method for coaching children to overcome problems, Elin decided to try the Kids'Skills approach with Mark. However, figuring out what skill a child with a given problem behaviour needs to develop is not always easy. Elin knew Mark would need to learn to control his temper, but she was not sure what skill he needed to learn in order to be able to control his temper. Having turned the question around in her head for some time, she figured that the skill he needed to have was to be more "resilient", or to be able to let go and move on when things didn't work out the way he wanted.

That was Elin's idea of what skill Mark needed to work on to overcome his problem, but she hesitated to propose that skill to him. She knew that children are much more likely to become motivated to learn skills if the idea of what skill they should work on comes from children themselves rather than an adult such as a parent or a teacher.

Elin asked Mark to have a talk with her at the end of the day. Mark agreed and the two of them sat down to talk. Elin showed him a copy of the illustrated Kids'Skills workbook and told him that she had taken part in a training course to use this method with children. Mark perused the pages of the workbook and appeared interested.

Elin deliberately kept her idea of what skill Mark needed to learn to herself. Instead, she asked him questions to help him figure out all by himself what skill he might need to become better at to get along better with his friends:

"What happens to you Mark when things don't go the way you want?"
"How do you feel in your body when that happens?"

"And then what do you do?"
"How do your friends respond to you?"
"What about your teachers?"
"What do you think your friends think about you when that happens?"
"What would you want your friends to think about you instead?"

Mark gave thoughtful answers to all these questions. He showed that he understood how his rage influenced others.

Elin then asked:

"What would you like to learn, or become better at, so that your friends would think good things about you all the time?"

Mark became thoughtful and then said that he needed to learn the skill of "cooling down".

"What a good skill to have!" Elin responded. She was delighted because she had succeeded in getting Mark to figure out what skill he needed to learn in order to overcome his problem. The rest of the conversation would revolve around building motivation and developing a feasible plan for Mark to learn that skill.

"What could help you to calm yourself down when you are about to become furious, Mark? What could you do instead of what you have been doing so far in those situations?"

"I think I need to learn to walk away, to be by myself for a moment and then go back, or go to a teacher to ask for help," Mark suggested.

Benefits of learning the skill

"How will that be good for you? What will you get out of learning that skill?" Elin asked.
"The others will not be cross with me", Mark said thoughtfully.
"What else?" Elin asked Mark to keep the conversation rolling.
"I can continue to play with the others", he said.
"That's great. Anything else?"
"I will be happy again", Mark said with a smile on his face.

It is often useful to expand the conversation of benefits to include others.

"What about your friends and other people who know you? Do they also benefit in some way from you learning the 'keep cool' skill?"
"They won't be cross with me".
"Sure, and when they are not cross with you, what good does that do?"
"They will think that I am a good 'bro'".

A discussion about the benefits of learning the skill helped Mark to develop what motivational psychologists refer to as internal motivation, or the will to achieve something, not merely because someone else wants you to, but because yourself see real benefits of learning that skill.

Supporters

"You can decide who you want to ask to support you in learning the 'cool down' skill", Elin said to Mark.

Mark's eyes lit up when he named his supporters: his mother, his father and his little sister.

"And how would you want them to support you?" Elin asked.

"They can ask me every day when I come home from school how my training has gone."

"That makes sense. What about your friends? Which of them would you want to support you at school?"

Mark named two of his classmates and then said that he also wanted Elin and another teacher he liked to be his supporters. When Elin asked him how he wanted the teachers to support him at school, he said that when needed, the teachers should remind him of his skill simply by saying 'snow'. That was the name he had given to his 'cool down' skill when Elin had asked him what he wanted to call his skill.

Imaginary supporter

In addition to human supporters, you can also ask children to think of an imaginary supporter, or power figure, that will help them learn their skill. This symbolic helper can be, for example, a favourite animal, a cartoon character, or a superhero. Most children like the idea of having a fantasy supporter and enjoy inventing creative ideas of how it can help them to remember their skill.

Mark wanted his imaginary supporter to be a superhero from his favourite computer game. He showed Elin a picture of the character with his smartphone. Later on, he printed out several pictures of this superhero, coloured them with crayons, and attached them in various places to remind him of the skill he wanted to learn.

Celebration

"When you have learned your skill, you will of course need to celebrate in some way by doing something nice together with your supporters at school or after school", Elin said to introduce the idea of celebration.

Mark gave it some thought and then came up with the idea that he would want to invite his two supporter classmates out for McDonald's and a movie.

"That's a nice idea", Elin said, "but you will of course need to ask your parents for their approval". Later that day, at home, he asked his parents. They gladly approved and thought it was good idea.

Setbacks

Elin introduced the idea of forgetting the skill in this way: "You know Mark when you try to learn a skill – any skill – it's not uncommon that sometimes things don't work the way you want because you sometimes forget the skill that you are learning. When that happens, you will need others to help you in one way or another. Do you have any idea of how we – your supporters at school – can help you in those situations?"

Mark understood. He said he didn't want anyone to remind him by criticising him, or telling him off, because that would only aggravate him and make him forget all about the skill he was supposed to learn.

"So how would you want us to remind you instead?" Elin continued.

"Say 'snow'. Just say 'snow'. That's all", was Mark's answer.

Elin wondered whether Mark's idea would work in real life. She wondered whether perhaps using the word 'snow' in the heat of the moment might add to Mark's fury rather than help him calm down and therefore asked him how he would respond if other people would use the word 'snow' to help him calm down.

"What will you do if any of us sometimes says 'snow' to you?" she asked.

"I will say 'stop' to myself and then 'sorry'", said Mark and looked quite determined.

To make sure that Mark would be able to do just that in the heat of the moment, Elin decided to let Mark rehearse this response in role-play. Together they acted out several scenarios, where Mark pretended that he was furious because he could not get something he wanted. When Mark was furious, Elin said 'snow' and he showed, time and again, how he could do what he said he would do, to say 'stop' and 'sorry'. Mark enjoyed the role-play and Elin had the feeling that this sort of rehearsal played an important role in helping Mark develop his new behaviour pattern.

Follow-up

During the next weeks, Mark put a lot of effort into learning his skill. Whenever Elin, or either one of his classmate-supporters, used the code word 'snow' to remind him to calm down, he knew what to do. In addition, Elin also sometimes reminded him of his skill beforehand, when she noticed that he was on his way to join the other children who were playing a game together. In those situations, Elin could say to Mark something along the lines of:

"Mark, remember your skill. Now you have a good opportunity to practice".

Mark enjoyed his discussions with Elin. "Can we do that workbook again?" he had asked Elin more than once during the time they worked together. Mark looked forwards to his brief one-on-one encounters with Elin.

Mark made rapid progress. In four weeks, he had made enough progress that everyone agreed that it was time to celebrate. Next Friday, as planned, Mark invited his two classmate-supporters out for McDonald's and a movie. The boys were excited about the plan during the day at school, and Elin found out later that the evening had been a great success.

Discussion

Kids'Skills is a set of guidelines about how to talk with kids, or how to coach them, and how to awaken their interest in figuring out creative ways to overcome their problems.

Using these guidelines changes one's relationship with children. You stop bossing children around by telling them how they should behave or think. Instead you learn to listen to children and to appreciate their own ideas of what skills they need to learn and how to learn those skills. You assume the role of a coach rather than that of a teacher or therapist.

Kids'Skills does not only help children change. It changes everyone around the child too. Elin, for example, feels that Kids'Skills has changed the way she views children. She says after learning this approach she no longer thinks that children choose to behave badly. Instead, she now thinks that some children simply lack some skills that they need to acquire to be able to behave well. This shift in her thinking, she feels, has been benefited her a lot, not only in her role as a teacher for children but also in her role as a supporter for their parents.

More information about Kids'Skills is available on the website. Also, a free app called Kids'Skills App is available at both Android and Apple app stores.

Chapter 6

From challenging to outstanding

Yasmin Ajmal

Formerly a primary teacher and educational psychologist, I currently work as a Solution. Focused and educational consultant on a freelance basis. The first Solution Focused Brief Therapy course I attended 25 years ago fundamentally changed my practice. My subsequent privilege to work as a member of the BRIEF team in London delivering training courses solidified my understanding of, and belief in, the empowering nature of a Solution Focused (SF) approach when working with young people.

Four years ago, I was asked to work alongside two talented teachers with a class in a deprived area of outer London as they moved into Year 5. I ran sessions with the class on a weekly basis over the course of a term. Through the language of possibility and success, the students were invited into constructive conversations about building the classroom environment that would bring out the best in themselves and each other. This chapter explores their incredible journey from the most challenging class in the school to an outstanding class who exceeded academic expectations and supported school developments.

> We are highly thought of in the school. It makes us proud. It makes us want to do better.
>
> (Haafiz)

Noticing and naming the good things

The currency of communication amongst the students was largely one of negativity where criticisms and arguments insidiously chipped away at the self-esteem of them all. Shaping a culture of mutual appreciation that could support change, difference and challenge was about shifting patterns of attention.

Several short (20 minute) observations were set up based on the WOWW model (Berg & Shilts, 2004) over a cross-section of activities including a maths session and settling after a playtime. The focus was simple: to write down all the good things that were happening. Feedback was both class-based, thus increasing group identity: 'This is a class that has some great ideas', and individually based, thus increasing individual confidence and competence: 'I noticed students quietly helping others'. The shocked response from one student after the first feedback session was: 'I didn't realise we were doing all those things!'

It was a short step for students to start describing the things that *they* had noticed and valued. Their observations, known as sparkling moments (White, 1998), became a regular feature in the classroom: short 5 minute slots for 'snappy sparkles', to create energy at the beginning or pride at the end of a day; 'predictive sparkles' as a fun way to build a picture of what a good lesson would look like; and a 5 minute 'sparkles audit' on all the good things they had noticed *so far*, hinting that there were more discoveries to be made, to help re-focus the class during an activity. There were also 'secret sparkles', where students were quietly nominated by the teacher to observe and then feed back what they had noticed. Consistency and repetition were important in gradually making their skills visible and encouraging the students to build on small everyday actions that were likely to be useful to them.

The staff welcomed the validation of the things they were trying to set up in the class: 'I had no idea that the children had been enjoying the lessons so much. It made me feel more confident in my abilities' (class teacher).

Over time, sparkles began to spread naturally in the classroom. Students often preceded a comment during class discussions with a statement such as: 'I am handing my sparkle to Adrienne today because she helped me with my maths'. The students had found a way of lifting each other up: 'When you hear other people's sparkles it makes you feel happy', 'When people talk about you it brings a smile'. It was like building a habit, which began consciously and then became a part of the norm with the students in the driving seat.

Building descriptions of what is wanted

The most pertinent sparkles to notice were those things which were most likely to support the future that was wanted. The class were well aware of the concerns about them and their behaviour. The students were invited into a different dialogue:

- 'Sounds like things have not been going so well recently for this class. Would you like things to go better?' *The closed part of the question established the context, the open part was an invitation for the students to step into the conversation.*
- 'Yes'.
- 'Suppose tomorrow things did go better and you are the dream class; what will you and your teachers notice different?' *The aspirational notion of a successful 'tomorrow' communicates a belief and confidence that it could happen.*

Building richness into the details helped the students to move beyond a reiteration of what they thought they ought to say towards their own unique ideas. Comments such as: 'We wouldn't be giving up when things are difficult' were first translated into the presence of something by asking: 'What would you be doing instead?' One answer, 'We would be resilient', was then explored further, for example, 'How would that show?' or 'What will you be *doing*?' to reveal tangible behaviours that would be a sign of 'resilience' in action. Exploring the fine minutiae of 'tomorrow' through key aspects of the school day, such as first thing in the morning or out in the playground, situated the picture in the reality of their everyday worlds and the students were encouraged to see, feel and hear what this will be like.

Multiple perspectives multiply possibilities, so the views of others were also included: 'What will tell the head teacher that this class is having a good day?' Occasionally the conversation was extended beyond school: 'How will your mum (others at home) know that it has been a good day in school when you get home?' Asking additionally: 'How will she respond? What difference will that make to you?' can help to create a context that supports the likelihood of more good days happening.

Follow up discussions used open-ended questions such as: 'What has sparkled today for you?' This allowed for new discoveries which might not have been said but had emerged through setting in motion a way of thinking that would support a better day emerging.

Once established, the 'at your best' framework can be applied to any aspect of school life, such as working well together, tidying up or being kind. On one occasion the class were sent back early from their music lesson because their behaviour had been so difficult. (Ajmal and Ratner, 2020). Rather than spending time on what had been 'wrong', a 0–10 scale was introduced, and the class were invited to:

- Describe what the best version of the class in music would look like.
- Look at where they would scale things today and the good things that had happened. Celebrating those desirable aspects of thought and action already present was an important validation for those students whose behaviour had been OK.
- Detail what would be different or what their music teacher would be noticing when the class were one point higher.

The teacher was surprised at how readily the students had participated in the discussion given that they were 'in trouble' and how much had been covered in only 10 minutes. The particular value of scales is that they can be returned to again and again: 'What number were you today? What good things were happening?' Students themselves would stop me in the corridor: 'Do you remember when we had the bad music lesson – you helped us to think about the good things we had done rather than the negative. Well we were a 7 today because we all got our instruments out and we were good at the beginning of the lesson'. A few months later the class were at their 10 when they gave a wonderful musical performance to the school.

Changing the interaction patterns

The social worlds of young people are important, and so we need to weave relationships into descriptions. As the students started talking about the changes that would be happening, so we began to enquire about how their actions would impact on others and how the actions of others will then affect them.

- How will your teacher or friend know that you are, for example, making an effort?

Asking students to describe what they are doing through the eyes of others can also help them to translate something they might think they are doing, such as 'making an effort', into more explicitly observable behaviours in the public social world.

- How will your teacher or friend let you know that they have noticed? What will they do?

The more the students outlined a sequence of actions and responses, the more likely it was that they would notice and attach significance to them.

- And if your teacher or friend did that, what effect will this have on you?

The intention was to expand a sequence of possibilities with many openings and doorways, each of which could lead to change and difference. It was not a set of carefully rehearsed moves but building an understanding of the reciprocal nature of relationships in which the students could have some influence in a different pattern emerging.

After a successful class assembly, one of the children commented that maybe people would think about them differently now. 'Sometimes we have our ups and downs, and some teachers would not have believed we could try our best'. We need to be prepared to harness opportunities as they appear:

Yasmin: What words do you think the teachers might use to describe the class now?
Students: Responsible – mature – epic – enthusiastic – helpful.
Yasmin: What difference will this make to you and what you do?
Students: They might think of us as a class who are strong in a good way. And then we can be stronger.
Yasmin: How will you know that they have noticed that you are getting stronger in a good way?

The class liked being under the microscope of praise rather than criticism, and the more good things they heard, the more they were predisposed to continue to notice things that fitted in with this version of themselves. They were no longer stuck in one reputation but were discovering an infinite number of possibilities in themselves and the agency they could have in shaping the world around them.

'What seems to have happened is that they were just used to negatives. This assembly has helped them to change their perspective on themselves and what people think of them' (class teacher).

Facilitating peer conversations

An activity was set up whereby pairs of students would 'interview' each other, using a scale structure, about a best hope they had for themselves in their learning or behaviour. A short demonstration at the front of the class enabled the students to see the flow of questions in action (describing the 10, locating current successes and exploring signs of progress). Occasionally the students were invited to try a 'detailing question' such as: 'How would that show?' from examples placed on their tables. Later we also watched a video of three students interviewing me about my own best hope. The 'interview' was stopped at various places and students were asked to consider what they had learnt so far, *why* a question might have been asked or what to ask next. In helping students to think about the process and intentions of questions, the desire was not to 'train' them to work in an SF way but to invite them into a different way of looking at things, a different language and how to build useful questions based on responses.

The students were allocated the role of journalist to emphasise the question asking aspect of their role and the value of curiosity in helping people to discover their own solutions. Within minutes, the classroom was buzzing as the enthusiastic journalists asked their scaling and 'What else?' questions with a total belief that their partner had lots of useful ideas. At the end of the interviews, the students were asked to give compliments to each other:

> I liked Dylan's questions. He was really thinking about the questions.
>
> (Sarah)

> I liked it when Sarah was answering because she had a strong thought in her head and the questions helped her to say it.
>
> (Dylan)

The teacher felt that the children had learnt that what they said was valued and the value of really listening. 'The detail questions challenged the children to ask more and it was nice to see them adding their own questions. We are always so speedy, slowing things down for even a few moments can make so much difference' (class teacher).

When we ask SF questions, we are 'meeting' the other person. The conversations opened up the opportunity for the students to experience and see each other in a different way, to learn things they didn't know. Several months later, the students were still commenting on the impact of these paired conversations:

> Talking about our targets has inspired people to take things on.
>
> (Imran)

> You have unleashed our intelligence and thinking. You have made us think properly.
>
> (Carly)

> The partner work has been helpful for me. When you work with a partner it is easier to think about things. And your partner is really listening to your ideas and your partner helps you think deeper.
>
> (Anthony)

The class teacher commented that she was now able to pair children with anyone.

The Learning Ambassadors

As the students moved into Year 6 and became Learning Ambassadors working with younger children, the SF ideas continued to support their best versions, the work they were doing and a belief in themselves.

At the beginning of the project the students outlined what they would do as an Ambassador and the skills they would bring to the role. It gave them the opportunity to paint a picture of the person that they were and wanted others to see.

The students met with the teacher they would be working with. It helped to build their confidence and competence in asking good questions such as: 'How will you know that we are doing a good job?' It was further evidence of how they could shape their environments and what they did through a clarity about where they were heading.

The students kept a learning journal recording what worked well and what they were learning. After several weeks, the Ambassadors interviewed each other in pairs about what they had been doing and the skills they had been using. Their comments were a testament to their continued journey of self-efficacy:

> You need to be persistent because if a child isn't getting it then you need to keep carrying on to help them.
>
> (Robert)

> You have to be enthusiastic and the reason why is that if little children see you have enthusiasm then it bounces back on them.
>
> (Samia)

You have to be optimistic that the children can do well.

(Millie)

You have to know how to deal with big issues and know how to solve them.

(Farouk)

The students thought carefully about what a good handover to the incoming Ambassadors would look like. They went to classes and talked about what they did. They held 'interviews' to find out about the skills of the new Ambassadors and their ideas: 'It will help them to take the role seriously'. It is striking the commitment that positions of responsibility can inspire. Joanna, an Ambassador who had experienced many ups and downs herself in school, voiced her concerns about the consistent misbehaviour of Hamid, and her suspicion he was just applying to be an Ambassador as a way of getting out of class. So, at the start of the interview Joanna explained: 'Before I ask you questions, I want to let you know that being an Ambassador is not just about the time when you are doing things. You are an Ambassador all the time and a role model. Imagine if someone sees you not following an instruction or being rude. It is not just about you, it is about the children you are working with. And just to let you know, that even if you are appointed, you can be asked to stop doing it at any time if you are not showing your best side'. After the interview, Joanna commented: 'I think we ought to give him a go, but we need to think very carefully who we put him with'. It was clear that Joanna took much pride in her Ambassador role and wanted an unequivocal maintenance of high standards to continue when she left for secondary school. However, in her 11-year-old way, she also showed an understanding that being able to 'step up' into a role of responsibility can change behaviour.

At the end of the year, every receiving class teacher talked about the dedication of the student Ambassadors, their time keeping, their preparation and their impact on the confidence of the children they worked with. The head teacher proudly showed the Ambassadors working to visitors. The dream class had arrived in the public social world! Back in their own classroom, the teacher talked about changes in the way the students managed themselves, approached tasks and took more responsibility for how things went.

Conclusion

Creating a culture of appreciation harnessed the energy of the classroom and created an ethos where all the children had a voice. In helping students to value their own uniqueness and the difference in others, they reconnected with a pride in themselves. Their responsibility and ownership grew organically through their experiences and importantly through the practical opportunities, built into daily classroom life, to continually reflect on those aspects of behaviour and thought which best supported the class that they wanted to be. In times of diminishing resources and over-full agendas, building conversations around the skills, capacities and belief of the class had a powerful effect on all the students. It gave them the tools to have their own internal dialogues so that, like dropping a pebble into water, the students could continue to build ripples of success.

> This has this boosted the profile and morale of some children who are now more integrated within their peer group. But they have all benefited. It was like taking the students on a journey where there were some things laid down about where they were heading, but they each had a say in how they wanted that journey to be.
>
> (Class teacher)

> It has been the best year ever. Our teachers have taught us how to be sophisticated.
>
> (Kieran)

My thanks to George Carey Church of England Primary School and to class teachers Naureen Akhtar and Yasmin Akhazzan for their creativity, skills and belief in the students, without which the success of this work would not have been possible.

References

Ajmal, Y., & Ratner, H. (2020). *Solution Focused Practice in Schools: 80 Ideas and Strategies*. London: Routledge.

Berg, I.K. and Shilts, L. (2004). *Classroom Solutions: WOWW Approach*. Milwaukee: BFTC Press.

White, M. (1998). *Re-Authoring Lives: Interviews & Essays*. Adelaide: Dulwich Centre Publications.

Chapter 7

Bridging cultural divides in international schools with Solution Focused approaches

Felina Heart

I worked for a number of years at Pechersk School International in Kyiv, Ukraine, as a school counsellor. It is an English-speaking school serving students from forty different countries. The families have relocated to Ukraine through big businesses, embassies, the United Nations, NGOs or personal companies. The Ukrainian students are from upper class families who are often involved in politics. Typical concerns that were brought to me included transition difficulties, impulsivity, aggression, anger management, not following directions, foul language, as well as difficulty focusing and paying attention. I worked with students, staff and parents through private meetings, conferences, in-service trainings, and collaborating with the learning support coordinator on setting up and implementing Individual Learning Plans. I found that a lot of the students I worked with are English language learners and often lead a very transitionary life, where they move from country to country and school to school.

The Solution Focused approach has been very useful in my position as a school counsellor. After my initial foundation training, I was very excited to put what I learned into practice with the students. After my first couple of individual sessions, I really wanted to figure out how I could expand the use of the Solution Focused approach in individual sessions to using the strategies school wide. I looked at the work of Linda Metcalf in Texas and Russell Sabella in Florida, continued training with BRIEF in London, and started to realise the wide-reaching uses for Solution Focused basic approaches. I slowly started looking at all aspects of my job and at how I could make small changes to reflect the ideals of the Solution Focused approach. Following are some of the ways I started to make changes.

Areas of implementation

- A counselling referral system using forms that incorporate the Solution Focused approach and wording
- In family meetings to help change the focus from problem focused to Solution Focused

- In staff meetings, especially when discussing students who displayed difficulties
- School and community education
- With staff during the development and implementation of new programmes and projects
- Adding a visual and interactive format to individual and group sessions with students

Building a counselling referral system based on the Solution Focused approach

When I first arrived at this school, there was not a process for referring students to the counsellor. In the first year, teachers often just dropped off students for basic classroom management issues (not listening, not staying seated, saying no, etc.) that could be worked on in the classroom. I knew regular meetings with the counsellor were only necessary after other strategies had been exhausted. So, using Russell Sabella's handout, I started to create a referral process for counselling services based on the Solution Focused approach (Sabella, 2014). I utilised his teacher referral forms and parent referral forms to create my own referral forms based on my school's dynamics and needs. I also incorporated a pre-referral checklist for teachers to use before students were referred to spend time with me.

In the referral process, I identified six forms of referrals to the counsellor. First were short term concerns. These are the times the students were in distress and needed immediate support. Second were emergency concerns, which dealt with child protection issues such as abuse and self-injury. These would follow our child protection policy and protocols, which I developed. Third were concerns brought to the table through a learning support referral. In these cases, I worked with the learning support team and through the student's Individual Learning Plan. As I worked with these students, I would do Solution Focused sessions with them. Fourth were concerns brought up by parents. As I spoke with the parents, I would ask some of the following questions:

- What would you like to see going better for your child?
- If this happened, what difference would it make for him/her, for you as parents and for the family?
- Scales dealing with where they are academically, emotionally and/or with the particular reason the parents came to see me.
- Follow up questions to the scales about what put them at a particular number, where they would like to see them and if they moved up one point how they would know.
- I would make sure that every time they focused on the problem or a negative behaviour, I would actively try to shift their focus to what the student was already doing well and what the student could do to achieve this success more often.

All this would be recorded on the parent referral form, and then I would work on a plan with the parents.

The fifth type of referral is the teacher referral. Before teachers even got to the point of completing the referral form, they had a pre-referral process where they had to look at the student's strengths and try strategies to use the strengths to address the concern, to speak with the parents and to meet with me. In the meeting with me, I used a Solution Focused approach to help guide the conversation and change the focus of the teacher's interactions with the student to solutions, not problems. Together we would come up with a Solution Focused plan, with strategies and conversations which the teacher could use with the student. If after a few weeks there was no progress, then the teacher could complete the referral form, which is designed with the following Solution Focused questions.

- Scales rating the child on things such as focus, impulsivity, work completion, kindness and so on. It is important to note that these items are on all referral forms due to my continued work with the learning support team. We worked together on our referral forms so that regardless of whether the student was referred for learning support or counselling, a clear understanding of the student could be achieved.
- What will the student be doing better/different when your concerns are resolved?
- What signs would you see of progress in the student, and what would the student see in you that tells them they are making progress?
- Are there times the student has already achieved success or been higher rated on the above scales?
- What was happening and can you explain any of these times?

The last type of referral has been the student self-referral. Students have been able to refer themselves by coming to my office with the counsellor pass, which is located in each class. There is also a locked mailbox outside my office where students have been able to leave notes or completed self-referral forms.

With this new clear and concise referral process, there have been fewer immediate referrals to the counsellor's office, which results in less academic time missed by the students. Teachers have been empowered to be the experts in their classroom, and students have been empowered to be the experts on themselves. It has also allowed teacher and students to work together for a better classroom environment.

Family and staff meetings to change from problem focused to Solution Focused

I further looked at parent meetings and how they could be approached differently. I noticed that I was attending a lot of parent meetings with teachers where the meeting turned into talking about all the things the child was doing wrong. The parent and sometimes the child would leave the meeting defeated, and there never seemed to be a good, workable solution or support from all parties. Looking back at my training notes and Dr. Sabella's handout, I developed a format for parent meetings that would have a Solution Focused approach and would also help teachers feel like their issues were being addressed (Sabella, 2014). In the meetings, I started with "What are two or three things the child does well?" and then, "What do you want to see the student do better?" (biggest concern) (Sabella, 2014). With these two statements, I asked for input from parents, teachers and the student. If all had different ideas on what they wanted to see the student do better (hopes), we would first discuss how we could consolidate those or narrow them down into one or two items. Then the meeting would move to what would it look like if the student did these one or two things better, what would the parents and the teacher see, and what would the student notice? Sometimes we would address specifically what success would look like to the parent, student and teacher. I found that this allowed us to determine whether we all had the same end goal in mind. Finally, we would end with what parents could do at home to support the student, how the school could help and what the student could do. Students were encouraged to attend these meetings. Sometimes the students would be hesitant, so I created the agenda on a Google Doc. The student would then sit in an adjacent room with a trusted adult. They could be viewing the Google Doc and see the notes of what was being said, and they could add to the Google Doc and this would be shared in the meeting. This was successful because it allowed the student to see that it wasn't just about problems but about solutions, they could participate in the meeting without feeling nervous or embarrassed, and it allowed them to have a voice and share their personal expertise on themselves.

I have used this approach with meetings with staff members when discussing students and difficulties in class. This includes individual meetings with individual staff members or large staff meetings with several group members where students were having behavioural troubles in various classrooms. The meetings had often turned into a very problem focused discussion, where lists of concerns about the student were recorded and no solutions to help the situation were offered. I decided that when students of concern were discussed, I would lead with a focus on what the student was doing well, what our hope was for the student, and whether there were times when the student had done what we want to see. If they had, what classes had we seen this in, and what strategies had that teacher used to help that occur? This changed the climate of the meetings, and we saw an increase in solutions being offered and different strategies that teachers would use with the student.

School community education

A large part of my job has focused on educating parents and the school community. I have occasionally presented small workshops to parents during what our school calls "Parent Education Tuesdays". I have done sessions on child protection policies, the child protection curriculum, ways for parents to have open dialogues with their children, the importance of family quality time and more. In all the sessions, if parents asked questions or focused on problems, I tried to use a Solution Focused dialogue to refocus their attention to solutions.

Another part of our community and parent education includes our *PSI Life Magazine*. It is published three times a year and the counsellors have a featured article in each edition. One article I wrote focused on using Solution Focused tools in parenting. In the article, I addressed four main tools or strategies which could be used, with examples of their use in a variety of parenting situations. The tools were:

- Helping their child to verbalise their hope and what it would like if it was achieved
- Helping their child to identify times they had accomplished their hope before and how they did that
- Using scales to help their child to identify where they are, what they are already doing well and what they could do to make things better
- Avoiding negative self-talk by refocusing their child on their strengths

The last form of parent education is through personal meetings. I often had parents come in and ask for advice on speaking with their children, asking whether their child was "normal" and what they could do to "fix" their child. They came in with the idea that I was an expert and could magically solve their concerns. Since my training, I often deferred to Solution Focused strategies when speaking with parents and discussed various strategies they might try with their student. This stopped me from being the expert in their eyes and allowed parents to see that they and their children were their own experts. Sometimes I gave copies of my "SF Parenting Tools" article to parents and we discussed it together, looking at the strategies they felt comfortable with or thought might be useful. Parents reported back to me that scales were very useful and that they enjoyed the conversations with their children in which they focused on the times their child had done what they (the parent) had hoped to see. They shared that these strategies had allowed for more open and positive communication with their child and more pleasant interactions.

During the development and implementation of new programmes

All schools that I have worked at have implemented new programmes, but there isn't always support from staff members or "follow through" by administration. In a recent school, the implemented programmes included one for literacy, math, a child protection curriculum and a student self-regulation programme. The self-regulation programme I have worked with is called the "Zones of Regulation" and was created by Leah M. Kuypers. The programme's main focus has been helping students to recognise their emotions and others' emotions. The emotions are classified into four colour categories which represent a low state of alertness, ideal state of alertness, heightened state of alertness and an extreme heightened state of alertness (Kuypers, 2011). Once students have identified their state, they have a variety of tools and strategies they use to help self-regulate and to return to the ideal state of alertness.

During the implementation of this in one school, we had an assembly for students, lessons in the classrooms, a bulletin board display with the information, a pamphlet for parents, and a presentation to parents during one of the "Parent Education Tuesdays". In addition, I worked with teachers to use the language and tools in their classroom. Recently, I needed to address staff in a faculty meeting about the programme and how the implementation has progressed. I didn't want it to be a lecture about what they needed to do, but more of a Solution Focused conversation about where we were and where we wanted to go as a school. I took an idea from Linda Metcalf's book *Counseling Towards Solutions* and started with a Solution Focused self-reflection form which the individual staff members completed (Metcalf, 2008). The form asked the following:

- What have you done well when it comes to "zones of regulation" and self-regulation?
- How have you done that or how do you do that?
- What would others describe as your most valuable qualities, specifically around zones of regulation and self-regulation?
- How would you like to have your use of zones of regulation and self-regulation be perceived by staff and students?
- On a scale of 0–10 how would you rate your current use of zones of regulation, where would you like to be in a month, in two months, by the end of the year?
- Based on how you have implemented new ideas before, how will you do this and what would others see that tells you and them that you have moved up to where you want to be?

This self-reflection sheet then led into a discussion and sharing of ideas. It really helped to open everyone's minds to their own personal expertise and how they could use that expertise to move forward with the programme. I was no longer seen as the expert on how to implement this in their class; instead, they could identify how they could make it work with the individual structure of their own class. They no longer thought of it as a prescribed programme where they had to follow certain steps, but something about which they could be creative and make work drawing on their own personal educational philosophy.

Adding a visual and interactive element to individual and group sessions

One challenge I originally faced was making the Solution Focused approach more interactive to address the younger students I worked with, the English language learners, and also the high number of students with difficulty focusing for long periods of time. I have accomplished an interactive active approach through an interactive scale, utilising my sensory walk in my office with Solution Focused lists and visualizing a path to move forward, and incorporating games such as "Uno".

The interactive scale in my office was made with Velcro that has a sticky back. I placed two strips of Velcro parallel to each other on my wall. On the one strip are numbers with a Velcro back and the other strip has tags to represent the student, teacher, parents and siblings. Students can move those tags along the scale as questions are asked. I also created plates with Velcro backs and squares with Velcro backs. These could replace the numbers and students could create their own scales based on the foods, games, toys or other items in a rank order.

I also have a sensory path in my office for students to come and use when they need a break or to relieve stress. The sensory path is colourful and is stuck to my floor. It includes letters and numbers in a hopscotch format, foot prints in various directions for the students to jump on, hand prints on the wall to indicate wall push ups and other decals for lunges, touching toes and star jumps. The sensory path is meant to engage the students' senses in an active fashion. I have started to utilise this in individual Solution Focused sessions with students. The end of the path represents their hope and as we go along the path, they answer list questions, scales questions, or questions about the preferred future. I found that when the student is active and moving, they tend to more easily be able to share their actual thoughts. They are less concerned with what they think they should say and just say what comes to their mind. I have utilised games such as "Uno" in a similar fashion. "Uno" has worked very well when I am trying to help the students create lists. As they placed a number down, they add that number of things to the list, and as I placed a number down I will add that number of things to a list I have created. It has become a challenge as to who will have the most items on their list by the end of the game.

Overall, the Solution Focused approach has been valuable not only in my counselling sessions but also in my other day-to-day work. Every time I do something, I think how I could make it more Solution Focused. Even with, for example, the forms of the referral process, or the strategies for parent education, I continue to think about their development and adaptation, depending on the needs of the school and my practice. I believe the Solution Focused approach lends itself to be adaptable to daily situations and makes daily interactions more palatable for all involved.

References

Kuypers, L. M. (2011). *Zones of Regulation: A Curriculum Designed to Foster Self-Regulation and Emotional Control*. Santa Clara, CA: Thinking Social Publishing.

Metcalf, L. (2008). *Counseling Toward Solutions: A Practical Solution-Focused Program for Working with Students, Teachers, and Parents*. San Francisco, CA: Jossey-Bass.

Sabella, R. (2014). *Solution Focused Brief Counseling: From Problem Solver to Solution Seeker*. Fort Meyers, FL: Florida Gulf Coast University.

Chapter 8

The butterfly effect

Elliott E. Connie

When asked to write a chapter for this book, I thought long and hard about how to share my thoughts on the Solution Focused approach and the way I am thinking about this way of working these days. Just as with anyone who does anything for a long period of time, throughout my career my thoughts about Solution Focused Brief Therapy have evolved, and it is my hope that in these pages I can share my current thoughts as well as how I arrived at this current way of thinking. I expect this to be a bit of a challenge for me, both because this will be my first time sharing some of these thoughts and also because sharing such material makes me feel a bit vulnerable.

For this journey, I would like to start all the way back at the beginning. Though I have been fortunate enough to have had some of the best professional mentors and teachers in the field of Solution Focused Brief Therapy, my very first lesson occurred long before I ever thought of being a psychotherapist. In fact, it was the way back in the third grade.

For whatever reason, I still remember that day as if it were yesterday; it was the day we studied the life cycle of the monarch butterfly. I remember the teacher announcing to the class that the next day this would be the topic we were going to study for the next several weeks. I was so excited because, just as I am now, I loved anything related to animal life and was thrilled that we would spend the next few weeks in science class focused on butterflies. Prior to this, I had not given much thought to butterflies, except for seeing them flying around as my friends when I played outside, so this opportunity to learn a bit more about the life of this beautiful creature was new to me.

At this time in my life, I was not someone who loved school or excelled at it, but the next day I couldn't wait to get to school. This is the first time I remember feeling that way, thankfully not the last. On this day, the thing that had me so excited was that I knew that this was the day that our science class was to start the epic learning about the monarch butterfly. Up to this point in this science class we had spent most of our time doing different kinds of experiments and learning about elements, but this would be the first time we would spend time focused on something I was interested in, an animal and everything about its life cycle. Little did I know, this experience would be so much more than I could imagine and the lessons I would learn over the next few weeks would stick with me for the rest of my life. They would be lessons that would guide my professional work for many years to come.

When I arrived at my class on that day, I discovered that each student had a Styrofoam cup filled with dirt with a caterpillar in it. The scene was disgusting, quite gross. I didn't even want it on my desk. I stared at this hairy squishy glob, crawling around the cup as the teacher taught us about how the butterfly actually began its life as a caterpillar. I could not understand how something as beautiful as the monarch butterfly started its life as such an ugly creature. If I hadn't known otherwise, it would have been easy for me to see this creature just as it was and nothing more. I would have missed the fact that locked within the caterpillar which I could see was a beautiful butterfly which I could not. It was so invisible to me that even when my teacher explained it, I did not believe it. I was only convinced once I watched a video that explained the process. I realized the trick to understanding the life cycle of the monarch butterfly was that I had to learn to see potential and to look beyond what my eyes could see.

Though I have had some of the best teachers in the world guide me in my learning of the Solution Focused approach, it was this lesson I received in the third grade that prepared me to view people as caterpillars waiting to burst into the world as beautiful butterflies.

You see, the techniques and common questions of the Solution Focused approach are important, and learning them is the easy part. The hard skill of this approach is knowing how to ask questions that are more likely to lead toward change. This is the true skill of the Solution Focused approach and, strangely enough, I think you can learn that lesson from the life cycle of the butterfly far more efficiently than it can be learned from any text about this way of working. I want to take you deeper, I want to take you into a realm of this approach that is not often discussed, I want to get to the core of the helping profession. The way we view our clients has a significant impact on the way we talk to them and how clients respond to therapy.

Here's an example of this idea in action. Not too long ago, I saw a client who came to therapy with his parents, who were desperate for help. Their son, the youngest child in their family, was a 10-year-old boy who was really struggling with anxiety and depression. He was having significant behavioral issues at home as well as at school, and his parents described him as "the problem" in the family. Their son, who I'll refer to as Joe, was completely unlike his older siblings, who happened to be well behaved children who were also successful students in school and followed all of the rules in the home. It was clear to me that the parents blamed the child, or at least the child's behaviors, for all of the issues that had been taking place in the family. The child's behavior sounded awful, and the way he treated the others in the family sounded awful. Joe had been kicked out of several schools due to his behaviors. Over the past few years, the parents had tried several things to address Joe's behavioral issues, including therapy. None of them had led toward change, the parents were clearly frustrated, and their son's behavior was clearly the issue. The way the parents described Joe, it was very easy to view him as "the problem" and treat him accordingly. However, when using the Solution Focused approach, we must not allow ourselves to fall into this trap. We must always remember that this is just a child, a young person who is trying his best to get on with life in a better way. We have to remember that Joe wants something, and if we can ask meaningful questions that are connected to what Joe wants his chances of success go up. We have to remember that Joe wants to be better, Joe is a future butterfly. To view Joe in any other way would make the task of helping him become more challenging, more complicated, more likely to fail.

Think about this in another context. Imagine you were a master chef, the kind of chef who runs successful restaurants and can cook just about anything masterfully. Many people seek you out to taste your delicious food and occasionally for you to teach your culinary skills. Imagine that you were hired to teach someone how to make a complicated dish and before you began your lesson someone explained all of the reasons your student would struggle to learn to cook the meal you are going to be teaching them. What would happen to the way you taught that day? How would the words you were to use on that day be impacted? If you allowed yourself to believe that learning would be hard for your student, then everything about the way you interacted with your student would be different. This is the very essence of the butterfly effect, maintaining the belief that the people that you meet with are budding butterflies, even though you may be meeting them as a caterpillar or perhaps even in a cocoon. It's about treating people as if growth and change are inevitable. I do understand that there is no guarantee that positive change will occur from every therapy session or cooking class, but I am advocating for this stance because it makes change more likely and ensures that the professional keeps the mindset that is needed.

As another example, I recently saw a video on YouTube that featured a former Navy SEAL and now extreme distance runner, David Goggins, explaining that what gets him through tough physical challenges is the belief that he is the "baddest man on the planet". When the interviewer asked him whether he actually believes that is the truth, Goggins explained that it doesn't matter whether it's true. He said that what matters is that he has to believe it in the moment, so that he can continue to endure the struggle involved with extreme distance running.

Let's apply this thinking to Joe and his family. If I were to allow myself to think of Joe through the lens of the problem as the parents described, then my job as helper becomes more challenging, just as teaching someone to cook would be a challenge if you didn't believe they could do it. The same is true for David Goggins, who would have a much harder time completing an extreme distance run if he viewed himself as anything less than capable. This is equally true for Joe and his family; it is crucial that I view them through the lens of capabilities and doing so will inevitably impact the way I interact with the client.

In the Solution Focused approach, the very task is to establish a desired outcome for the work, most often by asking "what are your best hopes from this session?" (Iveson et al., 2012). This question can only be asked if I first believe that the client has hope for change in the future and second if I believe the client has the capacities to achieve their hoped-for future. For this reason, it is important that a professional using this approach attends to the way they show up in the session as well having mastery of a particular approach.

When asked about his best hopes, Joe explained that he would like to get his anger under control and be a better student in school. He explained that he did not know why he behaved the way he did and that he really wanted to behave differently. Through the conversation, he clarified that he wanted to be happy instead of angry and wanted to make his parents proud of his behaviors at school. It can be easy to remember that Joe has been kicked out of multiple schools for explosive anger already as well as having many anger outbursts at home and, as a result, it can be easy to doubt his ability to achieve his desired outcome. That urge must be resisted. My first job is to believe that what the client hopes for is achievable so that I can do my job of asking about the presence of what is hoped for.

The next job in the session where the professional is using the Solution Focused approach is to ask the client to describe a world where the hoped-for outcome has become the reality (Iveson et al., 2012). In this case, working with Joe, I asked him to suppose he had woken up on a day when he was happy and completely capable of making his parents proud with his conduct at school. The rest of the session was made up of follow up questions to help Joe describe the changes that he would like to experience in his life, in as much detail as possible. He described what he would notice and what his parents would notice. He also described what his siblings would notice as well as what his friends would notice at school. Literally every detail was asked about, so it could be a part of the client's future picture to compile as complete a picture as possible. The reason this is important is that the details matter, and the professional has no way of knowing which detail will make a difference in unlocking the client's ability to change. So, I asked Joe about every detail possible that would occur on a day when he woke up and his desired outcome was now his reality.

By the end of the session, Joe had a bit of a glow in his eyes from describing such a world. Though there is no way to ever know whether the client is going to make changes once the session ends, there does seem to be a common positive experience from engaging in conversations where you are invited to describe the best of yourself making desired changes in your life.

Two weeks later, when Joe and his parents returned for the follow up session, it was immediately clear that something had changed in the client's life. The parents explained that it was as if they had a different child. He had been "perfect" in school and behaving very well at home. Joe was getting along with his siblings, completing his chores, and more. When asked what has led to such changes, he simply said, "it just seemed like my parents started believing in me".

The parents explained that they realized that they had allowed the trials from the past years to impact how they viewed Joe, and watching him respond to my questions in the first session reminded them how important it was that they believe in him always. As it turned out, that was exactly what Joe needed, even though he didn't himself realize it.

In moments like this I cannot help but think about that lesson I learned all the way back in the third grade. I cannot help but think about the life cycle of the monarch butterfly and how this beautiful and powerful creature starts its life as neither beautiful nor strong. In spite of that, the beauty is in there the whole time just waiting for the conditions to be right for those traits to flourish. Imagine if we are able to treat all of our clients and everyone else we meet in such a way. What a world this would be.

Reference

Iveson, C., George, E., & Ratner, H. (2012). *Brief Coaching: A Solution Focused Approach.* London: Routledge.

Chapter 9

Building co-operation and engagement with adolescents

Evan George

When Chris Iveson, Harvey Ratner and I came across Solution Focused Brief Therapy (SFBT) in 1987, we were working in an NHS Mental Health Clinic in North-West London, and it is undoubtedly the case that within a very short time we had fallen in love with – indeed if the truth be told, we had become somewhat obsessed with – the approach. We set up a clinical workshop to help us to learn the model, and we recorded our work and reviewed sessions over and over; we started, somewhat presumptuously perhaps, teaching the approach to other professionals. We were receiving visitors who were coming from far and wide to observe what we were doing and, within three years, we had written and published our first book (George et al., 1990). The reasons for this developing and abiding passion were various: clients seemed to enjoy sessions, the approach did not waste clients' time, clients experienced the work as 'empowering' and sometimes commented on this, there were no exclusion criteria and so we would work with whomsoever was referred with equal optimism and enthusiasm, and we found ourselves enjoying our work and liking our clients even more than before.

However, there was one additional factor which was of particular importance in drawing us to the Solution Focused (SF) approach. In 1987 Chris, Harvey and I were all working with a significant number of so-called 'mandated' clients, people who arrived at the clinic consequent upon considerable pressure often expressed in the form of 'unless you make changes you are unlikely to get your children back from care'. As Berg and de Jong (2001) indicate, 'mandated' clients are typically viewed as 'difficult', 'uncooperative', 'hostile' and reluctant to engage, and yet as we became increasingly competent in the Solution Focused approach we noticed that our 'mandated' clients engaged with us just as well as our so-called 'voluntary' clients. SFBT really did seem to have the potential to help us to find a way of working co-operatively with clients who in the past might have been written off as 'resistant', as 'unmotivated' and in summary as reluctant to change. Now it is clearly not the case that all adolescents referred to us are either 'mandated' or 'reluctant'; however, it probably is true that there are relatively few adolescents who initiate the contact with a helping professional themselves, however much they may have gone online to 'Google' their 'condition'. The initiative to refer in most cases comes from an adult in the young person's life, an adult who has become concerned about the young person, and thus many if not most adolescents arrive feeling somewhat criticised in their life choices, criticised in their ways of living, feeling that the adult world is disapproving and wishing to get them to change. The connection with the 'mandated' client therefore seems clear. This chapter will seek to explore what SFBT does and what SF practitioners can do that is associated with engagement and co-operation with adolescents.

The concept of 'co-operating' is built into the very foundations of SFBT. In 1982, Steve de Shazer proposed that every client 'shows a unique way of attempting to cooperate' and that whatever the client does can be read as an attempt to co-operate. This idea has been roughly translated by practitioners into the assumption that whatever clients are doing is the best that they can do in this moment and that therefore it is the therapist's job to 'cooperate with the (client's) way', as de Shazer put it (de Shazer, 1982, pp. 9–10), or more generally to co-operate with this 'best that clients can do'. Clearly adopting these assumptions is a clinical choice, they may or may not be true, but to choose to adopt them has therapeutic consequences, just as the choice to assume that clients are resistant and do not want to change will impact on the way that we connect with our clients. These assumptions feed into a stance, a position that we choose to take in relation to our clients, and this position is fundamental in facilitating the client's engagement in the process. Clearly, if we are assuming that whatever the client is doing is the best they can do, then we are neither evaluating nor judging their actions, which in itself seems to be an unusual, and welcome, experience for many adolescents.

There are a number of other chosen assumptions that influence the adolescent's experience of the SF practitioner. The SF practitioner chooses to assume that anyone who is prepared to sit with us, let alone talk with us, does so for a good reason, that they want something. Young people, indeed all clients whatever their age, are assumed to be motivated for something. The only challenge for the SF practitioner is to ask good enough questions to discover what exactly it might be that the young person is motivated towards. Finding out what the young person wants from us and being persistent in this process makes a difference. It is not unusual, and indeed it is rather sensible, for adolescents to take their time working out whether we are trustworthy and, during this time, giving relatively restricted answers that will not represent hostages to fortune which could subsequently be used against them. The answer that is particularly useful to any adolescent during this assessment process, when the adolescent is assessing whether we are people of good will towards them or not, is 'I don't know'. Since this checking out period often coincides with the point when the SF practitioner is trying to elicit a focus for the work, this can result in a somewhat awkward conversation.

'So what are your best hopes from our talking together?'
'I don't know'.
'So, what do you think might make this useful to you?'
'I don't know'.

'Take your time – have a think – what are you hoping that our talking could lead towards that would be good for you?'

'I don't know'.

'Of course – it is not an easy question – if our talking could end up being of use to you – in some way – what tiny changes might you see that could tell you that this had not be a waste of your time, maybe, perhaps?'

'I don't know'.

At this point, the SF worker has a choice either to persist, which might of course begin to feel oppressive to the young person, or to track back through the referral 'how come you are here?', which risks leaving the young person feeling criticised, or to explain, to be transparent, and this transparency often seems to make a difference.

'I am sorry that I am going on and on (apologising is almost always a good thing to do), it is just that I am trying to find out what you want, since if I don't know what you want it is going to be so difficult for me to try and get this right for you – so how could you know that our talking together had ended up being useful to you?'

Experiencing a worker, an adult, trying so hard to find out what the young person wants, trying so hard to get the conversation right for the young person, is again both unusual and welcome. Adolescents typically find themselves being required to fit into the expectations of the adult world, but naturally when the work is centred on what the young person wants, their own best hopes, the young person is more likely to engage. As Peter Senge puts it, 'People don't resist change. They resist **being** changed' (Senge, 2000), and adolescents are no different.

Having established what is wanted, the SF practitioner will, if at all possible, take it seriously, even when what is wanted does not coincide with the referrer's wishes. Let us imagine a young person who, after a self-protective period of 'I don't knows' finally says 'I just want the staff to stop picking on me'. This is always an interesting moment, as the young person watches us closely to see how we will respond. Are we indeed different or will we just blame the young person by asking 'so what do you do to get them to pick on you?' or more subtly 'so what would you have to do differently to stop them picking on you?' The SF practitioner of course asks neither of these questions, instead remaining right alongside the young person. We do not step away from the young person and ally ourselves with the adult professionals in the young person's life by undermining the young person's framing with an innocuous sounding but insidious 'you feel people are picking on you'. Instead we ask, 'imagine you go to school tomorrow, and people are not picking on you, what is the very first thing that you will notice?' The SF practitioner accepts the adolescent's answer, accepts the young person's 'best hopes' (George et al., 1999), without attempting to modify them, and invites the young person to describe the life that contains the desired outcome. As Steve de Shazer writes, 'The client's answer needs to be accepted fully and literally – this is where the art of the approach comes into things' (de Shazer, 1997).

There are times when even the young people with whom we are sitting recognise that they might have to 'fit in' with the adult world's expectations, so when we ask 'imagine you go to school tomorrow and people are not picking on you, what's the very first thing that you will notice?', the young person answers by saying 'yes, but they've said I'm not going back into school until I apologise for what I said'. The risk for the worker at this point is that we view the world through adult eyes, accept the necessity for an apology, and rush ahead, leaving the young person way behind; after all, education is important, as we adults all know, and the young person therefore clearly needs to apologise. However, the young person may well not have reached this point of either recognition or agreement, so if we were to ask, as many well-meaning professionals might, 'OK so how are you going to do that – to apologise', the young person, feeling pressured to apologise, responds with 'I won't apologise to him until he apologises to me for what he said'. The question 'OK so how are you going to do that?' implies and accepts the necessity for the apology, leap-frogging in the process the young person's decision and leaving the young person feeling disempowered. So an alternative response seems to open more possibilities:

'Yes but they have said that I can't go back in to school until I apologise for what I said'.

'That's really difficult – so the school wants you to apologise but you are still really angry and upset by what he said to you and by the way that he said it, and the school has said that you can't go back unless you do apologise. How are you going to decide what to do?'

Going slow centralises young people and their own decision-making processes and acknowledges the difficult situation within which they find themselves. This allows the young person to say, at some point, perhaps after discussion of the pros and cons for the decision:

'I'm just going to have to do it'.

The young person, their autonomy having been respected, has arrived at a relatively independent conclusion. At this point we can ask:

'So if you did decide to apologise, difficult though that may be, how would you know that you were doing it in a way that was acceptable to the school and also OK for you?'

Again, the SF worker resists the urge to rush ahead, acknowledges the difficulty, centralises the young person's own decision making – 'if you did decide' – and frames the question in an inclusive way 'acceptable to the school and also OK for you'. These inclusive framings make a difference, highlighting the element of control that the young person has, even in a context where they can feel constrained or compelled. Yasmin Ajmal, working in a school setting, typically found a way of recognising young people's choices by asking 'balance' questions: 'how will you know that you are getting the balance right between showing yourself a bit and doing it in a way that the school can accept?' Young people are likely to notice and to appreciate the interpersonal delicacy that we show when we ask these questions that allow them to save face.

We have already noted that very often young people sitting with professional adults are already feeling much criticised, and when people feel criticised they typically respond to criticism with self-protective behaviours, either denial – 'I don't do it' – or minimisation – 'I don't do it much – my friends do it much more than me' – or blame re-allocation– 'I do do it but it is not my fault'. So, when young people arrive often having already been identified as engaged in cutting or substance use or eating unhealthily, they are primed to self-protect since after all the pattern is a familiar one: adults criticise, and young people argue back. So if we imagine a young person referring to cutting themselves, the SF practitioner, who chooses to assume competence in all their clients, can inquire 'I guess that you must have a good reason for doing that?' This response is an interesting one. It not infrequently surprises the young person and, rather than the habitual self-protective response, can sometimes lead to 'no not really', which then allows us to ask 'so is this something that you would like to change?' If the young person assents to change, we can ask 'so if you were to do something different about (cutting) what difference are you hoping that this would make in your life?' Alternatively, of course, the young person may acknowledge the usefulness, 'cutting helps me to calm myself', a not infrequent response, and this allows us to ask 'if you had another way of calming yourself without cutting would that be good for you?' Although initially sceptical that anything else would work as well as cutting, if we politely and gently persist, 'if it could, maybe, perhaps', and the young person accepts the idea that it might be good, then we have opened a pathway to an alternative describing of a future of calm without cutting. The key difference is choosing to see competence 'you must have a good reason', rather than the incompetence evidenced in the sneaky thought 'there's something wrong with this young person'. The way that we think really does make a difference.

SFBT embodies a stance towards young people, a position, a way of thinking about them that translates, as we have seen, into the way that we talk, and this stance turns up in numerous more small ways.

1   Treating young people like partners in the process. We can demonstrate this respectful stance by asking permission: 'would it be OK if I ask you some questions about this?' and lots of 'thank yous'. Young people seem to appreciate this even more than adults, perhaps because they are more used to being treated as 'conscripts' in therapy rather than 'volunteers'.
2   Eliciting feedback. We can ask young people about the relevance and the usefulness of what we are doing by asking simple questions: 'is this making sense?' or 'are we talking about the right things?' or 'what if anything has been of use to you in this conversation that we have been having today?' or 'has anything been left out today – is there anything that you had in mind to say today that I have not given you the opportunity to say?'
3   Giving control of the content as much as we can to the young person. For example, we can say 'there is no need for you to answer any questions that you would prefer not to answer – you are in control of what you tell me'.

4 Giving control of who attends meetings to the young person, asking them whether they would like to bring a friend to the next meeting. As it happens, friends tend to be really useful in sessions since friends are often not embroiled in the same argument that a young person may currently be having with his or her parent, foster-carer, social worker or school. Friends really do seem to believe that going to school, studying and having good enough relationships with parents are all sensible things to do and their view-point can be explored, neutrally of course, during the course of the session. What a friend thinks can often be more influential than the view of critical, although of course well-meaning, adults.
5 Demonstrating our good faith. While sitting with young people, taking particular care to tune our listening constructively makes a difference. Listening for the young person's strengths and skills and competences and capacities, their resources and abilities, all those things that could give us the idea that the young person will be successful in moving forward, all feeds into our voice tone, our body posture and our eye contact and into the framing of our questions. As young people notice the external manifestations of our belief and trust in them, engagement and co-operation become more likely.

Conclusions

SFBT has a particular capacity for engaging reluctant attenders, and this is frequently true of adolescents. SFBT embodies a stance towards the people with whom we work, a stance that is communicated through all the questions that we ask. SFBT invites clients, including adolescents, to determine the direction of the work. SFBT takes what clients want, including adolescents, seriously. SFBT assumes competence in the client, including adolescents, choosing to assume that people have good reasons for doing what they do. SFBT practitioners frame young people as decision-makers, rather than decision-takers who merely accept the decisions that others have made about them. SFBT practitioners actively support young people in saving face in their worlds, worlds where they often find themselves the targets of the hopes, expectations and demands of others while they are trying to find their own best ways of managing their lives. SFBT practitioners take young people seriously and young people both notice it and appreciate it when we do!

References

Berg, I. K., & de Jong, P. (2001, October). Co-Constructing Cooperation with Mandated Clients. *Social Work*, 46(4).

de Shazer, S. (1982). *Patterns of Brief Family Therapy: An Ecosystemic Approach*. New York: The Guildford Press.

de Shazer, S. (1997). Radical Acceptance (comment on Giorlando & Schilling). *Families, Systems, & Health*, 15, 375–378.

George, E., Iveson, C., & Ratner, H. (1990, 1999). *Problem to Solution: Brief Therapy with Individuals and Families*, revised and expand edition. London: BT Press.

Senge, P. (2000). *The Art and Practice of the Learning Organization*. New York: Doubleday.

Chapter 10

Solution Focused practices in the assessment of learning problems
Panning for gold

Jeff Chang and Don Braun

Children and adolescents who are seen as not doing well in school often come to the attention of counsellors and coaches. Concerned, well-meaning parents and teachers may speculate about whether the student may have a "learning disability" or some other diagnosable problem that tells them why the student (in some normative sense) is not learning at the typical rate or in the usual way. Parents and teachers may request special education services, and many school jurisdictions require an assessment of a student's cognitive abilities (sometimes called *cognitive assessment* or *intellectual assessment*, but more inclusively called a *psychoeducational assessment* [our preferred term]) to support an *individual education plan* describing the special education services or accommodations to be provided. Some jurisdictions require a diagnosis from the *Diagnostic and Statistical Manual of the American Psychiatric Association* (APA), 5th edition (DSM-5; APA, 2013) or the International Classification of Diseases, 11th edition (ICD-11; World Health Organization, 2018) to assess eligibility for special education. A discussion about the western neo-liberal commodified approach to education that does not embrace diversity (Collins, 2019; Gergen, 1991; Hanushek, 1986) and the classification of individuals that springs from it (APA, 2013) is outside the scope of this chapter. Suffice it to say that in the western world, these assessment practices are, for better or for worse, well-established.

Using population-based norms to identify deficits and their potential causes, possibly leading to a diagnosis, appears to run counter to Solution Focused (SF) thinking. However, we (a school psychologist who has studied Solution Focused Brief Therapy [SFBT] and a counselling psychologist and SF trainer with assessment experience) have found that SF practices can help engage students, parents, and teachers; orient practitioners to what people are doing that works; and increase engagement, optimism, and accountability in children and youth, parents, and teachers. In this chapter, we will describe psychoeducational assessment practices; provide a Solution Focused framework for "data collection" in an assessment interview; provide an approach to standardised assessment that keeps an ear open for *what works*; describe how to discuss assessment results with students, parents, and teachers to elicit their expertise in supporting successful learning; and present a framework for developing and making realistic recommendations that are likely to be implemented.

Psychoeducational assessment

The practice of assessing and classifying cognitive abilities was originally driven by governmental needs, which is largely still the case to this day. Alfred Binet, the French minister of education, and his colleague, Theodore Simon, developed the first intelligence test, the Binet-Simon scale (Binet & Simon, 1905), to assess children with intellectual disabilities. The revised version, the Stanford-Binet (Roid, 2003), was considered the "gold standard" in cognitive assessment for several decades. Robert Yerkes developed two group intelligence tests for the United States Army, the Army Alpha and Army Beta (Waters, 1997), to screen World War I recruits.

There are well-known examples of abuses of so-called intelligence testing (Gould, 1981), in particular its role in systemically racist immigration policy (Snyderman & Herrnstein, 1983), involuntary sterilization of persons with intellectual disabilities (Grekul et al., 2004), and culturally inappropriate practice (Ford, 2004; Serpell & Haynes, 2004). Discriminatory assessment practices within Indigenous communities is a topic garnering considerable attention in North America (Canadian Psychological Association, 2018). Despite historical abuses, contemporary psychoeducational assessment provides useful information by giving a complex picture of the learner's skills and abilities. Current models for human intelligence recognise that cognitive ability is actually a complex collection of capacities. The widely utilised Cattell-Horn-Carroll theory, for example, contains at least 11 broad abilities, each with distinct components (Schneider & McGrew, 2018).

Typically, a psychoeducational assessment starts with interviewing parents, teachers, and/or the young person. A psychologist may do a classroom observation. Minimally, psychologists administer a test of cognitive abilities (in common parlance, but incompletely called an "intelligence test" [e.g., Kaufman & Kaufman, 2018; Roid, 2003; Wechsler, 2014]) and a test of academic achievement (specific academic skills, e.g., Wechsler, 2009a) to examine and compare cognitive capacities with domain-specific academic development. Other tests summarise teachers', parents', and/or the child's/youth's reports of emotional well-being, attention/hyperactivity, and behavior (e.g., Conner, 2008; Reynolds & Kamphaus, 2015). Other tests may seek to measure visual-motor integration (responding or reproducing visual information with a fine-motor response such as drawing or printing) (Beery et al., 2010), memory (Cohen, 1997; Wechsler, 2009b), neurocognitive function (Korkman et al., 2007), or language development (Newcomer & Hammill, 2019). The result is a detailed profile of the student's strengths and weaknesses in learning, enabling the psychologist to develop a comprehensive set of recommendations that leverage the student's strengths and remediate and/or find "workarounds" for weaknesses.

Solution Focused practices in psychoeducational assessment

Solution Focused practitioners tend to eschew a norm-referenced approach to problems. We prefer to focus on clients' preferred outcomes and "what works," as opposed to focusing much on the origins of problems or considering diagnoses. How can SF practices enhance the endeavor of psychoeducational assessment? We think that SF ideas can help from beginning to end.

Clarifying the referral questions

When parents or teachers request a psychoeducational assessment, they typically point to learning problems of some sort. Referral forms inevitably contain a great deal of problem description and place strengths or skills in second place. Psychoeducational assessments are often a search for causes of problems. For example: "Why does Keenan experience so many problems learning to read, write, or execute math calculations?" or "Does Amelia have ADHD or a behaviour disorder?" SF-informed thinking can transform these problem statements into descriptions of preferred outcomes and hypothetical solutions. For example, an SF-informed psychologist could transform these problem-focused questions into, "How can Ken experience maximum success with reading, writing, math calculations? How will we know that he is moving in the right direction?" or "How can we support Ella to maintain attention and experience positive interactions and relationships at school? What's the very first thing we'll notice when that starts to happen?" An SF-informed psychologist might review the referral request to orient themselves to how they might frame questions when they interview parents and teachers. For an SF psychologist, referral questions will naturally develop into inquiries about strengths and ways to circumvent problems and first signs of change. This way we can adapt and translate original referral questions to ones that enable the child and their adult supporters to notice change.

History detectives

An SF school psychologist inquires about the history of the individual being assessed. Informed by SF ideas, they will ask about some different aspects of history and do it differently than usual.

What we ask about

Interviewing clients for their history and background information can provide openings to incorporate a Solution Focused perspective into the assessment process. Traditionally, a school psychologist seeks information about the onset and history of problems, familial factors that might be associated with difficulties the young person experiences, and the effect of past interventions and services (Sattler & Hoeg, 2006). Parents seeking a psychoeducational assessment tend to be, understandably, problem-focused. They can usually describe the history of their child's cognitive, academic, and social/emotional problems in great detail, but often feel helpless about how to help.

An SF-informed school psychologist, while incorporating historical data, will invite a search for exceptions (de Jong & Berg, 2013) or at least irregularities in the problem (O'Hanlon & Weiner-Davis, 2004). Past instances of relative success are noteworthy. An SF approach to *history-taking* may actually be *history-making*, inviting recall of past exceptions and the circumstances that surrounded them. This can invite young people, parents, teachers, and administrators to think differently about the problem-saturated past. Whether we are doing therapy or assessment, clients, parents, or teachers are likely to focus on problems, but by using SF skills, we can elicit solution-based historical narratives. For example, scaling questions about the success of attempted remediation in school can help discover promising instructional strategies, asking for experiences with a favorite teacher provides insight into how to tap hidden resilience, and the miracle question provides powerful information about the entire direction of an assessment. We apply the same SF principles to file information and the review of previous reports. An SF school psychologist pays as much attention to high report card marks, gaps in reports of problems, and successful interventions as to the development of academic problems and psychopathology.

History-taking includes the present. We inquire about current exceptions to the difficulties the child is experiencing, when things seem to be better now, and strategies that help or even bring partial relief or temporary solutions. For example, in a referral for a student demonstrating impulsivity and verbal aggression, an SF psychologist might explore how the student is able to avoid enacting physical aggression. If a student acts out to damage property, we might ask how he is able to avoid injuring people. In almost every academic problem, some learning has taken place, providing clues into successful approaches. Students are commonly referred for assessment when experiencing problems with basic math facts, calculation speed, or particular operations. Almost all of these students have some understanding of math, be it their ability to name quantities or count. Their learning successes provide invaluable information about the way forward.

Mainstream school psychologists are becoming increasingly aware of the need for person-centred, strengths-based psychoeducational assessment (Climie & Henley, 2016). Incorporating a Solution Focused approach to historical interviews and background research sets the tone for a hopeful, personalized, positive, and empowering assessment experience. This is not to suggest that it is unnecessary to ask about family history of learning problems, the child's history of health conditions that could affect neurological functioning, or adverse childhood experiences, but this should be balanced with curiosity about the child's and family's history of solutions.

How we ask

It is our experience that they way we ask questions is as important as the questions themselves. Inquiring in a curious SF way, focusing on past and present real-life exceptions and potential future solutions, helps parents and children feel heard and understood. Listening in this way assists us to understand their motivations and desires. It is also important to listen carefully to what stakeholders are willing and able to do – what is doable and practical. We listen carefully to what the clients are *customers* for (de Shazer, 1988). As we are mindful of clients' motivations, desires, and receptivity for change, we can incorporate these into the written report. While SFBT is sometimes misunderstood as programmatic, the art resides in listening for openings (Chang, 2019) – what clients value and already know how to do.

Testing sessions

Testing sessions are, arguably, the most important arena in which to apply an SF approach. The hopefulness inherent in SF thinking may be contagious to clients, parents, and stakeholders. An SF practitioner, practising skillfully, displays an ethic of genuine care that continues throughout the administration of psychological tests.

SF practice, which emphasizes curiosity and prioritizing *what the client wants* supports practitioners to be engaging, relational, friendly, and kind, without compromising the reliability and validity of standardized tests. It is critical that the practitioner's communication style and non-verbal presentation match the values of SF practice. This involves determining the clients' intent and purposefully adjusting practices to reflect this intent. This past year, our referrals have included many preschool children whose parents wish to know whether their children are eligible for programming in a school for the "gifted." The parents' intent is to gather accurate psychometric data to support children's school applications which reflect their children's capabilities. On the other hand, their child's intent may be to do nothing more than play. To meet the intent of the parents, it is also necessary to meet the intent of the child, which usually means interspersing play and fun times between segments of testing.

Testing can identify strengths, both relative to the young person's other skills and/or abilities or relative to the population of his or her age mates. This can allow us to put an exclamation mark beside strengths that may escape the notice of young people, parents, and other stakeholders. Assuming a stance of curiosity enhances rapport and helps position the practitioner as a caring and accessible resource. Recently, Don supported a young person in Grade 5 experiencing reading, writing, and numeracy problems and social isolation. Through curious exploration, we discovered that the client could draw freehand maps of North America and the world with no visual reference. By navigating through Google Earth, he could locate his grandmother's rural home and many places he had been. Discovering this strength was tremendously validating for him and informative for his teachers.

At times, it takes creativity to locate exceptions and strengths. It pays to listen and observe carefully. When one has an inkling that a child might be good, or even great at something, it is helpful to find standardized evidence of this. For example, if a child loves and seems to be good at drawing, a test of visual-motor integration can provide valuable evidence about their strengths.

We consider being creative and flexible during testing to be an ethical obligation. To illustrate, during a recent parenting capacity assessment, a client scored very poorly on measures of her reasoning capacities using a standard battery of cognitive tests. In conversation, she seemed to be far more capable than the scores indicated. When we administered additional tests targeting day-to-day knowledge and problem-solving, the client obtained much higher scores. Had we not been curious and flexible, the original test results would not have captured her cognitive strengths, with the potential for serious ramifications in her life and family.

The report

In this section, we describe the typical sections in a psychoeducational assessment report. We provide some ideas for how an SF psychologist can use the report to provide a Solution Focused narrative to engage current stakeholders and future readers.

Reason for referral

We've suggested earlier that the assessment should start with a re-visioning of problem-focused referral questions. After the demographic information, a report typically opens with the referral questions, which should reflect that the assessment process is a solution-building, as opposed to a problem-solving, enterprise. Earlier, we suggested some Solution Focused framings for the reason for referral.

Relevant history

Earlier, we suggested that an SF school psychologist actively inquire about past exceptions, irregularities in the problem, and accounts of successful (even partially or temporarily) strategies. This approach transforms history-taking to *history-making*. Here, we document the history-making conversation we've already had, reminding the young person, parents, and teachers of what they have already told us about what's been better over the years, keeping the account descriptive and free of jargon. Reading all this in aggregate can have a profound effect on parents, teachers, and young people, inviting optimism and receptivity into the recommendations that follow. An SF school psychologist filters historical information by questioning whether the data is relevant to the referral question. While it is often necessary to document historical factors contributing to current challenges, we refrain from describing problems if we don't need to.

Clinical description/behavior during testing

This section describes the young person's presentation and behavior during testing. Here, an SF psychologist would highlight the young person's effort, cooperation, and strengths. Writing from a collaborative perspective, we positively connote the young person's behavior. In all our interactions with the young person, we note the client's positive qualities and efforts, which we describe here. This creates a context for receptivity for recommendations and can introduce new perspectives about the young person to parents and teachers.

Recently, Don was assessing an adolescent boy, who seemed disengaged from the testing process, yawning frequently, and performing poorly. Between and during subtests, he used the office supplies on the table to construct elaborate landscapes and structures. His focus and interest in this task provided an important contradiction to "off task" behavior described by his teachers. His talent for designing these structures led to Don to inquire about the strengths his parents and teachers have noticed.

Test results

In this section, an SF school psychologist reports the results of the tests they have administered. It goes without saying that that psychologists must be thoroughly fluent with the tests they use.

Using norm-referenced tests seems to contradict the SF nonnormative approach to human problems. As SF practitioners, we must decide how to position ourselves in relation to dominant normative discourses of diagnosis and testing. In independent practice, we may have the luxury of opting out of such practices entirely. However, in public sector systems such as primary and secondary schools, colleges and universities, and the public health system where funding for programs or individuals may rely on diagnoses or test results, we may need to relate to these practices as best we can. Taking a doctrinaire position may appeal to our ideological leanings and soothe our consciences, but may not be too helpful to clients.

Young people with so-called learning problems often learn in novel ways and exhibit unusual ability profiles. When reporting test results, an SF psychologist must be aware of skills or abilities that could be framed as strengths, both intrapersonal (i.e., relative to the young person's other skills or abilities) and absolute (i.e., relative to population-based norms). We suggest reporting test scores in terms of percentile ranges, as opposed to categories (e.g., "very superior" or "borderline"). This way, it is possible to draw finer distinctions when describing a young person's skills and abilities.

Understanding the statistical meaning of test scores, an SF psychologist can inject expectancy into a report, providing parents and school staff with openings to notice differences in the young person's skills and abilities. Even when a client's scores are low, an SF school psychologist communicates positively and hopefully using language that emphasizes their relative strengths. For example, "Kayla's scores suggest that her language reasoning abilities are better developed than her visual/perceptual capacities. Adults in her life may notice that when Kayla has difficulty understanding math concepts, she benefits from ample opportunity to talk about her math learning and to make applications to her day-to-day life." An SF psychologist should revisit and amplify these notable abilities in the consultation and feedback meeting with parents and school staff.

Some young people will demonstrate abilities and skills that are, in a normative sense, better developed relative to statistical means for their age. At the same time, other abilities and skills are not as well developed relative to statistical means. Some young people with uneven ability profiles are sometimes referred to as "learning disabled." The term "learning disability" is beginning to give way to the term "learning differences" (Learning Disabilities Association of New York State [LDANYS], 2008). Similarly, narrative therapists Epston et al. (2008) have referred to young people like this as "weirdly abled." In some jurisdictions the word "disability" has legal significance that enables access to resources and protects against discrimination (LDANYS, 2008). Irrespective of this, we suggest that adopting the view that a young person has distinct abilities and skills can invite us to be curious and, in turn, allow us to invite others to be curious about such abilities.

Formulation

Use the formulation section to tell a story. An SF school psychologist generates a narrative that is faithful to the various sources of data and provides a picture that is greater than the sum of its parts. The structure of the case formulation parallels the first two parts of the structure for feedback suggested by de Jong and Berg (2013): *compliments* and the *bridge*. The final portion of SF feedback de Jong and Berg describe are *suggestions*, which are contained in the Recommendations section of the report, described later.

In the formulation section of a psychoeducational assessment, an SF psychologist revisits the history, clinical presentation, and test results. As much as possible, while being faithful to the test data, a psychologist can give compliments to the young person, parents, and teachers. In addition to the compliments, one can highlight exceptions to prevailing ideas about the young person, describe what has worked (or is likely to work or work better) based on your assessment results, and pose questions that invite the young person's adult supporters to notice successes and be curious about further developments. For example, we have encountered many students who are not learning to read through the programming they receive at their school. In the formulation, we highlight the unique capacities of the child that are most amenable to reading, with examples (often exceptions to failure) that are realistic and repeatable in the classroom. We also endorse and encourage the school and family on positive aspects of their support that are almost always present. By framing the formulation in this way, we hope to share a contagious curiosity and hopefulness about the future.

De Jong and Berg (2013) suggest that in the bridge, the practitioner provides a rationale that links the compliments to suggestions. Practitioners should base suggestions or recommendations on a clear rationale. de Jong and Berg (2013, pp. 124–125) state, "The content of the bridge is usually drawn from client goals, exceptions, strengths, or perceptions. . . . When possible, it is important to incorporate client words and phrases." This is sound advice when producing a written report designed to invite the young person, parents, and teachers to experiment with new strategies.

Recommendations

In developing written recommendations, an SF psychologist should consider the capacity of the psychologist's relationship with the young person, the parents, and school personnel to support any suggestions. Early SF literature described *visiting, complainant,* and *customer* relationships (de Shazer, 1988), cautioning that these are descriptions of relationships, not classifications of persons or ascriptions of inherent motivation. These can provide a useful heuristic to assist school psychologists to frame recommendations. It is also useful to note that, as a practitioner, one can be in different relationship patterns with different stakeholders. With those who do not experience the situation as problematic, it is appropriate to simply give compliments. For those who may experience the situation as problematic, but not see themselves as able to contribute to solution-building, it is appropriate to suggest tasks of observation and prediction. In particular, it may be useful to suggest they notice strategies that are helpful. At other times, the relationship pattern supports asking someone to take concrete action or implement a specific strategy. Sometimes these are as simple as, "Keep doing what you're doing."

We frequently encounter clients we believe will benefit from counselling regarding emotions or behaviors that affect their learning. Many schools do not have the capacity to provide such support. In the recommendations, we compliment the parents on their efforts to access community services and encourage them to continue to do so. Being familiar with the capacities of the school, we may suggest that they focus on observation and communication, as well building positive relationships with the client and on facilitating successful experiences.

Consultation and feedback meeting

The final step in the psychoeducational assessment process is the consultation and feedback meeting. At this meeting, the psychologist typically describes the results of the assessment and the recommendations with the young person, parents, and school personnel. Doing this in an SF way, a face-to-face meeting of all stakeholders provides a golden opportunity to ask questions about the times when things are better and what seems to have worked and to express curiosity about what will change next and what will indicate that a strategy is working.

Conclusion

Psychoeducational assessments typically emphasize problems and their causes, potentially labelling and pathologizing young people. A Solution Focused approach to psychoeducational assessment can assist young people, parents, and teachers to notice what's going right, appreciate a young's person's distinct skills and abilities, and increase optimism.

References

American Psychiatric Association. (2013). *Diagnostic and Statistical Manual of the American Psychiatric Association*, 5th edition. Washington, DC: Author.

Beery, K. E., Buktenica, N. A., & Beery, N. A. (2010). *Beery-Buktenica Developmental Test of Visual-Motor Integration*, 6th edition. Bloomington: Pearson.

Binet, A., & Simon, T. (1905). *The Binet-Simon Test of Intelligence*. Paris: Ministry of Public Instruction.

Canadian Psychological Association. (2018). *Psychology's Response to the Truth and Reconciliation Commission of Canada's Report*. Ottawa, ON: Canadian Psychological Association and the Psychology Foundation of Canada.

Chang, J. (2019, July). *Listening for Openings: Amplifying Change*. Five-day intensive workshop organized by Athabasca University Faculty of Health Disciplines.

Climie, E., & Henley, L. (2016). A Renewed Focus on Strengths-Based Assessment in Schools. *British Journal of Special Education*, 43, 103–207. https://doi.org/10.1111/1467-8578.12131.

Cohen, M. (1997). *Children's Memory Scale*. Bloomington: Pearson.

Collins, S. (2019). *Embracing Cultural Responsivity and Social Justice: Re-Shaping Professional Identity in Counselling Psychology*. Victoria, BC: Counselling Concepts.

Conners, C. K. (2008). *Conners Comprehensive Behavior Rating Scales*. North Tonawanda, NY: MHS.

de Jong, P., & Berg, I. K. (2013). *Interviewing for Solutions*, 4th edition. Pacific Grove, CA: Brooks/Cole.

de Shazer, S. (1988). *Clues: Investigating Solutions in Brief Therapy*. New York: W. W. Norton.

Epston, D., Lobovits, D., & Freeman, J. (2008). Annals of the New Dave: Status-Abled, Disabled, or Weirdly Abled. In B. Bowen (Ed.), *Down Under and Up Over: Travels with Narrative Therapy* (pp. 41–60). Warrington: AFT Publishing Ltd.

Ford, D. Y. (2004). *Intelligence Testing and Cultural Diversity: Concerns, Cautions, and Considerations*. Mansfield, CT: National Research Center on the Gifted and Talented.

Gergen, K. J. (1991). *The Saturated Self: Dilemmas of Identity in Contemporary Life*. New York: Basic Books.

Gould, S. J. (1981). *The Mismeasure of Man*. New York: W. W. Norton.

Grekul, J., Krahn, A., & Odynak, D. (2004). Sterilizing the "Feeble-Minded": Eugenics in Alberta, Canada, 1929–1972. *Journal of Historical Sociology*, 17, 358–384. https://doi.org/10.1111/j.1467-6443.2004.00237.x

Hanushek, E. A. (1986). The Economics of Schooling: Production and Efficiency in Public Schools. *Journal of Economic Literature*, 24(3), 1141–1177. http://0-search.ebscohost.com.aupac.lib.athabascau.ca/login.aspx?direct=true&db=bth&AN=5290838&site=eds-live

Kaufman, A. S., & Kaufman, N. L. (2018). *Kaufman Assessment Battery for Children, 2nd edition normative update*. Upper Saddle River, NJ: Pearson Assessment.

Korkman, M., Kirk, U., & Kemp, S. (2007). *Developmental Neuropsychological Assessment (NEPSY)*, 2nd edition. Bloomington: Pearson.

Learning Disabilities Association of New York State. (2008). *Learning Disabilities vs. Differences*. www.ldanys.org/index.php?s=2&b=25.

Newcomer, P. L., & Hammill, D. D. (2019). *Test of Language Development – Primary*, 5th edition. Torrance, CA: WPS.

O'Hanlon, B., & Weiner-Davis, M. (2004). *In Search of Solutions: A New Direction in Psychotherapy*. New York: W. W. Norton.

Reynolds, C. R., & Kamphaus, R. W. (2015). *Behavior Assessment System for Children*, 3rd edition. Bloomington: Pearson.

Roid, G. H. (2003). *Stanford-Binet Intelligence Scales*, 5th edition. Torrance, CA: WPS.

Sattler, J. M., & Hoeg, R. D. (2006). *Assessment of Children: Behavioral, Social, and Clinical Foundations*. Austin, TX: PRO-ED, Inc.

Schneider, W. J., & McGrew, K. S. (2018). The Cattell – Horn – Carroll Theory of Cognitive Abilities. In D. P. Flanagan & E. M. McDonough (Eds.), *Contemporary Intellectual Assessment: Theories, Tests, and Issues* (pp. 73–163). New York: The Guilford Press.

Serpell, R., & Haynes, B. P (2004). The Cultural Practice of Intelligence Testing: Problems of International Export. In R. J. Sternberg & E. L. Grigorenko (Eds.), *Culture and Competence: Contexts of Life Success* (pp. 163–185). Washington, DC: American Psychological Association. http://dx.doi.org/ 10.1037/10681–007

Snyderman, M., & Herrnstein, R. J. (1983). Intelligence Tests and the Immigration Act of 1924. *American Psychologist*, 38(9), 986–995. http://dx.doi.org/10.1037/0003-066X.38.9.986

Waters, B. K. (1997). Army Alpha to CAT-ASVAB: Fourscore Years of Military Personnel Selection and Classification Testing. In R. F. Dillon (Ed.), *Handbook on Testing* (pp. 187–203). Westport, CT: Greenwood Press.

Wechsler, D. (2009a). *Wechsler Individual Achievement Test*, 3rd edition. Bloomington: Pearson.

Wechsler, D. (2009b). *Wechsler Memory Scale*, 4th edition. Bloomington: Pearson.

Wechsler, D. (2014). *The Wechsler Intelligence Scale for Children*, 5th edition. Bloomington: Pearson.

World Health Organization. (2018). *International Statistical Classification of Diseases and Related Health Problems*. 11th revision. Geneva, Switzerland: Author.

Chapter 11

A Solution Focused team conversation

Helping educators create lasting solutions with students

Linda Metcalf

When students develop behavioral or academic challenges in schools, they often speak individually with a counselor. During such conversations, the counselor and student who engage in a conversation may identify strategies that can provide relief for the student or the referring teacher (Metcalf, 2019). However, once the student returns to the classroom, armed with a bright outlook and strategy, the student can be derailed by the same context that previously helped to create the problem development. Without support from the teacher, who is left out of the conversation between counselor and student, the chances of lasting change for the optimistic student diminishes rapidly.

It has been documented that the Solution Focused approach is very applicable in school settings (Metcalf, 2010). However, once again, if a school counselor engages a student into developing a preferred future with steps to take and then sends the student back to class, again, the chances of change diminish. What has become more helpful when using a Solution Focused approach in schools is to involve the *system* that the student is connected with each day in a conversation. The *system* consists of administrators, teachers, teacher aids, parents and anyone else in the student's environment who plays a part in the student's education and daily life.

The conversation that can develop when adults and students in the *system* share their concerns and then their "best hopes" for the student can result in several opportunities. First, the *system* begins to see and know the student in a different context, often one where the *system begins* to recognize that the student is indeed interested in succeeding. Students involved in such meetings often appear quite different when engaged in a meeting where everyone is meeting to find strategies to be helpful. Second, the student begins to know his/her teachers differently, in a manner where the student often recognizes the teachers' desire to be helpful. The resulting new relationships begin to transform a *system* from one of maintaining a problem to one of providing an opportunity to achieve solutions together.

Beginning the process

The process is similar to a Solution Focused conversation, only it enlists responses from many individuals in the Solution Focused team conversation rather than one individual. The result is a collaborative effort where rich descriptions of strengths and exceptions dominate the conversation, rather than deficits. The Solution Focused team conversation is a radically new approach as instead of placing the educator in the role of expert, with traditional interventions, it invites the students and parents to assist educators in designing the solutions. Discussing problems is typical in education, but rarely does that primary discussion offer solutions that work for both students and staff. The Solution Focused team meeting amplifies possibilities for change through focusing less on the problem and more on the outcome.

The process found to be the most successful when forming and utilizing a Solution Focused team conversation includes the following steps here:

1 Teachers in the team receive a request to identify exceptions for the student a few days prior to the Solution Focused team meeting. The form on the next page can be used for the request. The form, *Solution Focused Team Conversation: Preliminary Observations of Success* prepares and suggests to teachers what the focus and climate of the meeting will be.
2 A Solution Focused team meeting process includes similar steps as used in individual conversations except that everyone in the meeting responds, including parent and student. The next form that is provided, *Solution Focused Team Conversation*, provides simple steps for the team leader or school counselor to use to facilitate the conversation.
3 As a follow up and consistent reminder of systemic support, the teachers visit with the student each week to complete the *Exception Findings* form, which simply allows the teacher and student to summarize and notice times when school went better. These exceptions can be presented as a team at the next meeting and serve as more information for helpful strategies.

Solution Focused team conversation

Observations of success

Dear Teacher,
There will be a Solution Focused team conversation for_____ on_____ at_____ in room_____. The conversation will consist of everyone involved in _____'s academic life, the student and parent. The conversation will not last longer than thirty minutes. Prior to the conversation, please watch for times when things go slightly better for the student academically or behaviorally and note what is occurring during that time. Consider lesson plans, activities, interactions with other students and teachers or any other actions that show slight success. Please write **only those** "exceptions" down on the lines below and bring to the conversation. Thanks!

1 _____
  _____

2 _____

3 _____

4 _____

5 _____

©Linda Metcalf, 2019

Solution Focused team conversation

Date:_____
Student:_____ Grade: _____
Team:_____
Attendees:_____

1 **Identify hopes:** The leader opens by expressing appreciation to those attending the meeting, then starts the conversation by asking everyone: *"What are your best hopes for our meeting today?"*
   (It is common for attendees to answer by saying what they do *not* want. Help those who respond in this way to develop a more workable goal by asking, "What do you want to happen instead?") Write the answers below:
   _____
   _____

   On a scale of 1–10, with 1 meaning not successful and a 10 meaning completely successful, where is the student currently:
   Parent:_____   Student:_____   Teachers (take average score):_____

2 **Set goals:** The leader thanks everyone for their responses and asks everyone, *"What will the student be doing in the classroom over the next three weeks so that the score increases and our concern decreases?"*
   _____
   _____

3 **Identify exceptions:** The leader asks the teachers about the exceptions that everyone present was asked to document: *"Looking at your Preliminary Observations of Success form, what have you noticed about the times when things are slightly better?"*
   _____
   _____
   _____

Direct a question to parent/student: "When have things been better in other classrooms, grades, or situations at school or even outside of school?"

_____
_____
_____

4 **Develop strategies:** The leader asks the student, teachers, parent, and staff members who are present: *"From our conversation today, which ideas do you think we might try out to move the score up the scale slightly?"*
Classroom strategies:

_____
_____
_____

Home strategies:

_____
_____
_____

5 **Summarize:** The leader asks for a collaborative agreement from everyone to experiment with the strategies for a certain time. (One to three weeks is recommended.)
Next meeting date:_____ Time:_____

©Linda Metcalf, 2019

Exception findings

Date:_____
Student: _____ Grade:_____
The documentation on this page is *only* for exceptions – times, situations, or activities when the student begins to be more successful in the classroom.
Week 1 Exceptions: List activities, situations, assignments:

_____
_____

Weekly score: (1–10) Student:_____ Teacher: _____
Week 2 Exceptions: List activities, situations, or assignments:

_____
_____

Weekly score: (1–10) Student:_____ Teacher: _____
Week 3 Exceptions: List activities, situations, or assignments:

_____
_____

Weekly score: (1–10) Student:_____ Teacher: _____

A case of school refusal

The following case is representative of a Solution Focused team conversation for a secondary student, Ben, who was experiencing a problem with going to school.

Ben, aged fifteen, came to therapy with his mother after Ben had attended only two days out of two weeks of school during the initial weeks of the academic school year. According to his mother, upon arrival at school, Ben would get into a fetal position in the backseat of the car, refusing to get out of the car due to severe nausea and stomach cramps. He would tremble and shake violently and declare that he simply could not go inside the school building. After a doctor checked Ben out physically, and it was determined that he was healthy, his mother sought counseling for Ben about stopping his school refusal.

During the initial session, I was curious about the two days that Ben had attended school. I inquired what was different in any way on those two days. I was also curious about how Ben was able to get out of the car and go into the building while he was still nauseous on those days. Ben began to recall that on those days he was still very nauseous but tried to go, telling himself that he just needed to get into a routine. He said that a coach, who made the subject so interesting that he often forgot about feeling anxious and nauseous, taught one of his classes. Ben also said that he did not feel under pressure to respond in the coach's class, as the coach allowed students to speak out on their own. The other class where he was more comfortable was an English class, which was located in a very quiet hallway. He liked that class because it had a very calm environment and the teacher allowed the students to come in and begin reading on their own before she started instruction. The other classes, Ben said, were so chaotic that he wanted to run out of the room. He said he had been home schooled the prior year, so facing so many students at once in the new school was too overwhelming.

After the first session ended, I received permission to contact the school counselor at his secondary school and then called to schedule a team conversation with each of Ben's teachers, Ben, his mother, an administrator and school counselor. I mentioned to the school counselor that the meeting would not last longer than thirty minutes. I asked her to email the *Preliminary Observations of Success* form to each teacher.

The conversation

When I met Ben outside in the parking lot the morning of the meeting, he was trembling so much that I was afraid he would not come inside. He scaled his own anxiety at a 10, recalling my use of the scaling question in our first session! I assured him that he would not need to do anything but listen. I had copied the exceptions to times when he felt uncomfortable in school, during the coach's class and English teacher's class, and had them ready to share with the team.

The conversation was a new experience for Ben's teachers, and at first, many were quiet. After I asked the "best hopes" question, however, many of the teachers had good things to express for Ben, such as getting to know him and to learn how to help him feel more secure in school. I looked around the room and spotted the coach, who had on a jersey and said, "You must be Coach___! I am so glad you are here. Ben told me that your class was easy to relax in due to your humor and instruction." I then asked about the English teacher. When she raised her hand, I said, "Thank you for making your classroom such a calm experience for him. He said that being able to walk in, sit down and read calmly helped him very much." Then I asked everyone else for his or her observations of those two days. Many of them did not have a lot to say since Ben had not been at school. However, then something important happened. I got the following responses from the individual team members:

Ben, my son had a little bit of trouble attending school. I eat lunch in my room each day. You are welcome to join me. That cafeteria is noisy!

(Teacher)

Ben, as your counselor, I have a comfortable couch that you can come relax on any time.

(Counselor)

Hey, Ben, you know, when you come into school each day, I could use help in the front office. Maybe that way, before you go to class, you can relax and walk to class with another student who helps me.

(Principal)

You know, I am out in the hallways all the time making sure the traffic keeps going. You can always hang out with me when I do that . . . no problem.

(Coach)

The conversation continued to be full of invitations, understanding and compliments to Ben for coming to school that morning to sort things out with them. I looked over at Ben, who seemed more relaxed, and I asked him where he was on the scale at that moment and he said, "An 8," and he smiled at me. I thanked everyone for the conversation and asked that they all continue to do as their team members had discussed. They agreed.

Two weeks later, Ben and his mom returned to my office to report that Ben had gone every day to school for the past two weeks except for one day when Ben said, "I really was sick!" I asked where he was on the scale and he said "a 5." He said he still got a little queasy each day, but once he got to school, he was better. He enjoyed helping out the principal in the morning and only ate lunch with the one teacher twice in two weeks. The other days he went to the cafeteria to eat with friends who encouraged him to try out for the football team.

A two-month follow up phone call to the principal informed me that Ben was seen smiling and laughing with students in the hallway daily, was on the football team and had asked a girl to a homecoming celebration dance.

Systemic approaches: efficient and effective

After over twenty years of providing Solution Focused team conversations with student clients, parents, school counselors/psychologists, teachers and principals, I have found that doing so has provided lasting change in 95% of my client cases. Typically, upon follow up after the team conversation, I find that the student client improves and continues to improve, as the system begins to see the school client differently and responds differently.

References

Metcalf, L. (2010). *Solution Focused RTI*. New York: Wiley.
Metcalf, L. (2019). *Counseling Toward Solutions*, 3rd edition. Kindle Direct Publishing.

Chapter 12

Put the numbers in! The value of scale questions

Harvey Ratner

Introduction

In the BRIEF approach to Solution Focused practice, the scale is used after exploring the young person's 'best hopes' from the work (Iveson et al., 2012) and the amplification of those hopes into a 'preferred future' description by means of the miracle question or the tomorrow question (Ratner et al., 2012). In this, our practice is close to that of Steve de Shazer, who in his later years was referring to 'the Miracle Question and its scale' (de Shazer, 2001). Harry Korman explains that 'moving from the miracle question to the scale is not a very good metaphor since the scale is actually a part of the miracle question' (de Shazer et al., 2007, p. 61). This means that the use of a scale should always follow that of the preferred future conversation in a first session and is designed to help client and therapist work out what the client is already doing that relates to movement towards the desired outcome. It is not an assessment tool or an evaluation of 'where the client has got to' but merely a doorway into an exploration of instances of success in their life.

I have heard the use of scales critiqued on the grounds that the use of an ascending order of numbers makes for an implicit pressure on clients 'to move up the scale'. However, whether the client actually does anything is up to them. Accordingly, after examining what the client has already done we refrain from asking 'what are you going to do next?' and instead ask 'what would be *signs* you are moving forward?'

The question of 'putting pressure' on clients could be the subject of a chapter in its own right. It can be argued that even a discussion with someone about their preferred future is inherently pressurising, giving them the message that they should do things differently or better in future, and we should be avoiding any such practice: insistence, as the saying goes, leads to resistance. However, if there is *no* pressure, will the client actually do anything? Is the articulation of a description enough of a self-motivator? There are even those who feel that not only is a sense of the future essential but that also without an action plan, you – or rather the young person – ain't got nothing. Steve de Shazer was not interested in detailed plans, but he held to the belief that the client needed to go away with some sort of homework 'as a reminder', he said while presenting one year at

BRIEF, 'that they have to *do* something'. He added that without assigning the client a task, he was worried the client would think they had just had a nice chat. My own position is somewhere in the middle. After developing a detailed preferred future description, I use scales both as a way to access descriptions of what they have already achieved and as a way (a form of 'benign pressure') to stimulate them – motivate them, if you will – towards further action. And, as we will see, scales are, I believe, invaluable tools for enabling young people to stay engaged in our conversation with them.

With all clients, we have to adapt anything we ask to fit to their understanding, and this can be a particular challenge when working with young people. In this chapter, I will show the use of the scale firstly with a primary age child, which shows how careful we have to be in making it clear what we are asking about, and secondly with an adolescent, where the use of different scales is demonstrated.

As my purpose is to explore the use of scale questions only, the reader is asked to bear in mind the point already made, that scale questions come after the therapist or coach has obtained a detailed description of the young person's or family's preferred future.

'I want to climb my way'

The teacher of a Year 4 (age 7) young man called Yasin had attended a course at BRIEF and told me afterwards 'I'm going to refer you my hardest student'. I have changed some details to protect the family's confidentiality. Yasin's mother Ayesha explained on the phone when making the appointment that he had had several short term exclusions and was on the edge of permanent exclusion.

I began the session, which also included Yasin's father Ashraf, asking about each person's 'best hopes' from coming, and then I used the miracle question to explore Yasin's preferred future in detail. He seemed to grasp the idea of a 'miracle' – I've known young people who haven't and where I've had to modify the question to a 'magic wand' or something similar – and I worked hard to make my questions as simple as possible; he spoke slowly and would often take a while before answering, and so I didn't feel I had the time to ask the other family members about their respective 'miracles'. Eventually I moved on to ask him a scale question. I took a sheet of paper and drew a line and marked one end with a 10 and the other with a 0. I considered giving the paper to him to draw the scale himself but the slowness of the session made me decide against that. I explained that the 10 stood for all the things he'd told me about in his 'miracle' and I wrote some of the key things above the 10, such as 'putting my head down', 'getting on with work', 'showing the work', his mother saying 'good' and his father rewarding him with money. I then said the 0 stood for the opposite, 'meaning you're no longer allowed to stay in the school' which I also wrote down. I then asked him to say what number stood for where he was 'now'. He thought for what seemed like a very long time and I tried to urge him on by saying 'what do you think?' and 'what number would you give?' After what seemed like an age he pointed to one end of the scale and said '10'.

Now, the usual rule about using scale questions in Solution Focused (SF) practice is that we should accept whatever the client says. As this is not an objective test, whatever number they give is 'right' for them. But my instinctive reaction was one of overt surprise verging on ridicule – '10?!' – and then I thought I had better repeat to him what the '10' and the '0' were, in case he had misunderstood me, and then added 'so it's not 10, is it?' He agreed, saying 'I need to improve more'. I asked him to give a number. He remained silent, stroking his chin in apparent thoughtfulness, and I said 'well, is it nearer the 0 or to the 10?' After a few more seconds of pondering, he pointed to the other end of the scale and said 'a 0'.

I was flabbergasted and sinking fast when his mother rowed to the rescue. 'If you put the numbers in for him. . . ' Ayesha said, hesitantly, as if it wasn't her place to advise the professional (maybe what she really wanted to say was 'put the numbers in, you dummy!'). I agreed immediately, telling her 'please help me here' and then I carefully added in the numbers on the scale, enunciating each one in turn, and then showed the paper to Yasin again. He pondered at length and I started to think he just couldn't get it, but now I had a co-therapist to help me and I turned to Ayesha and asked her if she had a better way of putting it for him. Before she could speak, Yasin blurted out 'I'd say 2'. I then put a circle around the number and asked him to say how come it was a 2 and not a 0. He drew a deep breath, I think of exasperation; after all, he'd answered my question and now I wanted still more! But he tried his best to comply, giving me short examples of what he'd done. At first these were on the vague side, such as 'I'm getting there' and 'I want to climb my way'. I wrote these down above the figure '2' and asked 'what else?' and he became more concrete: 'I walked away', 'I've been telling my mum if I've had a good or a bad day'. I then congratulated him on how well he was answering my questions, and directed a compliment to the parents for having a son who could work so hard and for so long in a meeting with me. Ashraf commented that Yasin's powers of concentration 'are getting longer'. I asked them where they would have placed him on the scale, and Ashraf said '2' and Ayesha said 'I'll give him a '3', Mum being kind'. And of course I wrote their ideas down on the sheet.

At the end of the session, a follow up appointment was made and they asked for and received a copy of the sheet to take away.

I reflected after the session that I hadn't done a good job. When I reviewed the recording of the session (the parents had given permission for it to be recorded for training purposes) I noted that I had asked them to rate where they put Yasin on the scale. This was in keeping with their view that the problem was entirely to do with Yasin's behaviour at school. However, when asking the miracle question I had been careful to try to make it a joint *family* 'miracle', for example asking what difference it would make to the family if they were hearing that things were better in school. However, when it came to the scale, I had omitted to make it a 'home plus school' scale. And then there was the way I'd made the scale so torturous for

Yasin, and how Ayesha, I suspected, would have left thinking I was incompetent. So when they didn't attend for the next appointment, I wasn't surprised.

I waited a week, but as there was no contact from the family I decided to call them. In principle I prefer to wait for clients to make contact (if they ever do), but sometimes there is a need to let the referrer know what has happened, even if it means admitting that I have failed in my job.

Ayesha answered the phone. Nervously I mentioned that they hadn't kept the follow up appointment. She apologised and said 'we were too busy to come'. That sounded vaguely promising, so I enquired as to how things were and she told me that things had improved enormously at school! She said Yasin was there at that moment and asked me 'would you like to talk to him?' I wasn't sure about that, and indeed when he came to the phone he was as 'slow' as before. He confirmed that things were better but I couldn't establish what he had actually done. I asked 'what has helped?' and after another long pause he said 'the list'. When Ayesha came back to the phone I said that he had said something about a 'list' and I wondered if he was referring to the scale sheet and she said 'yes, we've got it up on the kitchen wall'. 'Oh', I said, 'it sounds like you've carried on the work together!' She confirmed that that was indeed the case.

I never saw the family again. However, I had contact with Yasin's teacher over the next couple of years, as she continued to refer students to me, and I always enquired about Yasin and heard from her about his great progress!

Scales in school

Scales are an immensely valuable tool to use in schools They can be used by teachers with individual students, with groups and with classes (Ajmal & Ratner, 2020). I make liberal use of them in my one-to-one work as a life coach and counsellor (Ratner & Yusuf, 2015). The following case concerns a Year 10 (15-year-old) student called James. I have changed details for the sake of confidentiality and my thanks go to Headteacher Gary Moore and the staff at Regent High School. When I asked James at the start of our first meeting what his hopes were from seeing me, he said that he needed to talk because 'I'm not happy with the teachers'; he added that 'I'm a naughty boy' and 'I get into fights'. I spent some time exploring what would be different in future when things were going better. My sessions in schools are quite short – no more than 25 minutes – and I often don't use the miracle question or the tomorrow question but simply expand on the answers I have had from the best hopes question. It was hard to get firm detail from James, but I learned that he would be 'doing good in lessons, improving, not shouting out, trying to study, trying to learn, doing good in various different subjects, getting good phone calls home, with teachers and parents pleased with me'. After about 10 minutes, I decided to ask a scale question (the following transcript is taken from the video recording):

HR: So if I were to take a 0 to 10 scale, where 0 is how things were when Miss W talked to you about seeing me, and 10 is, we've done a good job here, things are fine, you've got what you want from seeing me. What number have we reached now, would you say?

HR: *(after a pause in which he said nothing)* So what number . . . is it still at 0? Or has it gone up from 0?

J: It's gone up a bit.

HR: What number would you give it?

Of course the actual number isn't important, but it enables the conversation to be more focused, the number 'standing for' aspects of living that can then be explored.

J: Erm, 3.

HR: 3?

J: 3 to 4.

HR: 3, 4 even? Okay, what tells you that? Tell me about improvements in the last week or two.

J: I'm trying to . . . I'm not like really getting in trouble these times.

HR: So, when you're not getting into trouble what are you doing differently?

J: I'm trying to behave in lessons.

HR: Okay. So, if I was one of those boys in the Maths lesson, what would I have noticed you trying to do?

J: I sit on my own in front of the teacher, with her favourites and everything.

I then asked him how he resisted the temptation to join in with the noise and disturbance that he had said went on in lessons, especially in Maths, and what positive effect it had on his friends when they saw him making an effort.

When working with clients, and young people in particular, I often wonder about what their motivation might be most directed towards, and I sometimes introduce further scales to clarify and, perhaps, to help reinforce the direction of travel.

HR: If I took another scale where 10 is you're doing the very best anybody could humanly do in Maths given the disruption and noise. 0 is you aren't doing anything to deal with it, you're shouting along with the rest, you're sitting in the back singing and shouting. Where between 0 and 10 would you say you're are at the moment?

J: Average 5.

HR: Okay. How do you do that? How do you manage to be a 5 and not a 0 in Maths?

J: I don't really make the noise and everything.

HR: How come? How have you changed things?

J: I try, because I'm doing badly in Maths. That's why.

HR: And why's that important to you?

J: Because my parents, they'd like me to get a good education. They want me to get good GCSEs [UK exams].

HR: They are encouraging you to do well in GCSEs? And what do you think about that?
J: I think they're right because I want to have a good future.

I continued to explore this, and revisited the first scale and asked some questions about how he'd know he'd moved up one point. His answers were still quite limited and I was aware that I was working hard to keep the conversation going. As our time started to run out, I decided a further scale linked to motivation was called for:

HR: One last scale before we finish: 10 is you're totally confident we can do a good job together and that you're going to get to 10 on the other scale. 0, not a chance in hell, we ain't gonna do it, forget it. What number represents your confidence?
J: It's about a 7.
HR: That's good, above halfway. What gives you that much confidence?
J: That I'm speaking to someone. And I can tell my problems and you can give solutions like to solve the problems.
HR: Okay. The talking and looking for solutions? So what solutions have we got at the moment?
J: Not sure...
HR: Well let's put it this way. What would Miss D see in the rest of this week, see you doing for her to know that you're making progress?
J: An improvement. That I improve in my lessons. Because I'm not getting that many bad reports now but still there's reports coming in.

Not having obtained his summary of 'solutions', I decided to round off the session with an attempt at a summary myself, which also enabled me to give further acknowledgment to what he was dealing with:

HR: Okay, would you like to meet again?
J: Yeah.
HR: Okay. What I've understood today is that you've been in some trouble and you want to do something about that now.
J: Yeah.
HR: Your parents are not very happy with the way it is. They want you to get a good education, and you think that's important. You're concerned that you don't have a good relationship with some teachers, and you want to be able to get on with work. And (*here a student walked unannounced into the room as they had the next appointment*) 'just a minute, just a minute' – and that you – 'Hi there, can you hold on a second please?' (*as the other student still tried to come in*) – and erm I lost my train of thought there. But you've moved up the scale even from when Miss W spoke to you, you've reached 3 or 4. You've got some really good ideas about what helps you to get on

better in the lessons that give you most trouble like English, Maths, sitting away from your friends, sitting at the front. It's tough obviously in Maths – the way you've described that class sounds really difficult – but even in that class you think you're about halfway towards doing the best you can. I'm really impressed with the ideas you've got. So it sounds hopeful and your confidence is good so that's terrific. What I'd like to do is meet with you in a week or two to review what you've noticed helps you to keep going forward.

The next session wasn't recorded but he reported progress and then we met for a third and final time:

HR: So bring me up to date because I've not heard anything. What's been better since we last met?
J: Yeah, it's been better. I spoke to a couple of teachers. And they're saying 'yeah, you've got a good report, keep it up'.
HR: Great, good. What do you mean by a good report?
J: That I haven't heard nothing bad.
Towards the end of the meeting I re-introduced the scale:
HR: 10 represents we don't need to meet anymore, we've done what we need to do here. And 0 represents when you first came to see me. Where would you say we've got to now?
J: A good 7, 8.
HR: About 7 or 8. Good, good. What tells you that?
J: I still do bad things . . . when I first came to you I was like, I was being 'bare' bad. Now I'm doing alright but I'll cut down on the bunking [cutting school] and I'll be alright.
HR: You can see there's still some stuff you've got to work on but you're doing a lot better than you were when you first came. That's the 7 or 8. And if we met again in 2, 3 weeks' time what would you hope that you'd be telling me that you'd done by then?
J: Erm, everything, like. . .
HR: What, coming in on time, not bunking? So you think when we meet you could be a 10?
J: Yeah.
HR: Wow. What tells you that you could achieve that in the next few weeks?
J: I dunno . . . it's like an aim ain't it.
HR: It's an aim, yeah. Well, what do you know about yourself that makes you think you can do this?
J: I'm not really sure but I'll try.

I was getting vague answers and was again aware that I was working hard – harder than him, probably – to keep the conversation going. Using different scales helps to fill out the talk. Of course, it's not just a matter of filling up the time – although this isn't a trivial matter when working in schools where there are allotted time frames. Scales make young people *think*. Even if they give vague answers, by giving a number they *commit* themselves – an example, perhaps, of a benign application of the 'pressure' that was discussed earlier.

HR: If I did another scale where 10 is you're going to try the hardest, you're going to put every muscle into a 10, and 0 is you're just going to wait and see what happens. Where would you say you'd put yourself in terms of effort?
J: 7, 8.
HR: 7 or 8 on that one. Great, great. So it sounds like this is important enough to you that you want to make a real effort at it.

I didn't of course know that this was our last meeting. In SF practice one rarely knows that. Sometimes young people will say they don't need to meet again but usually, as with James, I only learn later about overall improvements and that there wasn't a need for him to return.

Conclusion

When working with younger children, I no longer forget to put the numbers in. . .

References

Ajmal, Y., & Ratner, H. (2020). *Solution Focused Practice in Schools: 80 Ideas and Strategies*. London: Routledge.
de Shazer, S. (2001). *Conversations with Steve de Shazer*. Handout at workshop presentation at BRIEF.
de Shazer, S., Dolan, Y., Korman, H., Trepper, T., McCollum, E., & Berg, I. K. (2007). *More Than Miracles: The State of the Art of Solution-Focused Brief Therapy*. New York: Haworth Press.
Iveson, C., George, E., & Ratner, H. (2012). *Brief Coaching: A Solution Focused Approach*. London: Routledge.
Ratner, H., George, E., & Iveson, C. (2012). *Solution Focused Brief Therapy: 100 Key Points and Techniques*. London: Routledge.
Ratner, H., & Yusuf, D. (2015). *Brief Coaching with Children and Young People: A Solution Focused Approach*. London: Routledge.

Chapter 13

Dream ... believe ... achieve
A school in South Africa that has developed a philosophy based on Solution Focused principles

Nick Birkett and Merritt Watson

Background

School can be a scary and uncomfortable place for many people, from children, to teachers, to parents. In a formal school environment there are societal, organisational or governmentally prescribed standards and routines that often mould or force people into a particular box that they may not necessarily fit into. The stress, anxiety and negative feelings about school often stem from people's inability to feel competent or capable about fitting into these boxes for any number of reasons. When people are deemed to struggle in school either academically, emotionally or socially, it is measured by their inability to fit into these expectations.

Classical schooling in its nature tries to "teach" or prepare people to fit these prescribed expectations. The capacity of a person to reach these standards is often "assessed", which is in essence a judgement on a person's ability to fit into these boxes and can seem to be a judgement on their future ability to be successful and fit into the world. An apparent judgement of failure to meet these expectations is visible to those around the person and, more importantly, to the person themselves. This can be soul destroying and scary as it can seem to be a predictor of whether the person will live or lead a successful life.

A need for a new mindset

With all this in mind, it became apparent to us at the School of Merit that there was a need to find a way or strategy to shift these negative mindsets. The School of Merit is a small, non-denominational, mainstream independent school in Edenvale, a suburb east of Johannesburg, South Africa. It was started on residential property and, as the number of pupils grew, adjacent properties were purchased. Its unique attributes are the small classes and our support of "differently abled" children, meaning children who do not fit the normal school box. Unfortunately, children who are "differently abled" are labelled with negative comments. These often become a "self-fulfilling" prophecy, with schooling becoming a nightmare for parents and the children, with the "labels" being reinforced continuously.

The School of Merit decided to embark on a Solution Focused journey and change the philosophy of the school from that of a "dumping ground" for children who do not fit in to rather a Solution Focused school that accommodates all children and gives them hope.

A Solution Focused approach allows an opportunity to use positive language as a focus. When people are focused on the negative aspects such as what they "cannot" do and where and when they didn't meet the standard, this becomes the dominant mindset. Solution Focused thinking and strategies attempt to shift those views and allow people to develop a positive self-image, to focus on when and how they are amazing. You may not fit the standard required, but everybody has unique and individual talents and strengths. A Solution Focused approach makes your strengths the focus and allows you to realise and be proud of your individuality.

Shifting a mindset in an individual is challenging, let alone shifting a mindset of an entire institution. The challenge of doing this was made easier as the principles, practices and ideologies that are involved in a Solution Focused approach are inherently positive. We found that when our staff were introduced to the ideas in Solution Focused principles, each teacher had a moment where it 'clicked'. Many of the ideas relate back to good teacher training models of positive reinforcement, which may contribute to our teachers grasping the skills with relative ease.

There is, however, a need to facilitate, train and introduce people to the Solution Focused way of thinking. As a school we began our Solution Focused journey at the beginning of 2013 through a series of ongoing workshops and training sessions, conducted by Dr Jacqui von Cziffra-Bergs of The Solution Focused Institute of South Africa. We introduced staff to the principles of Solution Focused thinking, along with strategies to implement the thinking into practice.

As mentioned earlier, despite a school's positive intentions, negativity can often prevail. We therefore aimed to employ Solution Focused skills, ideas and use of language to see children differently; to look at children's strengths, both in and out of the school environment; to assist them to reach their best hopes; to look for exceptions and times when the problem is not present; to set collaborative goals between child and teacher; and to use the "problem" to overcome the challenge.

Best hopes and goals

We hoped that by introducing the Solution Focused approach focusing on the positive aspects and on the strengths of children and teachers, the talk and atmosphere would change to one of positivity, excitement, vibrancy and hope for all the stakeholders. Instead of discussions being about the hard times, the "naughty" child and the child's poor results, it would change to when the child did well in an activity and how a weak and seemingly "naughty" child was actually a very enthusiastic child. When the "problem" gets minimal to no airtime, we hoped that the focus and atmosphere would become more positive.

In essence, we wanted a school atmosphere and reality that mimicked all the teacher's best hopes and aspirations. We wanted an institution filled with joy and happiness where quality teaching took place. Our goal was to create a school where learners and teachers were not burdened by negativity and stress but motivated and excited by possibilities. Under the leadership of Merritt Watson, the head of school and owner of the school, we decided on the following goals (Watson & Von Cziffra-Berg, 2015):

- The staff had to look at alternative ways of helping children to reach their goals.
- Staff had to find a positive way to deal with children when other teachers had given up.
- There was a need to bring humour and laughter back into the classroom.
- Children needed to feel empowered and needed to take more responsibility for their own actions and their learning.
- Teachers needed to engage parents in a more positive manner and ensure that they were all working towards the same expectations and goals.
- There was a need for a way to encourage parent and school collaboration.
- Parent meetings and the approach, namely the interview forms and language, had to be restructured.

Strengths of the situation

As we embarked on our Solution Focused journey, we had no doubt that we would be able to change the energy and attitude in the school. As a school, we are in a very fortunate position as our teachers are well educated, have a great range of professional expertise, are dynamic and creative and have that innate love and compassion for children that one would expect of any teacher. The introduction of Solution Focused principles was so successful due to the amazing teachers at the school. They had an immense eagerness to learn, a staggering amount of creativity and, very importantly, a recognition and understanding that there was a need to make education and our school environment a place of happiness.

Johnny Kim states (Kim, 2008) "Schools can be places of solutions, strengths and successes", which was ultimately what we wanted to achieve. We are, additionally, blessed with strong and supportive leadership that pushes and encourages excellence and innovation.

How Solution Focused principles are applied

How do you create a Solution Focused school philosophy? Where do you begin? We found that the best way to do this was to start with the teachers and allow them, through their actions, to model and act out Solution Focused strategies. We were hopeful that this would filter through to all parts of the school.

The teacher workshops presented by the Solution Focused Institute of South Africa introduced our teachers to the new way of thinking and using language. After each workshop the teachers were given tasks to implement in the classroom to enact or practice what they had learnt. They were encouraged to create and come up with their own exciting ways to implement what was covered in each workshop, often in the form of an entire class goal. This is where the teacher's creativity and grasp of the concepts shined.

It must be stated that, despite teacher enthusiasm, implementation of any new concept can be met with reluctance and apprehension. It was therefore important that the tasks the teachers needed to do with their learners at the end of each workshop were enforced. This encouraged the teachers to grapple with the concepts and develop a personal understanding through implementation of class goals and activities. It allowed them to see the challenges and strengths in each of the strategies that were covered.

The main principles that have been taught and emphasised in the school through the workshops are as follows (Watson & Von Cziffra-Berg, 2015):

- To use a Solution Focused lens to see the child differently, see their strengths as resources, and find their exceptional abilities. This allows the teacher to assist them to notice these strengths in themselves.
- To become able to make Solution Focused diagnosis and be able to identify the problem and turn it into a strength.
- To find exceptions to the problem. To look for times when things were or are working.
- To be able to set goals with children and help them find a way to reach "their best hopes", and help them to notice small achievable tasks that proved they are reaching their goal.
- To use scaling in class conversations to help children move toward a goal.

As the teachers used Solution Focused language with the learners in the creation of the class goals, so the learners began to hear and become accustomed to the language and strategies. The workshops moved into using more specific strategies to deal with individuals, such as how to help them find their strengths when they had challenges and how to reframe their problem as a solution. In these instances, many learners who had otherwise been cast aside by other schools were now receiving positivity, encouragement and most importantly hope. This kind of interaction for a learner can be life changing.

Positivity spread and it was a mindset and practice that people enjoyed and appreciated. This allowed the school to become a Solution Focused school in a "natural and organic way". Through the training, the staff began to use and model the Solution Focused language and strategies, and a Solution Focused philosophy was embraced throughout the school.

A case study of George Messenger, a 16-year-old school boy, from Johannesburg, South Africa*

Initial meeting with George, his parents, Merritt Watson (head of school) and Debbie Schamrel (head of the high school)

George Messenger and his parents came to the School of Merit at a time of extreme turmoil and anguish. George had been asked to leave the prestigious school he attended because he had been found to be in breach of the school's code of conduct at the end of his Grade 10 year, having tested positive for illegal substances. His parents had heard about the School of Merit and its philosophy of treating children with respect and dignity. An initial interview was established to ascertain what his parents' best hopes were for him and more importantly what George's best hopes were for himself. This enabled the school to help him plot his "journey".

The Messengers immediately started describing the negative behaviours of George and the negative experiences at his previous school. They described what had been going wrong and how tough it had been, with their focus on the negative labels that had been given to George. They found it exceptionally difficult to focus on George's strengths and to recall "good" times when George was a "model" son. They seemed to feel completely overwhelmed and to think that there was absolutely no hope for this young man's schooling career. They were shocked, and they found it challenging to be asked, instead of questions about his current behaviour, attitude and mood, questions about what they wanted to see instead, what these expectations would look like, and what steps might be taken to reach them (the "miracle question").

It was almost as if the parents were so accustomed to problem talk that it was regarded as "rude" to ask about George's strengths and what positive attributes he could bring to the school, rather than the incident that had occurred. The conversation had to continuously be redirected back to George and his strengths and positive characteristics.

During the first interview, George was also invited to share what he perceived his strengths to be both in and out of school. No reference was made to his misdemeanour. His parents often tried to interject and comment about what had happened, but the focus of the conversation remained with George. The conversation was steered to his strengths at school. He was asked why he should be given a second chance and what he would bring to the school and why we should be considering him. It was remarkable to note his honesty and insightfulness. He was willing to share his strengths as well as his challenges and to take responsibility for his misdemeanour. He noted that he found school hard and never seemed to "fit in" at his previous school. As a part of the acceptance agreement/process, and because of the fact that George had seriously breached his previous school's code of conduct, he was asked to draw up his own contract with the School of Merit. He was also asked to attend personal Solution Focused therapy sessions with a Solution Focused psychologist. No guidance and/or structure was offered to him when drawing up his contract, other than asking him to specify the behaviour that his teachers and peers would notice and compliment him on. He was also asked to specify a "consequence" should he "slip or transgress", because life always has consequences and choices. However, the focus was always to note the positive behaviour and to strengthen this with praise and acknowledgement.

Second meeting with George and his parents

At a second meeting, George and his parents met with Mrs. Schamrel, the principal, to discuss his enrolment. Once again, George was asked about his best hopes for joining the school. Immediately, his parents began talking about how the previous school had let them down as a family. The principal had to carefully steer the conversation back to George and his strengths and what he could bring to the school, explaining that his previous school had a very different ethos. It was very difficult to avoid problem talk.

George and his parents appeared taken aback that the principal was asking George the questions, and they were definitely not used to empowering the learner to take the responsibility for his education, actions and consequences. When asked about his best hopes and strengths, George seemed to be placating the adults by providing answers he thought they wanted to hear, but when he had to note the details of **how** he was going to "walk" his journey and what his behaviour would look like, George took more sincere responsibility, especially when it was explained that the details would assist the teachers to compliment him when they observed the behaviours that he would have to list.

George was given the time to write up his own contract with the school. It was interesting to note that George took this process to heart and became immersed in how his strengths were to be actualised.

In summary of his contract: he included aspects of punctuality, regular school attendance, respect, diligence with his studies, attentiveness and obedience. He, additionally, listed consequences like demerits and detentions should he regress or not meet the criteria he designed.

George commenced his schooling career at the school in Grade 10, eight weeks before the end of the school year. He had four weeks left of class contact time with his teachers, before the end of the academic year, in which he needed to catch up work and prepare all his learning materials for the examinations. It had been strongly advised that he consider repeating Grade 10 the following year because he seemed to have missed many vital skills and concepts. George noted that he "would succeed and pass the year" if he was given the chance. George was committed and the school believed in his strengths and was willing to allow him to take his Grade 10 examinations. As part of his acceptance, George was asked to write a reflective story to the school.

Here are details of some pertinent extracts from his essay:

I've never really felt in tune with my old school. They were like, "You fit in? Cool. If you don't, well then that's tough for you".

I was often separated from the herd and felt left out. I used to be bullied even if the school says "zero tolerance for bullying".

I've had trouble coping with the school's standards all my life. It's caused me major stress, anxiety and depression, a real feeling of worthlessness.

I was an active sportsman yet after an injury my sporting career came to a halt. All of my coaches were so involved and "worried" about me. But as soon as they realised I could no longer participate, I was no longer worth anything to them and I was tossed to the dirt.

When leaving my old school, I felt relieved – like the weight compressing my chest and lungs had lifted. At the School of Merit, I instantly felt invited and comfortable, not in a constant state of worry. I could actually concentrate and understand the work being done.

> *I'm so grateful for the opportunity for a new start at the School of Merit and for the support I'm receiving from the pupils and teachers. I'm part of a new school. I feel I have worth. I'm an individual. I'm treated with respect. Teachers and fellow peers recognise that I too have strengths. I feel at home in this community and welcomed into this family.*

George completed his Grade 10 examinations with full commitment and enthusiasm and was promoted to Grade 11 in 2018. Everyone at the school was very proud of his positive commitment.

George's mother's letter

Mrs Messenger seemed to have the need to put pen to paper to try to verbalise her account with the "different approach" used by the School of Merit. Both Mr and Mrs Messenger seemed overwhelmed that in their time of crisis there was hope. There were positive attributes, regardless of how bad the misdemeanor was, and George was still valued as a young man who had much to contribute and/or achieve:

A summary of Mrs. Messenger's letter is here:

> George's academic career started at his old school but the end of George's academic career at this school brought to light many hidden truths with which we had unknowingly lived with for so many years.
>
> After having entrusted him to this school since the tender age of five, the manner in which it ended was despicable, since we had been led to believe that they had the best interests of my son at heart.
>
> We believed his development in this environment would give him the opportunity of growing up to be a confident, well-rounded young man with a good education. I did not understand that the focus of the school was on its own success rather than the individual learner's. It was the lack of individual care and attention at school that was leading George to regress.
>
> At our last meeting at his old school, the deputy headmaster's words to George were: "I see you as a square peg trying to fit into a round hole". These words brought everything into perspective! They had failed in their endeavor to mould my son into what they needed and took advantage of George's transgression of a conduct rule to get rid of him. They highlighted the disinterest in George as a person and us as a family.
>
> During the transition from his old school to the School of Merit I was dumbfounded. From the moment we stepped into the School of Merit reception, we were received with such warmth by people we had never met. You spoke "with" us not "to" us. You were interested in my son and the positives and strengths that he possessed and would bring with him to a new school.
>
> Hearing that:
>
> - It is fine to be who we are;
> - Everyone has strengths and that it is on those strengths that we build our success;

- Weakness can be addressed;
- It is okay to fail but to stand up again is more important – to do differently – small change leads to bigger changes;
- You would hold our hand and not let go; and
- You believed that he could be successful.

You knew what your school had to offer but you took the time to rather understand whether it would assist my son in achieving the success that he so wanted and believed he could achieve.

What was even more astounding to hear was that you believed in George.

Subsequently, you gave us insight into George's strengths and weaknesses together with guidance and direction to assist George to utilise his own strengths to overcome his challenges.

It was very exciting to walk this path with you. It gave me renewed hope that there was still a possibility that George would receive what I had always wanted for him from his first day in Grade 0.

A simple thank you will never express the gratitude I have for everything that you have done and undertaken to do for my son and for us. Thank you.

Summary

George has given of his best to try to uphold the respect and belief that he received from his teachers and his peers. He has said that he was taken aback that the initial interview was not about parental concerns only and that he was not excluded, but part of the negotiation process. The School of Merit strongly believes in the *collaboration* of all those involved. Each person's opinions and thoughts are considered, and a negotiated way forward is discussed.

The school believes that by empowering this young man to believe in himself, he was given the opportunity to show his worth. The approach seems to create an environment that allows a child to develop a sense of belonging and self-worth. George's success is a testament to his drive and the philosophy that positive language and Solution Focused goals can lead to result that may surprise even the most experienced schools or minds.

Some names and identifying details have been changed to protect the privacy of individuals.

References

Kim, J. (2008). *Solution Focused Brief Therapy in Schools*. New York: Oxford University Press.

Watson, M., & von Cziffra-Berg, J. (2015). *Doing Differently*. Johannesburg: The Solution Focused Institute of South Africa.

Chapter 14

Solution Focused practice in a British University

Peter J. Eldrid

Solution Focused counselling is well suited to the university student community (referred to as higher education in the UK) and can provide an important source of brief intervention as part of a network of other student support services addressing student well-being, including practical concerns such as housing and finances.

The way in which I use the Solution Focused approach is not greatly different whether I am working in a university or in another setting, such as a private clinic. However, there are some adaptations to practice which must be made to accommodate the responsibilities and requirements of higher education.

Duty of care

Universities have a general, common law, duty of care to students. As Universities United Kingdom (2015) recommend in their Good Practice Guide to Student Wellbeing in Higher Education, this duty includes the provision of pastoral support and taking steps required to protect the health, safety and well-being of students. It encourages universities to provide well-being services, including counselling, and also implies that they must take measures to assess and manage risk, such as the risk of suicide and self-harm. So as a counsellor at Brunel University London, I am required to abide by a risk assessment process which is not a part of Solution Focused practice.

Universities are now also more likely to be more proactive in relation to their duty of care for two reasons: firstly, in the UK recently there was much publicity and concern about an unusually high number of student suicides, implying that there was a higher rate amongst students than the general population, even though the actual rate amongst the general population is twice that of students. In addition, as a result of 'widening participation programmes, there has been active encouragement for a greater diversity of students to attend university, including those with mental health difficulties. It is therefore now more likely that there will be students attending university with pre-existing mental health issues who would previously have been excluded or may not have even considered themselves suitable for university life despite their obvious academic talents.

Within this context, universities will conduct a preliminary assessment when students request counselling so that the level of risk to themselves or to others can be determined and appropriate action taken if needed. At Brunel, CORE is used – a validated assessment tool used by the NHS and many other universities which provides information both about the client's current mental well-being and their risk of suicide and self-harm when they start counselling. This is then compared to their scores at the end of their counselling to measure the levels of change and to provide a further risk assessment. Within the Solution Focused framework, in addition to problem focused means of assessing risk, it is also important to explore signs of safety, as Turnell and Edwards (1999) have proposed, which involves exploring and acknowledging what a client may be doing to resist or minimise harm to themselves or others. In the absence of these signs, robust action must be taken.

Sessions

The Solution Focused approach fits well into what modern university well-being services are looking for. They are attracted by the flexibility of the Solution Focused approach, which can include comparatively fewer sessions while not insisting on the 50-minute hour or the same time on the same day of each week, which some approaches expect. Most university counselling services will limit the number of sessions a student can expect to receive to six 50-minute sessions, a model also used frequently in the NHS.

Solution Focused practice generally fits well within this model, and the clients I see have an average of three sessions. However, what is different within the Solution Focused approach, compared with other approaches, is the treatment of every session as if it is the last session (Ratner et al., 2012). This means trusting that the client will know when to finish counselling, and busy students may well prefer to engage with counselling on a session-by-session basis. Universities may prefer shorter sessions to cope with demand, but I have also found that flexibility around the scheduling and length of sessions can mean counselling will fit better with the student's timetable. Students may also choose not to use all the time allocated for a session, which fits in with the Solution Focused model of treating things at face value and allowing clients to make decisions about what is useful for them.

How to begin

What I try to do as a Solution Focused counsellor is help my clients identify the changes they want to make by asking some very careful questions. I always start with 'What are your best hopes from our work together?' (George et al., 1999). In this way, the focus is already on the outcome, or preferred future, not the problem, on what they want rather than what is wrong for them.

I also ask questions such as 'What are you doing already that is working?' and 'Have you had any glimpses of how you would like things to be?', which draw the client's attention to the fact that noticeable change has probably started to happen already, often before the therapy has even started. This is what Weiner-Davis et al. (1987) identified as pre-treatment change.

Other important questions include 'What difference would it make to you if your best hopes were realised?' and 'What does your preferred future look like?'. This begins to draw the client's attention to noticeable change, which might also be noticed by others and makes progress towards this preferred future more describable to themselves.

Using technology

I have found that Solution Focused practice lends itself well to changing modalities from face-to-face, to Skype, email or phone. There is no inherent need to be in the same room as the client, or indeed the same country, and for some clients the slower pace of, for example, emails may be beneficial. Using remote technology accommodates international students and those who live off campus who often have to travel and not be fixed in one location. With no interest in interpretation or searching for what is below the surface, the Solution Focused counsellor is able to focus on the face value of what the client is saying. In addition, there is no attempt to read body language, so the Solution Focused practitioner doesn't need to see the client.

Case 1

A young male client (A) wearing an Arsenal football shirt came into the counselling room and sat down. (I remembered hearing during my training that we don't have to share our client's views in order to help them, which was just as well as I have a fondness for Chelsea F.C.).

A: I don't have much time.
   Counsellor (P): What would be your best hopes from the time we do have?
A: I am in my final year and think I am going to fail my degree. I was doing really well but it's my dissertation. I have to hand it in next week and it is not finished.
P: On a scale of 0 to 10 where 0 equals you fail this degree and 10 means you get your dissertation in on time and pass with flying colours, what sort of number are you on now?
A: I am two nil down.
   Rather than answer the question directly he provided a football metaphor, which I could then mirror in the questions I asked:
P: How long before the game ends?

A: About 15 minutes (which he had explained meant next week)
P: Is this a game you really need to win? (i.e. How much does this degree matter?)
A: Yes, very much so.
P: What would get you back to 1–2? (This is equivalent to asking: What would move you one point up the scale and get you back in the game?)
A: Well if I could just sit down and write the end of chapter three.
P: Wow, so you have written nearly three chapters already!
A: Yes.
P: How did you do that?

He started talking about what he had already done successfully, and then he remembered watching Arsenal come back to win 3–2 having been two nil down.

This seemed to boost his confidence and help him see that changes which can lead towards a good outcome were possible even when previously all appeared to be lost.

He left after about 10 minutes, saying he didn't have any more time for counselling as he needed to get back to finish his dissertation.

Case 2

A Chinese student presented with concerns that she would not be able to complete her dissertation as her stress regarding her dying mother was interfering with her capacity to study. Her CORE assessment indicated she had felt suicidal at times but was not currently at risk and had no active plans for suicide. I asked her what her best hopes were, and she said that she wanted to complete her degree and cope as best as she could with her mother's illness. Her mother's health had deteriorated, and she needed to return suddenly to China which she feared would mean she could not complete her degree. However, such was her determination that she managed to negotiate an extension and continue with her studies, despite leaving the UK. I agreed to continue offering her counselling by email. Time differences made Skype less practical. After a couple of email exchanges, she told me how for her, communicating via the written word was preferable as she found expressing her emotions in English difficult. Writing allowed her to look words up in the dictionary and express herself more clearly and accurately. During these email exchanges, she told me that she could not understand why I would not give her advice; however, she did agree to my request of asking her to notice what she was doing when things were feeling better for her. She came to realise that she could not stop her mother from dying, but she could manage the feelings about it in such a way as to continue with her degree within the given time frame.

When her mother died, her grief and distress caused her to question her own sanity and she was reassured when I commented on the normality of these reactions. This acknowledgement of her pain and emotions was reassuring to her and enabled her to notice how well she was coping under extremely difficult circumstances. This interaction shows that the Solution Focused approach **can** acknowledge the emotions and problems that clients bring and is not 'problem phobic', as it is sometimes assumed to be.

Best hopes for students

The most common problems presented by students are depression, anxiety, relationship difficulties and academic worries, though it is rare for students to present solely with academic worries as they usually have other concerns. This is reflected in the fact that the most common response to the best hopes question from students is to be happier **and** to finish their degree/studies.

Depression and anxiety may lead to students not going to lectures, staying in their rooms and avoiding socialising, and inevitably impacting on their academic progress. Disabling anxiety stops students doing what they want to do – in their personal and in their work lives.

Much of my work involves looking at how life would be for the student without these problems and what they would be doing instead. I explore the times when they do manage to attend and focus on a lecture or when they are able to socialise and relax with their friends. Looking for instances of change in this way is important, as even noticing very small changes can enable the client to begin to feel empowered and more optimistic.

Helping clients look for and notice signs of change, however small, can begin to make a significant difference. Solution Focused practice is not so interested in how change happens but in recognising and noticing that change is happening all the time. The task of the Solution Focused counsellor is to help clients to notice this change and the significance it has for them.

On occasion, a student's description may indicate what appears to be a major positive shift or where their best hopes begin to be realised. I consider that it is important for me, as the counsellor, to take care not to appear excessively enthusiastic about what I regard as a significant change, in case the client doesn't see it that way or notices no impact of such change. This would merely be cheerleading my own agenda. (de Shazer et al., 2007). It is tempting to lead from the front but far more effective to support from one step behind the client, as Cantwell and Holmes (1994) suggest.

Scaling is a very effective tool that Solution Focused practitioners use to help clients identify visible change. Students are very familiar with marks out of 10. The question I pose is 'Where 0 is the worst things have been for you and 10 is that your best hopes are realised, what sort of number are you on today?' 'Sort of' makes room for between 2 and 3 or half numbers, which helps clients make better descriptions of where they are. The most common answer from my clients at the start of counselling is 3. I then ask, 'What are you doing already that gets you to a 3?' This invites description of their strengths and their capacity to cope, which can be important in empowering the client.

Buddies and Ambassadors

At Brunel, we train second and third year students to be 'Buddies' to new students, offering support and information during their first six weeks. The training is similar to *mental health first aid* training (a programme being developed to raise mental health awareness amongst the British public). The Buddy is trained to recognise when someone might need further help, to signpost to other services and to offer a crucial first point of contact with someone who is familiar with many of the challenges new students encounter.

The training involves role-playing how to acknowledge difficult feelings while looking for strengths and possibilities, a technique described by O'Hanlon and Beadle (1994). So, rather than discuss all the things the new student is anxious about and give advice about what to do, the Buddy is encouraged to ask questions which indicate the new student's strengths and how have they dealt with new things in the past. They may also ask about what the new student is pleased to notice about themselves already, since arriving at Brunel. This encourages a sense of empowerment for the new student. There is a similar training for student Ambassadors who live in halls with new students offering mentoring support and signposting to other services throughout the academic year. They can help with anything from students having a mental health crisis to a group of flatmates having a kitchen dispute over who stole the milk. For example, a student might say 'I am really anxious because I have never been away from home before.' An Ambassador might be tempted to say, 'Oh my that sounds terrible, what is it that you are anxious about?' The student would then be likely to describe the nature of the anxiety in more depth and connect it to specific examples of current circumstances which are, in their view, causing the anxiety. This response is problem focused and likely to result in an escalation of the anxiety. This in turn would soon have the Ambassador feeling out of their depth and sensing that they lack the expertise in how to respond. It could also lead to them rushing to signpost to another student service which could leave the new student feeling the Ambassador is overwhelmed or even uninterested.

To avoid this scenario and to continue to be useful to the student, I encourage Ambassadors to say something along the lines of 'You sound worried, can you tell me what you have done when you have felt anxious in the past?' This will lead the student down a path of describing what works for them and reminding them about their strengths and how they have managed previously. It will also potentially draw their attention to how they have already found ways to cope with their new environment.

Staff training

I have trained university staff, ranging from security officers to academics, to help them exercise their duty of care and to offer appropriate support to students who they assess as being at risk or having major mental health issues. Staff can be anxious if a student has a mental health diagnosis and may then underestimate what they can offer the student.

I boost staff confidence by helping them see that if a student is raising issues with them, the student clearly considers that they can be helpful. I encourage them to focus on what the students says and remind them that a Solution Focused approach is only interested in what is on the surface. This can be very enabling for staff who are expecting to have to dig deep to be really helpful to their students. I help them be clear about how and when to signpost to other services. I encourage them not to become over-involved and to recognise when they might be overwhelmed. However, as with the Buddies and student Ambassadors, they need to take their time before signposting to other services. This will ensure that the new student will be more likely to feel they have been heard rather than that they have overburdened the member of staff.

I also try to give staff more confidence by encouraging them to see students as resourceful even when distressed. This is an important part of Solution Focused practice that I introduce, and it shifts staff's perspectives so that they know their role is to help enable a student's own resourcefulness rather than have to solve the problems for them.

It is important that within the training the worst fears that staff or students have about supporting others are explored, and they always raise concern about talking about suicide and self-harm. I try to demystify some of the assumptions about these topics and advise on other services within the university to which they can signpost. Talking about such sensitive issues can help staff be more empowered and confident to respond while recognising their limits.

Conclusion

In conclusion, the Solution Focused approach is, in my experience, a very effective and economic way of working in a university counselling service because it plays to the strengths of its clients, recognising their resources for change and their uniqueness in managing difficulties in their lives. Modern students are often too busy meeting deadlines to spend a lot of time in counselling. The Solution Focused practitioner wants to help the client to change as soon as possible and is expecting this rather than assuming long term work will be required. Indeed, the most likely number of sessions students attend is one. This suits many students who simply want to get back on track. The approach also does not rely on diagnoses or ideas about normality and pathology.

When the impact of counselling at Brunel is evaluated through comparing CORE scores at the start with those at the end of counselling, the Solution Focused approach performs consistently high in comparison with other approaches and requires fewer sessions. This enables greater turnover of clients while maintaining the quality of service. Moreover, Solution Focused counsellors are much less prone to burn-out. All of this is very important when demands on university counselling and well-being services are greater than ever before and budgets are continuing to be stretched.

References

Cantwell, P., & Holmes, S. (1994). Social Construction: A Paradigm Shift for Systemic Therapy and Training. *Australia and New Zealand Journal of Family Therapy*, 15(1), 17–26.

De Shazer, S., Dolan, Y., Korman, H., Trepper, T., McCullum, E., & Berg, I. K. (2007). *More Than Miracles: The State of the Art of Solution-Focused Brief Therapy*. New York: Haworth Press.

George, E., Iveson, C., & Ratner, H. (1999). *Problem to Solution: Brief Therapy with Individuals and Families*, 2nd edition. London: BT Press.

O'Hanlon, B., & Beadle, S. (1994). *A Field Guide to PossibilityLand: Possibility Therapy Methods*. London: BT Press.

Ratner, H., George, E., & Iveson, C. (2012). *Solution Focused Brief Therapy: 100 Key Points and Techniques*. London: Routledge.

Turnell, A., & Edwards, S. (1999). Aspiring to Partnership: The Signs of Safety Approach to Child Protection Casework. *Child Abuse Review*, 6, 179–190.

Universities UK. (2015). *Student Mental Wellbeing in Higher Education – Good Practice Guide*. London: Universities UK.

Weiner-Davis, M., de Shazer, S., & Gingerich, W. (1987). Building on Pre Treatment Change to Construct the Therapeutic Solution: An Exploratory Study. *Journal of Family and Marital Therapy*, 13(4), 359–363.

Chapter 15

Coaching for youth offenders in an institutional setting

Joe Chan

In Singapore, according to the Singapore Police Force's Annual Crime Brief for 2015 and 2016, the youth arrest figures for persons aged between 7 and 19 years old is on a steady decline. Of the total of 2788 youths in 2016, there is a number of these youths who, despite being in some kind of diversionary and community sentencing orders, still go back into offending behaviours. Youths aged between 14 and 21 years old, who are repeated offenders, will be subject to a recommendation to go through more structured regimes of rehabilitation care and programming. Many of these youths, when discharged from these institutions, will still be expected to be on a mandatory supervision order of varying duration to the institution as part of their aftercare programme. However, if they are found to be not complying with the orders of the supervision, then they can be recalled back to the institutions for re-detention.

Since early 2018, my team of social workers and youth workers from REACH Community Services and I have been going into such an institution to work with male offenders aged between 18 and 25 years old who have been recalled because of breaching their supervision orders. Knowing that this would be a group who would be very challenging to work with, I felt the need to think carefully about what we were going to do with them which was different. In general, we know that the youths in this setting would have already gone through various rehabilitative programmes and also different sentencing options, and yet when they are given a taste of freedom during their supervision phase, they still end up coming back into to the system.

According to N's perspective, "I feel that there is this disconnection between what everyone is doing, whether as an SSO (Social Service Organisation), counsellor or school counsellor, and whatever the 'institution' side is doing. So, you guys think we have never been through this before, so you need to give us this targeted thing. But in actual fact when we have been in and out of 'the system', been in and out of school counselling, been in and out of disciplinary side, I think pretty much we know the answer already."

Thus, this chapter is really just a reflection and description of my curiosities, my thought process, a brief description of the plan and my experience of our engagements. This chapter will be in no way evaluative of the work of the team or this institution; instead, it's really just an exploratory account of my curiosities in working with such institutionalised settings and trying to do things differently. It is my hope that my sharing here will spark off even more discussions and reflections amongst Solution Focused (SF) practitioners who are doing this sort of work, so that we might all become even more effective.

Programme design

As I proceeded to plan for the first run of the programme with the youths, I thought about taking them through something different from what the institution was offering, something that would be complementary and maybe even refreshing. For the youth offender population, many of the youths would have gone through programmes which emphasise rehabilitation or are corrective in nature. In such a setting where they are being assigned counsellors, caseworkers and officers to ensure they are compliant with the regime, often the focus is on what they need to change based on their assessed needs and risks.

So I decided to adopt a more collaborative and empowering approach where we would go in and pay attention to what possible outcomes they would like to work on themselves during the sessions. I was particularly keen to see the effect of us positioning ourselves differently in our work with the youths. So, for example, instead of the more usual talking about the pitfalls which had resulted in them coming back into the system, we might use a coaching approach where we showed interest in where their energies lay for themselves.

According to the International Coach Federation, coaching is defined as "partnering with clients in a thought-provoking and creative process that inspires them to maximise their personal and professional potential." So for this platform, it would mean that we would enter into the sessions with as few judgements and assessments as possible, while we listened and explored their best versions of themselves, starting from the rest of the time they had inside. I also decided to take the different Solution Focused coaching elements which would typically happen in one session and separate them out into the different sessions of the programme, with the youths as the focus of each session. The format of each session was a group, run in an open group fashion for about 1 hour and composed of about 20 youths. In each session, there were about 5 or 6 facilitators who would then help to facilitate together with me.

My thoughts around the structure of the sessions were that I wanted to see whether we could break down the segments of a regular coaching session into bite-size parts and expand on each segment during each session. Given that the context was an open group setting, I also wanted to see the outcomes of such a design and particularly whether each individual session could stand alone and still be useful for participants.

A breakdown of the I-Coach programme of 1 hour each session

Table 15.1

Session	Topic	Objective
1	Perspective taking	Introducing the power and effects of having new perspectives in life especially in repeated circumstances
2	Goal formulation	To facilitate the process for the youths to clarify what they want for themselves at this point of their lives
3	Scaling for success	Momentum to achieve what they want and how this can be built on the positives already present rather than starting from zero
4	Celebrating small steps	Learning to focus their energies on affirming to themselves what has gone well and expanding from there
5	Peak performance	Handling complacencies and cultivating a mindset to hit the next level

Reflections and observations of the sessions

Generally the sessions were quite smooth as the youths were happy to be out of their cells and to come together for the sessions. With the collaborative stance that we adopted, the youths felt comfortable and at ease in relating to us. Throughout the sessions, we also threw in lots of interactive activities and games to bring out the objective of the session. The youths generally tended to open up more in the small group settings where there were about 5 or 6 participants in each group.

Both the future focused nature of the topics, focusing on things the youths could work towards, and the small group setting enabled the group to build on its dynamics where many ideas and points could be explored and expanded further. One of the hopes that I had was that the youths would be able ask themselves the same SF questions even after the sessions. However, this part was a bit challenging to track because of the nature of this profile of youths and the fact that we were unable to track them over a longer period of time. This was because different youths left the institution to return to the community at different times depending on their individual sentencing.

As I reflected back on the sessions, there was definitely a lot of learning opportunities, especially in terms of engaging with this clientele group. For such youths who have been through so much of the system, sometimes just hearing a different set of questions from a different space seemed to be really refreshing for them. In the first session when I introduced myself and my team to the group, I actually told the youths that we were there as coaches, and we drew the parallel of a sports coach, which they could immediately relate to. This initial staging, where we positioned ourselves differently from their usual caseworkers and counsellors, was helpful, because each youth could relate to an experience that they had had, often positive, with a sports coach in the past. In the sports coaching context, it's also often about becoming better as an individual or as a team, which sets a platform to discuss different concerns.

In the second session, we looked at goal formulation towards the youths' preferred futures, and we invited them to list as many details as possible about their best hopes and miracle pictures. For the staff, it was particularly exciting to hear the youths' aspirations and hopes for themselves, and our role was to show no doubt or judgement, but just to provide them that space to put it out there in a written form on paper. It was here that we found out that some of them wanted to be athletes and fitness instructors, which then become further talking points in subsequent sessions.

The SF approach is a particularly useful approach in such an environment, where we often see a mixed profile of individuals coming from different educational backgrounds, and particularly skewing towards the less educated. It seemed that using many of the simple SF questions and techniques such as scaling, exceptions and doing more of what worked really helped the youths to grasp the sessions better.

As I reflect and look back on the contents of the programme, it was also helpful that the SF approach doesn't have a theory on how change happens for the clients, so we put more emphasis on the applications of the approach in that particular setting. With such a profile of clientele and in a group setting, it was really useful to go in without a narrow perspective of how change will happen, particularly so with these youth offenders who had already been told so much about what they needed to change and what they needed to avoid doing. Instead we went in and invited their sense of agency into the sessions, which seemed to be refreshing and engaging for them.

Key summary points of what is useful for youth offenders in an institutional setting based on 2 interviews with N, male, 22 years old, and H, male, 21 years old

Overall, intervention that focuses more on skills and knowledge, and which is tied to concrete plans with small steps for when the institution is left, is deemed as more valuable.

1 In an institutional setting, negative behaviours are viewed through a disciplinary lens where young people are expected to comply with the rules, and there seems to be a high level of behaviour compliance. However, affirmations of their efforts to exhibit positive behaviours, rather than rule compliance, in this setting were still helpful in encouraging a sense of agency in the youths.

2 Young people's preferred mode of learning is experiential and hands-on with activities. Lecture-style interventions seem less engaging and boring to participants.
3 Assessing and designing an intervention programme based on risks and needs alone is not enough for young offenders. We need to consider the personalities, cognitive levels and individual profiles of the young person as well. Having 2 people committing the same offence doesn't mean that a standardised intervention will have the same impact for both people, even though their risk levels might be the same.
4 When an intervention has worked well with a small group, it doesn't necessarily guarantee that the same outcomes can be met if we try to scale it up to a larger group. Outcomes can be affected by the personal characteristics of a facilitator and by the openness to change of a particular client group.
5 In an institutional setting, we need to process the youths' idea of change further and break it down into much smaller steps which can inspire hope in them. According to N, sometimes the experience of going through programme after programme without seeing any change can make that experience feel meaningless after a while. Instead, as Michael Durrant (1993) puts it, by teaching young people to "watch the grass grow" we help them to focus on and to notice the small steps and successes, even when they are affected by being in an institution.
6 In an institution, we have to be mindful that the power of socialisation is happening all the time with youths. We take the view that our interventions are able to tap into the strengths of the different individuals and groups inside the institution and can encourage them to take charge of the pace and scope of their change. This can be really helpful, both to them as individuals and as influencers in their social groups. We are really not the experts of their change; these young people are experts on themselves. In this way, we can harness the power of socialisation for hope and for positive change.

In conclusion, I hope that this chapter has sparked certain interests and curiosities for practitioners on the ground on how we can carry out our practice differently so as to complement and effect change with our young offenders today. I think that especially for coaches working in such institutional settings, we can leverage the coaching approach to hold a different set of conversations with our young people today.

References

Annual Crime Brief. (2014, 2015). *Singapore Police Force*. Source: *Police Government News and Publications Statistics*.

Durrant, M. (1993). *Residential Treatment: A Cooperative, Competency – Based Approach to Therapy and Program Design*. New York: W. W. Norton.

Chapter 16

Solution Focused "injections"
Solution Focused working in acute paediatric settings

Harriet Conniff

Introduction

Holding a Solution Focused (SF) stance to working with children and young people with chronic health conditions and serious illness is useful and vital to me, professionally and personally, as a psychologist working in acute health settings. In such contexts, the children and young people are patients; undergoing life-sustaining medical treatment is a reality of their everyday lives. An important role for the SF practitioner in physical health contexts is to support people to "live well despite chronic health difficulties" (Simm, 2012).

Reports of SF working with children in acute inpatient healthcare are absent from the literature. The work described here is with children and young people (aged 0–18 years) with chronic health conditions that are life-threatening/-limiting and has occurred in various UK hospitals. Names and identifying information have been changed to protect confidentiality. I will focus here on the "Solution Focused injections" more common to my inpatient working, shorter interventions far removed from the "traditional therapy hour in a room" typical of my outpatient work.

An SF stance

An SF stance is fundamentally useful in my work. A central aim of the approach is to create a context for clients to notice and then use their own strengths to move forward in their lives: "building homes for solutions" (Steve de Shazer, 1988). This stance is illustrated by the common response to hearing that I work with children in hospital: "that must be so difficult". Of course, children being sick and suffering is not easy for anyone, least of all the child and family. I tend to reply with something like "of course it can be hard and I am only human. I find it useful to focus on how people *do* manage in the face of adversity and am privileged to have conversations with people at this time about what is important to them". This stance or focus on what people *are doing* to get through sustains me to do my job and allows me to ask (hopefully) useful questions.

Solution Focused "injections" 109

SF does not have an overarching explanatory theory as to why it works or not (Ratner et al., 2012, p. 21). Instead there are some general assumptions informing the stance:

Clients are the experts on their lives

"You're not seeing us as failing – you see us as parents. Yes, we have a sick child in hospital but we are still parents" (Father of baby on life support). This father's quote followed a bedside conversation where I assumed that he and his partner still held expertise as parents while their child was in intensive care. They told me that continuing to be parents was important to them, so they requested to take part in their child's care where possible such as assisting nurses, washing their child and having cuddles despite all the tubes.

It is useful to listen for resources rather than deficits

Problem-free talk as a means of gathering strengths and resources can be particularly relevant in medical contexts where the focus is, understandably, on treating health conditions and what is wrong. Asking the father earlier about what was important to him revealed a whole history of the importance of fatherhood and being present as a father.

Every problem has at least one exception

In multidisciplinary team (MDT) meetings, sometimes discussion about a child's adherence to treatment can become problem-saturated. I try to shift the focus to what child and family are managing to do: "so they are coming to clinic appointments and manage evening medicines sometimes, what would you need to see next to fit with the treatment plan?"

"The greater the problems a person has survived the more rich the hidden history of achievement and possibility is likely to be" (BRIEF, 2012, p. 2)

I hold onto this assumption when staff are worried that a parent has previous contact with mental health services. I may say to the team "I imagine that this parent may have good experience of getting through challenging times".

Diversity needs attention

I have added this assumption to my SF working. As chronic health conditions cut across all aspects of society, I work with people from varied backgrounds, cultures, ethnicities, races, faiths, classes, ages, genders and sexual orientations. SF could be said to incorporate diversity, as the model allows for describing details from people's everyday lives and the myriad forms these details may take. However, diversity is an area that much of the SF world has not paid explicit attention to (Connie & Frohn, 2018 personal communication).

Families live in contexts of discrimination, prejudice and uneven access to resources. This inequality can become more pronounced when a child has a health condition requiring hospitalisation. I find the following question useful: "If I were from a similar cultural background to yours (or was male/shared your religion/ etc.), what questions might I ask that could be useful to you?" Of course we must not assume that if someone appears similar to ourselves that they will have a similar outlook, so arguably we can ask these questions with all we work with. Placing the onus on individuals and families when there are broader issues of discrimination and inequality might be questionable though. Thus, Walsh (2010, p. 100) proposes going beyond the remit of the traditional SF model to work ethically cross-culturally, which may include interventions at an organisational and structural level and considering issues of power. As a psychologist, I may make use of my professional title to ask questions and advocate for marginalised groups in MDT meetings, by writing letters and raising issues of power and inequality with management.

2) SF in health

Chronic health conditions that require frequent and long hospital stays are known to have a negative psychological impact on children, young people and their families (Edwards & Titman, 2010, p. 57). Children with life-limiting/-threatening conditions are more at risk of experiencing poor mental health, as are their families, with factors such as loss of control and feeling different to peers commonly cited (BPS, 2015, p. 74).

Using an SF approach in physical health has been described in the role of physician (Giorlando & Schilling, 1997), as an oncology consultant (1990s BRIEF trainings – Ratner personal communication) and as a hospital speech and language therapist:

> the hospital environment offers good examples of how important it is to listen to clients. You are not going to rush in with solution-building without first having heard and acknowledged clients' pain in distressing circumstances, but there are always opportunities to reflect back strengths and discover possibilities as to how to move forward.
>
> (Burns, 2016, p. 20)

Insoo Kim Berg and Steve de Shazer regularly worked with people with drug and alcohol issues that clearly impact on physical health. Generally though, the SF literature has focused on its application in mental health, social work and education.

There is published evidence for SF being useful in health: Ford (2014) reviewed SF working in healthcare which predominantly refers to adults. Elsewhere the efficacy of SF has been demonstrated in adult health conditions as varied as chronic pain (Simm et al., 2013) and post stroke (Burns, 2016). Literature is emerging on SF interventions in paediatric contexts being effective (Baldwin et al., 2013; Christie, 2008; Viner et al., 2003).

What is it that might make SF so effective in healthcare settings? Carr et al. (2014) researched the experience of SF from the perspective of adult clients with long-term physical health conditions. They highlighted SF as especially useful in long-term conditions where patients and families commonly experience a loss of control over their lives: "the way the psychologist worked with participants increased their feelings of empowerment, control and confidence, and enabled them to uncover their own solutions to difficulties and feel better able to manage their illness following therapy" (Carr et al., 2014, p. 390).

Baldwin et al. (2013) reported the success of children's rehabilitation using SF. Participants' feedback suggested co-constructed goals in SF makes those goals more meaningful to patients who then are more likely to work on rehabilitation at home compared to more expert-professional approaches where goals are directed. Burns (2016, p. xii) raises how valuable SF is in physical health beyond "clinical recovery" as it pays attention to relationships, thus aiding "personal recovery". My own clinical experience fits with these analyses and that an SF stance is also effective in health settings as it is protective of clinician burn out.

SF Language in health

Occasionally I come across professionals who have some knowledge of SF approaches but perhaps misunderstand it as being Pollyanna therapy and not to be used for "serious problems". Sometimes people have concerns about using SF language of miracles and best hopes with health conditions that do not go away and may be life-threatening or palliative, fearing 'unrealistic' goals. Like Burns (2016, p. 33), I have used the words best hopes and miracles in such contexts and people do not respond with "getting better" or "not dying". In the context of children's hospitals (where there are often stories about miracles), I may sometimes use an alternative to miracle day such as "Let's imagine that tomorrow turns out to be a good day for you. How will you know that it's going well?" Or in a scale: "So, if 10 is you are feeling better in yourself given the circumstances [stuck in hospital/limited mobility/breathlessness/etc.] and 0 is the opposite, where would you say you are on the scale now? How will you know you have moved up?"

3) The medical context and SF Injections

In acute settings, the child's medical condition and treatment can rapidly change. Knowing about the medical context is useful. This may be unlike other SF therapy settings where challenging contexts may not be known. Awareness of the medical context is not the same as knowing about the problem. In healthcare settings, there is a difference between awareness of some of the medical challenges people face and what people then choose to talk about; I would not assume, say, that any medical update becomes the basis for a best hope, yet it is an important context. In the case below, a mother (P) updates me that her baby daughter has to have a PEG (percutaneous endoscopic gastrostomy tube that goes straight into the stomach for feeding), and she is frightened. In this instance, using an SF approach when hearing about a medical difficulty, I do not ask why it is difficult for this mother to see her baby have another procedure, how hard it was before, what worries her most. Here knowing what a PEG is, what is involved in inserting it and maintaining it means we can use the small amount of time to focus on what is important to the mother, then for me to ask what might be the first small sign she is coping with the idea of a PEG:

P: It's been so tough to see her going through all these procedures and she has nearly died so many times, I am not sure whether I would be able to cope with her having to have another thing done to her even though I know she needs to have it.

Me: What would be the first small sign that would tell you that you were coping with this, her having to have the PEG?

P: I think, well, I would be able to speak about it more with my husband and my family. I mean he knows but he's at work so he has not had the full update yet – he is coming on Friday but, yes, I would make time to have a conversation with him.

Me: And if you were having that conversation, when would it be?

P: Well, Friday most likely Friday evening when we get back to the room.

Me: And on Friday evening as you arrive back in the room what would you be doing that was fitting with your version of coping, coping with this information and having this conversation?

P: I think I would be in the room and not go off and have a bath, I would be in the room. Yes, and I would ask him what he thought about what the doctors said, as usually I wait for him to bring it up or just carry on with having a bath and getting to bed – I mean I am really exhausted. . .

Me: What would your husband notice about you that would tell him that you were coping and that you were having a different kind of conversation?

P: Well, the fact that we were having it in the first place! Yes, and I wouldn't be chatting on about anything else avoiding it, I would ask him and listen to what he had to say.

We get interrupted by ward round and only resume our conversation the following week when the parents have consented to the PEG being inserted. They let me know they were reassured by meeting the PEG nurse and talking with another parent of a child with a PEG. The mother reports that the decision to meet this parent came as a result of the conversation she had on the Friday with her husband. It is important to note that my role is not *to make* children and families have medical treatment or procedures; the mother had said "I know she has to have it", which gave me permission to have a conversation about coping with it.

SF injections

Time for therapeutic conversations can be squeezed on the ward. Conversations are frequently interrupted by observations taken, drugs administered and clinicians doing their rounds, as we saw earlier. Walsh (2010, p. 144) discusses the potential for SF talk across different types of contact. Inpatient work takes place in "untherapeutic" clinical locations, sometimes having the luxury of a treatment room for privacy if the child is well enough to move or at the bedside speaking quietly. When a child or family are in crisis, my intervention may be just one question: "what keeps you going right now?"

Staff were worried about G, a 12 year old girl who was not taking essential medications. On first meeting G and her mum on the ward, we only had 10 minutes before she needed a scan. I asked what her best hopes were for her admission:

G: To not have to come into hospital so much, take my medicines better.
Me: Jump forward a few months, say you were taking your medicines better and wake up one morning, what would be different about you as you walk into the kitchen on this day where you are taking your medicines?
G: I'd be more independent.
Me: How would this show?
G: A cheeky smile and just doing it [taking medicines].
Me: How would your mum and sister react?
G: Sister would say what's going on??!! Mum would smile and think I was being responsible. . .
The porters arrived. We met for an outpatient appointment a month later. I asked "what's better?"
G: It's all been good.
Me: Great! Tell me more.

Responding to my "what else?" questions, she told me about "good things" which included: "Completed treatment for a month – the physiotherapist could tell as I was less crackley, feel more able to do things like activities with my family which makes me happier, more confident to talk to others about my conditions (at school and home), knowing where to go for help, taking breaks regularly. . . ". In our first conversation, we had begun to build a picture of how she might be in herself on a taking medicines better day. This short "injection" may have been useful in the beneficial clinical and personal outcomes that followed.

When children are unwell they can have reduced concentration. Parents are likely to be tired and stressed, and therefore also less able to take part in long conversations. One 10-year old boy was recovering from a long intensive care stay and had after effects (poor concentration, attention and memory with active hallucinations). We had a 5-minute session about what helped him to cope when he got confused and wrote a list. The list was relayed to his family and staff so they could remind him to look at it. Next time we met, he reported feeling better about "confusion" and had been relearning to walk, although he expressed fear about trying the stairs. I asked him how his physiotherapist knew he was ready, which produced an even longer list of his skills in successfully walking again. SF therapeutic letters can also act as a memory aid for families and help the system view progress and strengths in families.

In working with staff, there can be time constraints too; MDT ward rounds are fast paced with multiple teams present and many children to discuss. I selectively chip in with questions about progress or small exceptions. In discussing a young girl with learning disabilities who was in hospital to get used to having oxygen to breathe at night, I asked: "how did you manage to get her to try the mask even for 5 minutes? What difference did that make?" Elsewhere I have consulted with staff around how they might share information with families in a useful way, for example starting MDT updates with "what are your hopes for this meeting?"

4) Summary

In inpatient working with children, the setting can limit time for therapeutic conversations. I have found that even a few Solution Focused questions (a quick SF 'injection') can be effective in bringing ideas to life about where children and families want to be and developing thick description of what's working already.

References

Baldwin, P., King, G., Evans, J., McDougall, S., Tucker, M. A., & Servais, M. (2013). Solution-Focused Coaching in Pediatric Rehabilitation: An Integrated Model for Practice. *Physical & Occupational Therapy in Pediatrics*, 33(4), 467–483.

BPS. (2015). What Good Looks Like: Delivering Psychological Services for Children and Young People with Physical Health Needs and Their Families. *Child & Family Clinical Psychology Review*, 3, 71–83.

BRIEF. (2012). *Solution Focused Working*, 1–2. www.brief.org.uk/assets/documents/the-solution-focused-approach-an-overview-09-12.pdf.

Burns, K. (2005). *Focus on Solutions: A Health Professional's Guide*. London: John Wiley & Sons.

Burns, K. (2016). *Focus on Solutions: A Health Professional's Guide*, revised 2nd edition. London: Solutions Books.

Carr, S., Smith, I. C., & Simm, R. (2014). Solution-Focused Brief Therapy from the Perspective of Clients with Long-Term Physical Health Conditions. *Psychology Health and Medicine*, 19(4), 384–391.

Christie, D. (2008). Dancing with Diabetes: Brief Therapy Conversations with Children, Young People and Families Living with Diabetes. *European Diabetes Nursing*, 5, 28–32.

De Shazer, S. (1988). *Clues: Investigating Solutions in Brief Therapy*. New York: W. W. Norton.
Edwards, M., & Titman, P. (2010). *Promoting Psychological Wellbeing in Children with Acute and Chronic Illness*. London: Jessica Kingsley.
Ford, G. (2014). *Solution Focused Practice: A Brief Summary of the Health Related Evidence Base*. British Heart Foundation Booklet.
Giorlando, M. E., & Schilling, R. J. (1997). On Becoming a Solution-Focused Physician: The MED-STAT Acronym. *Families, Systems, & Health*, 15(4), 361–373.
Kim Berg, I. (2003). *On Solution Focused Therapy*. Interviewed by V. Yalom & B. Rubin. www.psychotherapy.net/interview/insookimberg#sectionlivinganddyingwithmeaning.
Ratner, H., George, E., & Iveson, C. (2012). *Solution Focused Brief Therapy 100 Key Points and Techniques*. London: Routledge.
Simm, R. (2012). *Living Well Despite Chronic Health Conditions*. Presentation at the Lyme Disease Association Conference.
Simm, R., Iddon, J., & Barker, C. (2013). A Community Pain Service Solution-Focused Pain Management Programme: Delivery and Preliminary Outcome Data. *British Journal of Pain*, 8(1), 49–56.
Viner, R. M., Christie, D., Taylor, V., & Hey, S. (2003). Motivational/Solution-Focused Intervention Improves HbA1c in Adolescents with Type 1 Diabetes: A Pilot Study. *Diabetic Medicine*, 20(9), 739–742.
Walsh, T. (2010). *The Solution-Focused Helper: Ethics and Practice in Health and Social Care*. Maidenhead: McGraw Hill Open University Press.

Chapter 17

Using the Solution Focused approach within New Zealand Police to create happy endings for young people and their families

Emma Burns

I am a registered psychologist, having worked in a variety of settings since becoming registered in 1996. This includes mental health, education, traumatic incident response, and suicide bereavement. Since 2010 I have been employed by New Zealand Police, where I spent eight years working with "child offenders" before moving into the family harm team in late 2018.

My work with young people has changed dramatically since I began in 2010. Back then, I had never heard of the Solution Focused approach and worked from the expert model that I had been taught back at university. However, to be honest, I never felt comfortable with this. In 2011, I attended an initial training run by Michael Durrant. I must confess that I had mixed feelings when I left. Part of me was inspired and delighted to have found such a simple approach that just made sense. But part of me was sceptical – this might work for "easy" problems, but I worked with young people, often from generations of issues such as crime, drug use, violence, and gang affiliations. How could this work with them?! All I could imagine was being laughed out the door when I asked the miracle question! But, I realised, the only way to know is to try it. So, try it I did. And I have never looked back.

Attending that one-day training (and others since) changed not only my practice but my enjoyment of my work and indeed my whole life. The doubt I had about using this approach with young people on an offending pathway was blown away. I quickly discovered something that has remained a central tenet for me – people are people. Having worked in a variety of settings, it became apparent that regardless of the service used, or the "problem" identified, a person's preferred future is consistent. Focusing on this has also led to much better collaboration on cases where there are multiple agencies involved, because the shared focus is the preferred future, rather than agency goals.

Over the ensuing months, I had my eyes opened to the incredible creativity and resourcefulness of the children and young people who I had previously thought needed to learn strategies from me – they were already streets ahead! Indeed, those stories would provide an entire book in themselves.

I very quickly fell in love with the difference that the Solution Focused approach made – for the young people and families I spoke with but also for myself. While I had always loved my job, using this approach enhanced that immeasurably. No longer did I come away from visits feeling like I hadn't helped. I looked forward to each and every visit, and it helped me see people as competent and resourceful. I have been blessed to be part of people's lives and witness some absolute miracles. The Solution Focused approach is not something I do at work – it has become my whole way of being in life.

The following is one of many stories of magic that I have been blessed to experience in this role. All names have been changed to ensure privacy.

Once upon a time, there was a nine-year-old boy. This young boy lived, mostly happily, with his grandmother in a small kingdom in New Zealand. Like most tales involving magic, the hero of the story was not without his difficulties and sorrows. The little boy – we will call him James Hartley (a name he chose himself for this chapter) – had been in the care of his maternal grandmother (who I am sure is secretly his fairy godmother, but don't tell anyone) since he was a baby. His birth mother struggled with a number of issues, including drug use, and was not able to look after James.

One day, I received an email from the senior sergeant who works in our District Command Centre. There had been an incident the previous night involving James, who had been the subject of a police callout, having become aggressive towards his grandmother. This had resulted in a heavy police response, and the purpose of the call was to ask me whether I thought the response had been excessive. Having read the incident report, I felt compelled to make contact with the family, at the very least to see how the little boy and his nana were feeling after what must have been a difficult and stressful evening.

My initial phone call to the grandmother only increased my sense that there was huge potential to put in some support for the family. She was very open to a visit, but made it extremely clear that "James will not talk to you – lots of people have tried, but he won't engage with anyone." I assured her that it didn't matter – if he didn't feel comfortable speaking with me, he didn't need to, but I could speak with her regardless. A visit was scheduled for later that afternoon.

When I met with the fairy godmother – oops, I mean his grandmother – James was in the room, but immediately hid behind a couch. I made it clear that he absolutely did not need to speak with me if he didn't want to and gained his permission to speak with his nana about the previous evening, to see whether there was anything we could think of that might help things get better for him.

A very short time later, James emerged from behind the couch, sat beside me, and proceeded to talk at considerable length about his view of the world. It was immediately apparent to me that James was an exceptionally gifted child and that his preferred future was considerably different to most children of his age. The problem wasn't his – it seemed to be the inability of the world around him to accommodate his unique traits and abilities.

At the time, he was also being assessed by the local child development service. I must confess that my heart sank when I heard this – I was deeply concerned that this boy would emerge with one or more deficit-based descriptions. At that moment, it became even more important to explore what the Solution Focused approach could offer him.

When asked the miracle question, James was able to give a rich description of his preferred future, and several key themes emerged – he felt strongly that he needed his nana to help him manage his feelings, he wanted to spend time creating and inventing things, and he wanted to be able to be himself and be accepted by his peers and others. James was acutely aware of feeling "different from the other kids" and desperately wanted to be just like everyone else.

During this conversation, James showed me some things he had made and used them as metaphors for what happens when things don't go well for him. One of these was contained in a suitcase that he retrieved from upstairs. Inside was a contraption resembling a pinball machine. James showed me how it worked and said that it represented what happens for him. Each "lever" was an opportunity to make a good decision and use a strategy to prevent the "ball" from dropping further. In the meantime, his grandmother was incredulous and expressed disbelief that her grandson was still in the same room, much less engaging in conversation. I was also amazed – this young boy was incredibly easy to speak with, and the nearly two hours of conversation seemed to fly past. With a clear picture of his (and of his nana's) preferred future, and solid evidence of his many and varied strengths, we parted ways with the agreement to meet again in a few days' time.

Over the next few months, James made steady progress in tackling problems that had been getting in the way of him achieving his stated preferred future. And all his successes belonged strictly to him – he was able to come up with creative and clever strategies with which he took on and conquered many difficulties that had been troubling him for some time. One of my favourite ones was when James used the analogy of a chess game to succeed. He would approach each emotional challenge as a match and plan ahead for this. He also chose to keep a record of these matches and reflect on what had worked and how he had managed to do these things. We also talked about how you can only play one game of chess at a time, which helped him feel less overwhelmed by things.

At every visit, exceptions after exceptions were discovered. This identifying and highlighting of exceptions and successes was backed up by his amazing nana, who readily took to the Solution Focused approach and likely had been using many elements of it for some time. James would often joke that his nana was "doing an Emma" – for example, asking him "how did you do that?" following instances of success. James and I had had many, many such conversations following identifying exceptions.

Early on, there were still a number of incidents – six in eight weeks to be precise, many of them quite serious, including terms such as "predominant aggressor", "assaults police" and "arson." One incident was attended by a particularly fabulous police officer, who instinctively knew how to connect with James. This officer (who requested that he be known as Reinardo Gonzalez) emailed me the following day, saying the following:

> James actually calmed down somewhat when dealt with and spoken to quietly and rationally, my experience with him was overall a pleasant one, we spoke about Dr Who (which I know nothing about but he was happy to tell me), how good he is at maths (which is his favourite school subject), his dream of becoming a robot builder, and his love of dogs, and he enjoyed a warm milo at the station. I know this sounds like cheesy stuff but in the bigger picture it is talking about these things that really helped build rapport with him.
>
> James gets upset when adults are being "bossy", I told him just to imagine I was a big ginger baby with a beard (bit of kid humour) which made him giggle a bit and took away from the bossy adult thing, talking about his nana who he misses and asking questions around why he isn't with her, she could also be a fond topic depending on what was spoken about her (he loved talking about their Friday night fish and chip dates in front of the fire). Yelling also triggers James, not that he was yelled at by me but from what I gathered, talking to him calmly and sitting beside him in a non-threatening way was a quick agent to dispel any anger. Apparently the kids at the address had yelled at him which panicked him more.

Reinardo told me all this, but then said that it was probably "cheesy" – I told him that it was far from cheesy – what he had identified was what mattered. He had managed to build a connection with James at a time of distress, which had provided huge support for James. Reinardo went on to make further visits to James, which was incredibly powerful for James, who always carried a strong sense of remorse and shame following incidents. These further visits gave James the opportunity to "put things right" and also allowed for more positive information to flow back to police, to help them develop a more balanced picture of James (and indeed to begin to think differently about "child offenders").

Amid all this, the "assessment" from the child development service continued. During one of my visits, James was talking to me, and his nana took a call from the service. James was curious about what was being said, and his nana told him that he "did not quite fit the boxes." James sat thoughtfully for some time, then uttered the most fantastic sentence – "That must mean that I am a very special kind of human that they have not seen before". This outcome was immediately framed in an exceptionally positive light, and we all agreed that this indeed reflected the fact that James' "differences" were actually unique strengths. This helped James to reconsider his view of himself, and from that point forward was able to embrace that which he had previously considered to be negative aspects of himself. He now believed that the things that made him "different from the other kids" were in fact unique talents and ways of seeing the world.

Over the coming months, James continued to make quite incredible progress. Having been excluded from school around the time I first met him, he has commenced at a new school, and despite being very nervous about this, he is thriving and continuing to manage in his unique way, using incredibly creative strategies that he has found work for him. I am often questioned at work as to whether he still lived in town, as police were baffled as to how he had gone from being considered a "high-risk child offender" to suddenly dropping off their radar!

In addition, James is now able to talk quite openly about how he is feeling. Whereas he previously would react with anger at times of hurt or fear, he now can tell those he trusts how he is feeling and talk through things until he has gained peace. This was no more evident than in recent days, following a visit from his birth mother.

Over the years, the lack of relationship with his mother has been a source of much sadness and distress for James. While he logically understands the history, he has remained upset and carried a strong sense of abandonment as a result. James is now ten years old, and until very recently, had not seen his mother since he was five. When he knew she would be visiting, he experienced severe anxiety and was extremely worried that it would go badly. James was able to talk about this, and he reflected on all the things he had overcome in previous months, which gave him some confidence that, whatever happened, he would be OK.

The visit had some good moments and some very difficult ones. After his mother had returned home, James asked to meet with me to talk about how he was feeling. This was a huge step for him, and he openly shared his thoughts and feelings about this – particularly the disappointment that she was not who he had wanted her to be and the mixed feelings towards her as a result. We talked this through until James indicated he felt that he felt better – he knew from our first meeting that I was raised by my maternal grandparents, and I wonder whether this helped strengthen our connection. James also spoke about other things, including some that he had not previously opened up about. After I left, I received a message from his fairy godmother stating that James had said that he felt something that he hadn't felt for a while. When she asked him what that feeling was, he said "relief" and burst into tears.

When reflecting on my conversations with James and his nana, what stands out to me is the importance of identifying the strengths and abilities that James already possessed. It was absolutely evident from the very first meeting that he was a uniquely talented child, with extremely high intelligence and the ability to think and process information at a level far above most children his age. I strongly believe that it was the Solution Focused approach that opened the door for this young boy to make the decision to speak with me and to begin to form what has become a very special and strong connection. I equally strongly believe that it is likely that taking a deficit view has been a huge barrier in the past – understandably so!

It was also apparent that he was at high risk of being characterised by his supposed deficits. For me, one of the biggest successes in this case was that working with him in a Solution Focused way saved him from the system. I believe that a diagnosis would have been extremely damaging for him and would likely have led to no meaningful support. I am hugely blessed to be able to work using the Solution Focused approach, to build relationships with young people and their families, and to work towards THEIR preferred future.

I recently asked Reinardo what he thought had made the difference in his interactions with James. His response was

> All the negatives I had heard before even meeting James already had me thinking about what I would do differently if I got the chance. I have James to thank because I took a chance on him, I trusted him to make good choices and he hasn't put a foot wrong. He showed me that when we have a little faith, big things can happen. The only ingredients I provided in his recipe for success were time and understanding, he did the rest.

When I asked his nana what she thought had been helpful, she said

> Through your and Reinardo's positive contact with James, his perception of anyone in authority other than me has changed. Previously he would react if anyone other than me talked about personal stuff/feelings/choices in behaviour. He now sees it as helpful, not as pointing out deficits – a benefit of the SF approach that I hadn't realised would happen.
>
> The other is it helped me to focus on what was good in James rather than focusing on the horrible things going on (of which there were many!). I was constantly focused on his bad behaviour and unable to see the good, so my mind-set had to change to provide an environment where he could see more positives and the focus was on the future/what was working well etc. No excuse but I was stressed to the point of not seeing anything positive, horrible to reflect on now.

When I asked James that same question, his initial response was "Things are better now because I have a lovely psychologist friend." I told him that I needed to disagree with him on that one and reminded him that HE is the one who has made the changes and who gets the credit for being awesome. After pondering this for some time, he said

> I just set my mind to it. I love my nana, and I realised that my behaviour was hurting her. I realised that what I had been doing had been hard on her and was hurting her heart. So I changed my attitude. Basically, to change your actions, your brain needs new input. So I made the decision that I didn't want to hurt nana, so I set my mind to it. And once I decide something, I do it. And whenever things started to go wrong, my nana would 'do an Emma' and remind me of how well I had been doing. That gave my brain the input it needed to change my behaviour. Then nana would 'do an Emma' again and ask me how I had managed to do that.

From having six police call outs in two months, police have now had no dealings with James for seven months (and counting). They see him as my "success story" but I am quick to correct them on this – yes, he absolutely is a success story, but his success belongs to him. I have had many Solution Focused conversations with him, but all his strategies have been his own, and he has flourished far beyond anything I have done.

Recently, I asked James how he had decided to come out from behind the couch that very first day I visited. His response was this – "Well, I could tell that you were a very lovely person, and I believed that God had sent you to help me". He further reflected that it was hearing good things being said about him, and my asking questions about how he would like things to be for him, that had helped him realise that this was not "just another person looking for what is wrong with me." As mentioned, James has struggled with feeling different from other children his age, and it is my belief that the Solution Focused approach provided the perfect antidote to that. James is, and always was, an exceptional child, and I am certain that he will continue to do well. He reports that being back at school is going very well, and he feels like he is "the same as everyone else". However, James will never be the same as everyone else – he is far too talented, intelligent and insightful to be so. And I secretly hope that he stays that way, and I am absolutely certain that he will continue to thrive and achieve all his hopes and dreams. He is already well on the way!

I think it is important to note that, while James is a child with exceptional intelligence, my experience is that being "clever" is not a requirement for things getting better. In fact, I have worked with children considered to have intellectual disability, but this has not been a barrier in any way. In a similar way to the Solution Focused practitioner not needing to be "clever", neither does the child or young person need to have high intelligence to benefit from this approach. It is about a joining of hope and optimism, building a strong relationship, and travelling together towards the preferred future – with lots of smiles and celebrations along the way.

Chapter 18

Trusting the child
Using the Solution Focused approach with children and young people on the edge of care

Luke Goldie-McSorley

Working with children and young people using the Solution Focused approach is brilliant; it is exciting, inspiring, educational, fun, ever-changing and the best job in the world. I have been extremely fortunate to have worked with hundreds of children between the ages of 5 and 17 years using the Solution Focused (SF) approach in a vast and varied number of situations and contexts, and I remain totally enthused and inspired by it as a means of having a conversation and inviting change in people's lives.

I have worked as a social worker in a local authority Solution Focused edge of care service for 6 years, and using SF to support children and young people to remain living with their families has been my core practice. Over those years, my practice and understanding of the Solution Focused approach has grown and developed, and I have sculpted my own ideas about the work I do and the approach. Predominantly, I meet with families as a whole in their homes, and I have also spoken individually with many young people, met them outside of the home and in school, and also had conversations with them in the presence of their parent(s). These will be the examples I touch on in this chapter, and I will combine these together to ensure confidentiality and protect those I've been lucky to speak with.

My practice has always revolved around the core processes of the Solution Focused model; I will ask the best hopes question, invite a description of a future where the clients' hopes are realised, and make use of scaling to invite thought of what is already working and further description of change. I will shape follow up conversations on what has been better or is already working, amplifying the resources and abilities of the client, asking questions related to coping and managing the harder and more difficult moments in the client's life (Iveson et al., 2012). This has been the same throughout my time entwined with the Solution Focused approach in conversations with children and young people, though over the years with practice and continued development I have sharpened and honed my skills and expertise. Something I have found to be particularly powerful in the development of the craft in a Solution Focused way has been how I have connected to and in many ways embodied the principles and assumptions I have learnt about Solution Focused approach.

The principles and me

In most ways of working with people, there tend to be core values and principles that are attached and inform a way of being that goes along with the approach. The SF approach is no different and, I would say, goes a step further as in my practice those principles and assumptions inform and drive the way in which I practice Solution Focused work and approach people in an extraordinary and exceptional way, creating conversations filled with hope, admiration, belief and empowerment, especially when working with children and young people.

Some key principles:

1 The future is both created and negotiable
2 People have their own good reasons for doing what they do in that moment
3 Trusting the client to find their own best way
4 Clients are the experts of their own lives
5 Believing in your client's capacity to achieve their change

Whilst every single assumption has a power and merit that makes it essential to the approach, I feel that numbers 2 and 3 are particularly outstanding to me and require specific mention in relation to my SF work with children and young people:

A belief in the client doing the best they can in that moment, with their own good reasons for those decisions, and a trust in the client's ability to change and find their own best way. These are particularly interesting principles when working with children and young people and, whilst they pose a great challenge to many practitioners to accept in working with this client group, they are the bedrock of my SF practice and therefore the essence of this chapter.

Trust and where it fits

It is from these principles that I nurtured my thinking about the concept of trust in my practice. In particular, I have been interested in how this can benefit clients and how different practitioners working in different contexts can keep this idea of trust in their mind. This led my thinking towards what trust is and how traditionally it is understood or explained.

Trust is defined as reliance on and confidence in the truth, worth, reliability and so on of a person or thing (Collins, 2003). In many conversations with colleagues and other professionals when talking about or teaching the SF approach, the notion of 'trusting the client' presents as alien or at odds with some extremely well thought of and effective methods of working with people. I am asked *"How can you believe that they can change without assessing them? Surely you can't believe people mean what they say? How can you provide the clients with solutions if you are just going with what they say; what if they don't know how to change? They are children and clearly don't recognise what they are doing or how to get out of this situation; how can you trust them when they are making such bad choices?"* and *"Surely by trusting them you are condoning their negative behaviours or decisions; therefore, nothing will change?"* It can be a very complex and delicate interaction in response to these statements/questions. Each response must be taken on merit and by the very virtue of the principle of trust, a position adopted that practitioners have good reasons and thinking to raise that point. I look to explain from my perspective that trusting a client isn't one of the principles you can contest, although it isn't easy to do, a lot like Solution Focused practice in general. I would explain that, unless immediate safeguarding/safety concerns are raised, the client has the ability to find their own best way; therefore, speaking with them in a manner that trusts that and cooperates with the client in that way is far more useful to the client. My trust allows me to loosen the shackles of doubting every client's capability to change, and I start from a point of trust and belief in their skills to change, rather than of doubt. I would talk about how freeing it is as a practitioner and how this freedom gives me the opportunity to place my focus on making each period of time with the client as useful as it could possibly be, with the best version of me as a practitioner. I would acknowledge the challenge of trusting a client whose situation and actions are escalating the fears and worries of many around them, and this fear and concern can very quickly turn to doubt and cynicism about the client. I maintain a position of one foot in acknowledgement and one in possibility (O'Hanlon & Beadle, 1994). Whilst it is difficult, I believe that in most situations the client has heard practitioners' worries about situations which are not deemed good enough and has had their poor choices highlighted, and therefore a practitioner presenting those issues again doesn't make it any more likely that change will magically happen. I would also try to elucidate the nuances of trusting the client and believing the client has a good reason for what they do in that moment. Acknowledging this principle in our minds does not eradicate the understanding of an issue of safety or the condoning of choices which have more than likely led to us being in contact with the client. What I argue, however, is that it can create a space within the conversation between us and the client, where our questions can invite a shift in the client's attention, towards their ability to overcome their challenges, and towards their hope for what could happen instead, in their own best way. This is, however, a challenging point for many practitioners and yet as a social worker operating in a safeguarding context, this assumption is my favourite one and the most meaningful one that I hold.

Trust in action with children and young people

The principle of trust and belief, in my practice, flows through all of the core processes of the approach and I think benefits clients in every aspect, and this is never more so than with children and young people. In some situations, I have met with a teenager and asked them:

"So, what are your best hopes from our time meeting together?"

To which the response was;

"I dunno".

So I have then continued with a different, possibly more suitable, question:

"How would you know us meeting like this was useful?"

In so many instances this small interaction, which can and has continued with many more "I dunno's" is an example of the trust I have for the client in this situation. I trust that, no matter what factors or influences are in place, they are facing me and willing enough to say "I dunno" because they have their own good reason to be there. Therefore, it is my absolute duty to stay with them in that moment and trust their good reason, trust that they are thinking, and trust that whether they answer the question or not, they are trying to get in touch with how these conversations could be useful to them. I have found that my belief that the young person is working hard to become attuned to their hopes can allow me to accept the fact that they may not be able to specify what their best hopes are from our talking together. On many occasions, I have talked for over an hour with various teenagers about trust, relationships, things being better, having a life, being happier and being safer and, in those moments, I have never once forced or influenced the young person to choose one of those topics as their hopes. I have even allowed myself the error of thinking ahead to my next few questions when asking:

"So, if from our talking you were being happier, would this be useful?"

Only to be told, "No", so I then continue my stance that I totally trust that young person, that I don't need to force them to agree to a desired outcome from something they have said, and instead I ask again,

"So, what might tell you this was useful?"

This can continue, sometimes for the whole session, and then I reflect with colleagues afterwards that maybe I didn't find the right questions for them or I didn't pick up on something they said, and my own practice is in doubt, but not the trust for the client. On countless occasions, the very next session with these young people has been progressive extensions of the last conversation we had, and the client has proved how much of the work is done in between sessions and why trusting their ability to find their own best way is also our best way. Teenager after teenager has returned to our next session with a picture of where they hope to be, an outcome they desire from our talking, and even an outcome from their future. There have been thoughts of travel, of living more independently, of pursuing further education, of achieving in current education and of strengthening positive feelings and bonds around them, all of which encompass resolutions to the worries and concerns relating to their need for support. This, I find, can be some of the most powerful moments we can have with teenagers, a group who strive to be heard, acknowledged and trusted by adults, yet who seldom experience this. Therefore, if they interact with someone 'sent to help' who asks what it is they, as a teenager, hope for from the conversation, and if this practitioner stays with the question to show they mean it and stays close to what the teenager is saying – that is something which breeds collaboration with teenagers as they can sense the principle of trust.

As I move into descriptions of a time when best hopes are happening (preferred futures), or the first tiny signs of these best hopes being achieved, again there is trust within this process. With children as young as 5 and with teenagers up to 16 or 17 years, I have asked in various ways about the small signs of their hopes being realised. I have asked these questions, traditionally denoted as preferred future description questions, in relation to a catalogue of hopes. Sometimes these take the shape of a normal conversation, sometimes I use pictures to help the conversation, or I might encourage a very young child to compose a story about themselves at their best, including a cast of the people who are close to them. At all times, I keep in mind the principle that they are the experts on their own life and their own solutions, and I maintain a belief that they can describe this preferred future with the detail that is useful and unique to them. I focus throughout on questions which invite descriptions of observable and concrete details, bolstered by questions about interactions and multiple perspectives, and laden with questions which slow down the process to zoom in on the smallest of moments, to invite thought about the detail of that future moment. It is no surprise to me that 5-year-olds through to 17-year-olds can produce imaginative and detailed descriptions of their future. From details of how they might be in the playground or respond to a teacher, to passing a sibling in the corridor in the morning, to a conversation with a parent during a disagreement, to what friends would notice which is ever so slightly different, it is all already there, begging to be asked about, showing off the boundless capacity and possibility of the client and demonstrating another reason to trust.

In many situations, when meeting a teenager for follow up sessions (any session after the first), I have found instances where trust has elevated my questioning to a greater level of usefulness and I feel humbled and amazed by the teenager, in a whole variety of situations.

There have been wonderful instances where I have arranged to meet a teenager on their own, either through my edge of care service, or through parents or school staff, and before my session I've been 'helpfully' provided with information about what hasn't gone well or lists of how bad it has been, as well as warnings that the teenager may not tell me everything. This is a test of our ability to hold on to the principle of trust as a Solution Focused practitioner.

I have regularly arrived at school gates, homes or offices or even collected young people in the car with an unwavering belief in their ability, so that my first question is almost without fail:

"So, what's been better, or gone well since we last spoke?"

For countless young people I have found, especially for teenagers, that this tends to be quite a peculiar moment for them, as they are being invited to slow down in their thinking and asked to amplify and explore small moments of success. I have seen some young people flourish week by week, as they are invited to share their successes, and asked questions about what it took, how they managed it, how they sustained it and what it said about them. They often then spoke about the harder moments, and the moments when they weren't at their best, though these conversations also included questions from me about their hopes for the next time and about what they may have learnt about themselves and, often, how they had stopped things from getting any worse. I noticed that the belief in themselves developed as they recognised their own agency and thinking processes as the best tool to achieve and realise what they wanted and what was good for them.

I have also had much more challenging scenarios in follow up conversations where there is concern about risk relating to suicidal thoughts, high levels of anti-social community involvement, or a mixture of additional needs, violence, and traumatic past experiences, all occurring within the period of adolescence. In these moments my best partners have been my Solution Focused approach and my belief in the young person's abilities. In conversations relating to suicide and self-harm, alongside my immediate safeguarding priority, I have asked hope- and belief-filled questions of the strengths and skills of that young person in having reached this far. I have trusted them to know themselves and their own mental health better than anyone on the planet and trusted that they would be best placed to know what would make a difference to them and what the smallest signs of that difference taking shape would look like. I have taken the traditionally Solution Focused and, still to many, uncomfortable position of entirely positioning the young person as the expert, in control of where our conversation led, with my place to be in control of the process by following up on each of their responses with questions. I have found that, in many situations, this has been a memorable moment for young people, one they reference back to at later dates and sometimes well into the future. I think this is because this stance and brief approach to their grave situation is so different from many of their other experiences relating to emotional and mental health challenges and something I truly believe to be attractive and useful to young people experiencing those challenges.

Some of the most wonderful conversations I have had have been based on following the thread and pace changes of unpredictable conversations with teenagers who have not perhaps had their answers acknowledged before or been asked questions about what they were thinking. Questions can often be filled with the agenda of the worker/professional, with the aim of leading the young person in a particular direction. However, I have found that a belief in sticking with their thread in a respectful, delicate, acknowledging, tentative way, allows for the practitioner to invite the rich detail of the teenager's thoughts, skills, resources and experiences, all in a way that fits with their hopes or good reasons for speaking in the first place. When working with apparently 'hard to reach' young people, I have tried to remain focused on their expertise and resources. This includes following through the highs of them telling me what is great about them or their strengths and the lows of them telling me that that question was "stupid", when I would move to the next and hopefully more useful question. I have found that at the times where the young person doesn't find explicit talk of 'strengths' or 'feelings' useful or comfortable, we have detoured around those with an alteration to my language, whilst I continue to regularly check in with the young person about whether the conversation is useful or whether we are talking about the right stuff. For example:

"And would that be a good thing for you?"

To which, if given permission to continue via a "yes", I can follow with:

"And what difference would that make?" or "What would that mean for you?"

In conclusion, I think that the purpose of any SF conversation with a child or young person is to be useful in a way that fits with them and, where necessary, with those around them. It is to invite them to view their life should their own hopes be realised and to recognise what they are already doing that fits with those hopes. It is so important in a conversation with a child or young person to ask questions that invite them to amplify their brilliance, strengths and successes. Being a child of any age is hard and it takes, I think, a monumental degree of inbuilt resilience that I think can be overlooked by many. Children and young people are inherently strong, adaptable and resilient humans. They navigate through daily moments which, without such strength and resilience, would halt them in their tracks. Although sometimes there are stoppages, I believe that through the conversations we have with them, where we trust that inside them, they have the solutions, resources and thinking capable of starting the engine again, they can begin to move towards the next chapter of their lives.

References

Collins. (2003). *English Dictionary & Thesaurus, 21st Century Edition*, 2nd edition. Glasgow: Harper Collins.
Iveson, C., George, E., & Ratner, H. (2012). *Brief Coaching: A Solution Focused Approach*. London: Routledge.
O'Hanlon, B., & Beadle, S. (1994). *A Field Guide to Possibility Land*. London: BT Press.

Chapter 19

Facing new challenges using a Solution Focused approach

Creating a supportive learning process for Roma adolescents in a volunteering project in Hungary

Árpád Bárnai and Viktória Sőregi

Background to creating the learning process

The Élményakadémia (Academy of Experience) Association was founded at the end of 2005 by 12 volunteers who dedicated their future to the development of individuals by non-formal education. We have experienced first-hand the beneficial effects of this special experiential learning method and decided to help others to discover that they have more virtues and talents than they believe.

Experiential learning can be specifically defined as "learning through reflection on doing". Going through a direct experience will teach different behavioural responses, self-control, and self-knowledge. Reflection is a crucial part of the experiential learning process. A skilled facilitator, asking the right questions and guiding reflective conversation after an experience, can help open a gateway to powerful new ways of thinking.

After several successful national and international programmes with youth, young adults, and social workers, we began to brainstorm ideas on a learning method that would have the potential to help underprivileged young people to launch themselves and begin to navigate a life of their own. We already had some experiences working with Roma youth, but we did not have a full training dedicated only for them.

We wanted to contribute to the first steps of young people with hardships in starting their adult lives. The new training was aimed at youth who began their lives with much less support than most Hungarian teenagers, either because they grew up in an institution, without a family, orphaned or simply abandoned by their parents, or in very difficult circumstances in remote villages of Hungary where the standards of living can be as low as in the poorest developing countries of the world.

For example, in some segregated Roma settlements, residents live in conditions of extreme rural poverty: no indoor plumbing, no reliable electricity, no reliable heating. Children have no light to study by, and educational opportunities are limited. These Roma communities don't have the means to organise themselves, and they can expect little sympathy from the rest of the population. Their rich and beautiful cultural heritage is being gradually lost amid the overwhelming deprivation and everyday tragedies each family has to deal with.

We intended to create a supportive learning environment using the tools of experiential learning, volunteering, and Solution Focused coaching.

The programme – "From Us to You"

In 2010, we organised the very first series of programmes titled "From Us to You", the structure of which was based on volunteering work where we used team building techniques with around 20 young Roma people as a means of experimental education. The name of the programme – which refers to the hope that it's possible to make the world a little bit better by responding on a small scale, interpersonally, to an actual need – was invented by the members of the first team.

Based on our former encounters with these young people during one-off sessions like the outdoor challenges we sometimes organised, we already presumed that much could be achieved in this field by using the means of explorative pedagogy and non-formal education. At the same time, we theorised that this arbitrary approach did not present a substantial solution because of all the extraordinary challenges that young Roma people have to face, which needed more time and structure for an upcoming programme.

However, we noticed something important which would be helpful in designing the programme. There were unexploited resources in these young people, like their exceptionally strong drive and eagerness to help, which were often overlooked by their environment and by themselves as well. Those young people who experienced what it was like to be in need and to ask for help themselves were well aware of the difference that help can make in their lives and the lives of others.

The trainers' aim with the programme was for the participating youth to gain experiences that they would be able to use in leading their own lives: listening to other people's ideas, planning and working together, making decisions, taking responsibility, delegating tasks, and reflecting for themselves. At the end of the first training, we have seen that they changed a lot: they were more open, communicative, and brave enough to take initiatives; they could work together as a team and give feedback to each other. These results were so promising that the programme, which was originally only a pilot event, has been organised every year since 2011. An ever-growing team of trainers, educators, and facilitators have participated in the programme, slowly transforming the humble "From Us to You" name into a recognisable "brand" amongst other non-profit initiatives. We did not recruit a whole new group of participants each year, because some of the former members had the chance to come back the next year and participate again.

The structure of "From Us to You"

Over the last few years, we have formulated a well-tried framework which has evolved into a long-term learning process that is composed of several sessions. In its original form, it takes 16 days stretched out over a 6-month period. Participants come each month for a few days, we work together, then they go home; meanwhile, we can be in touch via the internet. The training days are very intense, and it takes time to internalise new skills and reflect on everything that has just happened. The programme is made up of 4 bigger modules (team-building, planning, volunteering, and closing) and a few optional shorter meetings (site inspections):

Team-building exercises for volunteers participating in the programme (3 days).

Planning sessions of volunteering action – Participants have to choose a place (usually one of the settlements which some of them are coming from) where they can do a voluntary task, planning the activities, defining the different roles in their groups, and thinking about the materials – all facilitated by trainers (4 days).

Site visit – Preparation for volunteering (1 day).

Volunteering – They go to one of the Roma settlements in Hungary which they have visited before. They realise various activities together with the locals: playing with the children, cooking, painting the walls of the common bathroom, planting flowers, collecting trash, playing football, building a football gate, and so on (4 days).

Closing with participants –Evaluation of the half-year learning process and feedback from each other (4 days).

"From Us to You Extra"

In 2015, the young people from the first programme asked for our support to start coordinating the programme themselves with our assistance as their mentors. Perhaps the most important affirmation that we were going in the right direction was the following sentence said by them: "Please, do not be upset with us, but we'd like you to step back a little bit". It was a clear signal that they were beginning to grasp what it was like to take responsibility and make decisions, and the prospect of doing something "important" appealed to them. They felt that they got control over a certain part of their future which so far had been completely out of their hands. So, the experienced participants who would have liked to take the responsibility to lead the programme and the group became "junior trainers", and we, their former trainers, had the new role of "senior trainers", supporting their work throughout the whole process. Thanks to the financial support of different grantmakers, who also appeared to be encouraged by our previous achievements, the programme could extend to 30 days throughout a whole year with over 30 participants.

This new programme came to be titled "From Us to You Extra". Additionally, we invited social workers who had already served in the Roma settlements where the participants came from. These professionals were incredibly important supporters of the learning process as they could be the witnesses to how skills and competencies unfold, how a young person finds a new role in their group. Our goal was to show them a way to upgrade their existing methodology to include our approach into their everyday work. In return, they offered us their extensive knowledge and unique perspective on the inner workings of these settlements. Thanks to their input, the programme could evolve into this jointly created learning process. Our idea was that the youth could also support the work of the social workers.

Formally, "From Us to You Extra" expanded with trainer courses where junior trainers and social workers received foundational training of trainers. The extra time spent in this training made it possible for the junior trainers to get comfortable with the practice of communicating and collaborating, so when they were thrown into increasing challenges during the volunteering period, doing something they had never done before, they knew who to lean on when facing a particular problem. Each group of volunteers was supported by a team of junior trainers who had undergone the mentoring organised by the senior trainers.

It is very important to note that this is a recurring opportunity for young people to leave their familiar home environment and try themselves out in increasingly difficult tasks. Like the youngest child in fairy tales who grows from being labelled a loser to taking part in shaping the world by fighting challenges and persisting against all odds, these young people go through a model version of their own hero's journey by participating in the programme. Moreover, it is also imperative that, upon returning home, other members of their communities can also get inspired, hopefully, by the signs of change they see in them.

Just as in all good processes of learning, participants learned at least as much from each other as from their trainers. Course leaders also received a remarkable amount of inspiration from each and every one of the participants.

Fingerprints of the Solution Focused approach on the programme

Our approach and assumptions

Over the course of the programme, we also investigated the very exciting idea of turning experiential learning upside-down. We not only used learning by doing, learning from past experiences, or experiences from the present, but we also built on the description of preferred future experiences. The way we approached the participants of the programme has been shaped by the Solution Focused approach. We consciously incorporated the following SF assumptions into the design of our programme:

These young people are the experts of their lives

We assume that it makes sense to be curious about them because young people have good reasons for how they behave. Instead of the clichéd question that their adult family members or teachers so often pose – "What's wrong with this youngster?" – we'd rather say: "She must have good reasons for this behaviour. What could they be? How does this behaviour help? How is it useful for her?"

They want to help others

The young people participating in the programme often faced criticism and disbelief regarding their intentions. When they said they wanted to participate, some said that their true motivation was "just to have fun" or "get out of the settlement and be with other teenagers". We didn't think that there is only one source of motivation, and so we listened and believed them when they expressed their willingness to help. This showed not only in words but in small gestures too (e.g. when they see someone being hungry, having trouble lifting something up, or crossing the road, they immediately help). They often have strong empathy since they themselves have also gone through some hard times. (This deep level of empathy showed when somebody shared a personal story or expressed a need that was not met, and their response was to pay attention, listen with empathy, and try to provide comfort.)

They can help others; they just need to notice and appreciate the impact

In spite of the young people themselves needing help, they have a lot of resources that can be useful in helping others. Some of these resources they have despite all the difficulties of their lives. Others they have exactly because they went through all the challenges they faced. But they need to be aware of all these resources and actively look for opportunities to utilise them.

Some of the social workers and facilitators in the programme felt unsure about the young people's ability to put into practice the volunteering they had planned, and so they were trying to control this by holding their hands too much. They would tell them how to do certain things in volunteering and give them advice without being asked for it. What helped us to let go of the need to control the outcome and quality of the volunteering was the inspiration we got during our SF training: desires/hopes are the forerunners of capabilities/abilities.

They want to take responsibility

They often face responses from their environment, in school and in the broader community, which communicate a message of mistrust, exclusion, or racism. When an opportunity is presented to take real responsibility, they will be actively involved in volunteering and they will enjoy it.

In general we tried to support the young people in a Solution Focused manner through using the following tools and approaches during the programme.

We were building on strengths, paying attention to the kinds of behaviour and resources we see in young people which we are glad to encourage. Our starting hypothesis was that patterns of promising behaviour and talk to which we paid attention would gain more importance, since what you pay attention to gets bigger.

We not only treated the young people as experts of their own lives, but we addressed them as **experts of the local reality of their settlement**, because they were born and raised there. When visiting a settlement, the local young people were not ashamed of showing us their neighbourhood, and we asked for their help in finding our way around it. We kept asking ourselves: Where are we? What have they achieved during the programme? What would we do similarly in the future? What would we do more of?

Generally, we worked with what we had, We aimed to practice the solution-oriented attitude in organizing the programme itself, too, by working with what we had, even if it was unplanned or presented challenges. What if the child can only join the programme later? What if something happens during volunteering that we have not planned? What should we do if a young person's life presents grave difficulties?

Small and positive changes began to happen during the programme, and the question was whether these young people noticed them. Every so often it happened that a bad moment or a problem got blown out of proportion which caused them to ignore small but important signs of development.

By **turning the participants' attention back to positive differences** and encouraging changes, we were successful on many occasions in helping them notice their own improvements and their ability to strengthen those of others.

Focusing on differences also gave us an opportunity to take a look at the following question: **What are the signs of making progress?** We did not formulate a long-term strategic plan with them; rather, we created a detailed plan for taking the next few steps. This practice proved increasingly efficient when not only the project management part of volunteering was discussed, but the circumstances of young people's lives, vision for the future, or lifestyle was concerned, too.

Signs of being useful

We have organised the programme every year in the past 8 years since we saw a lot of signs of its usefulness. The participating youngsters gained more confidence and became more competent in several life skills. In order to get a better sense of the impact, we asked about 30 of our former participants the following questions. They were young Roma people aged between 15 and 19 years.

Q: What is important in the "From Us to You" programme for you?

A: "Making friends, you will have more confidence because you meet people you've never known, and in the end, you almost treat each other like brothers and sisters".

A: "Wow, as a participant, having new experiences, getting to know new people, and do something together with other people which we plan and execute by ourselves".

Q: In which field have you made progress or improved thanks to the programme?

A: "I improved my organizational and communication skills, working in a group, collaborating with new and already known people. It's easier for me to assess, identify problems, and find a solution".

A: "More patient, more understanding, kinder, I got better at working in a team".

A: "I got better in pretty much everything, I pay more attention to others, I try to help more people, and my speaking ability got better".

A: "I have more confidence, my vocabulary became richer".

A: "I became braver and more skillful".

A: "In my driving skills, now I can not only drive the car well but also drive people, and I've become more patient with others".

A: "I'm more expressive, more honest, braver, more talkative, more direct, more interactive, more relationship-building, and I've learned to love the presence of people around me and I've become a very social person".

Q: What is the impact of taking part in the programme on your life?

A: "It helps me a lot now with my oral exams, the communication, I can express myself better. I tell others a lot about my experiences and the programme itself, what it's really about, and I try to make other people go in the right direction, too".

A: "It had a positive effect on my future! I am more direct with people, and I can think about the solution for a thing in more detail, what is the most appropriate and practical".

A: "Before the program, I did not want to go to high school but since I took part in it, I have attended two courses and I want even more. It pointed out that you always have to learn and it's good, too".

Q: **Which parts of the programme helped you to get the most out of you? Which parts helped you to improve the most?**

A: "I improved in the planning phase and managed to get the most out of myself in the volunteering part".

A: "It was learning from start to finish".

A: "I don't think I could choose. Each time I learned more and more. In team building and planning, I learned to give room to others, to trust others, and to work with people. In volunteering, I learned to give a second chance to others, and I learned that everyone can be helped to get their life going in the right direction, and we have to accept if something goes wrong and we have to try again, we cannot give up if we want something a lot, and we have to see the good in everybody. Last time, I learned to confess to myself and others and accept what I was making mistakes in and what I could have done better, maybe, and what I needed to improve. I owe a lot to the program. :-)".

A: "The discussion and the volunteering . . . that I could help others because it's good to see that they help me and it was good to give back".

A: "I was pretty lazy, so I was really happy with the programs, and also, it felt good!! They were imaginative and creative programs, so they really got the most out of me!"

A: "The sympathy and the faith that was put in me".

Informal and non-formal ways of learning supported by a Solution Focused approach

Compared to a more formal coaching conversation or a team coaching process, our programme has built upon the informal elements. It could be described as a **non-formal learning process** with a **strong focus on informal learning** possibilities. What were these learning possibilities?

We tried to put more **emphasis on the co-creation** of the programme: both the formal and the informal part of it. Everybody could share their ideas and it was possible to give us (and also each other) constant feedback in a safe environment. We, as trainers, were working on putting more trust in the process and the group, we tried to let them experience the feeling of being competent, being able to shape their lives, to exercise agency – even if it was only about taking a 10-minute break or not. The level of trust on our side and the focus on co-creating the process increased by every year.

Frequent appreciation of tiny steps taken, small signs of progress – we really tried to celebrate their attempts and proposals to shape the programme, as this was a very empowering experience for them. These young people were coming from a background where they have rarely been asked about their opinion and being noticed for something they did well.

We were asking an extraordinary number of questions, many more than they had ever been used to. We were **asking instead of assuming**. To their surprise, we seemed extremely curious about them. They found it hard to handle in the beginning, but after a while, they discovered the power of the questions and the possibility of opening up to someone else and started having long conversations amongst themselves as well. We focused more and more on creating space for useful interactions within the group of participants. Our intention was to create a community that saw the potential in its members and provided a chance for the girls and boys to see their peers, not unlike themselves, in an attractive role, taking responsibility – one day, hopefully, they would like to achieve the same. We tried to help them to create a better self-image.

The most popular tool ever was positive gossiping. They were hungry for the feedback but not from us, the trainers and other adults, rather from each other. In positive gossiping, we are talking about somebody, we are gossiping, but we can only share pleasant feedback, stories, and insights. The person who is talked about is also present but cannot react to the feedback; they just take it all in or let it go.

For opening or closing each shorter part of the programme, we frequently used "time travel" as an exercise. We asked them to sit together in pairs or trios and imagine what would happen during the programme in 5 days and in their lives in 10 years. We could easily jump back and forth in time; our imagination was the only limitation. This exercise proved to be a very useful tool for creating the future together. When they had the chance to talk about it more and more, suddenly, it became real and achievable. They realised that they could set goals and let themselves dream about something they had imagined.

The venue was always a new place for everybody, somewhere close to nature. The young people had to leave their homes, and for many it was the first time in their lives being alone, without their families. We encouraged them to take care of themselves and their needs and create a safe place for the group. It was something to be shaped, complemented, and completed; it was freedom and responsibility, a chance to exercise agency and creativity. We could live our lives in the way we wished to.

We were focusing on small differences and signs of progress and also encouraged the young people to do the same. It allowed us to let go of perfectionism and high expectations that would put too much focus on the outcome we hope for, and instead helped us to concentrate more on the growth of the young people.

Conclusion

The programme expanded in 2019 due to its success in having attracted European grants. We plan to run the international version of this project in Romania, Slovakia, and the Netherlands, where there are Roma communities. This programme impacts on everyone who is involved with it. For the Roma youth who participated in it, we can see that they developed a bigger willingness to go for challenges. For the young people and the trainers, it helped us all to step over so-called social-cultural filters and build good working relationships together. It also had a huge impact on us as trainers, as we found it easier to notice any kind of improvement and all the small successes too.

Chapter 20

Figuring Futures
The art of reframing challenges

Elke Gybels and Rik Prenen

When it comes to helping vulnerable and troublesome children and their families, a lot of interest and practice is focused on verbal language and introspection. These verbal skills are very important in coaching and therapy. Both client and practitioner are challenged to express themselves unequivocally by finding the right words.

Imagine. . .

Sitting at a round table . . . the practitioner on the other side takes a Lego® doll, representing you, puts it right in front of you, in the middle of the table, and asks "What are your best hopes from our talking together? What else?" While you describe your preferred outcome, a bright blue treasure chest is put a few inches away from the doll. You keep talking about your life, how you want it to be, about the things you want to keep, to achieve, to change . . . the conversation feels safe and familiar. The questions you are asked all sound logical and point in a direct way to the changes in your life that you want to notice. They encourage you to talk about your goals in life, your perspectives, the dream you dream. Your strengths, your skills and your resources come into view . . . a second treasure chest is put on the table. Right in front of the Lego® doll.

Figure 20.1 A Visualisation of a Client's Story and Their Best Hopes

Figuring Futures (Gybels & Prenen, 2015) is a distinctive method, an extra tool that enables a strong and meaningful dialogue using three kind of treasure chests, Lego® dolls, building blocks, colourful pads, and so on. In the hands of a skilled Solution Focused practitioner, the use of creative tools highlights, amplifies, reinforces and empowers the clients' strengths and coping skills. The setting on a table represents a visualisation of the client's dreams, the significant others in their life, the bump in the road . . . and invites client and practitioner to an externalizing overview as from a helicopter perspective.

Introducing creative tools

Mary (14, blond hair, ponytail), referred by her mother.

"Hi Mary, nice to meet you . . . have a seat. . .

Maybe a good place for us to begin is to tell you how I work. If you have any questions then, let me know. Usually, when I meet somebody, I use creative techniques during the talking. It helps me to ask the questions that help me to know you better and to find out what you are hoping for from your visit. OK?

So, here you are, on an early Saturday morning. I can imagine you do different things on a regular Saturday."

Mary smiles and says she always gets up early on Saturdays to help at the riding school. She is passionate about horses, likes to take care of them, and feels responsible for cleaning the stables. On Saturdays she always has lunch at grandma and granddad's place. They enjoy her company and she loves spending time with them. Back home, upstairs in her room, she studies and does her homework. Mary likes to study. And yet, it takes a lot of effort to go to school. Playtime is like hell.

As the conversation proceeds, a Lego ®doll with blond hair and a ponytail, and a sparkling square treasure chest are put on the table. Touching it:

Figure 20.2 Mary's Sparkling Treasure Chest of Strengths Right in Front of Her

"It's amazing the way you take care of horses and feel responsible for cleaning the stables, the way you keep your grandparents' company on Saturday, the additional effort for school during the weekend. Sounds like you are a busy bee. How do you manage?"

Mary smiles: "That's what I like most, taking care of others and of the horses of course. A good plan does the job! No big deal . . . I would like to become a good vet, that idea keeps me going."

"Awesome! Sounds you have it all figured out. Tell me. . . "

After talking a while, bending the doll a little forward:

"You also mentioned that playtime at school is hard. Your mom also told me when she called last Wednesday."

A doll, representing Mary's mom, is put right behind the blond ponytail doll.

From the very beginning of the conversation, we listen with great interest to the client's insights and competencies. The *client's treasure chest* represents all these resources and invites them to remember and to talk about their unique qualities. What are they proud of? What keeps them going? How do they tackle the bumps in the road?

The treasure chest of hope

While talking about the client's goals, "the treasure chest of hope" is put on the table, a few inches away from the Lego® doll. It invites the client into a consideration of the hoped-for outcome. We encourage the client, patiently and curiously, to vividly describe their goals, located in their current life. We invite them to describe their preferred outcome within their realm, we challenge them to picture the life they would like to be living and the process towards that future, and we ask them to specify what they will do differently.

- What are your best hopes? What else?
- What does your preferred future look like?
    - What difference are you hoping that that would make to you?
    - What will be different? What else?
    - What are you hoping that that would lead to?
- How will you notice things go better?
    - Who else is going to notice that changes have taken place?
- . . .

Figure 20.3 The Treasure Chest of Best Hopes

The metaphor of the treasure chest helps to describe and understand the client's overarching hoped-for outcome. We invite and bring forth a rich description, a detailed picture of what the future would look like if those best hopes were to be fully realised. Again, the practitioner is a dogged detective seeking out the clues to what is helping positive change take place. In fact, the way clients describe their best hopes from life legitimates every other question we ask.

The client's treasure chest

Quite a number of clients experience a sense of powerlessness in their life. They often feel disempowered and tend to focus on the problem and/or what they would like others to do differently. Placing a treasure chest close to the doll representing the client, the dialogue uncovers achievements that relate to the client's preferred future and the good things they have been managing to do. Furthermore, it helps to elicit a detailed description of significant alternative behaviour that leads to change. We deliberately invite them to describe more instances, current and past activities, and behaviours that recognise elements of that future already happening. Looking at the dolls and treasure chests, pointing at them, touching them and using the client's name enable both of us to pay attention to their resources. It helps to avoid the pitfall of the practitioner taking over and trying to impose a solution built on expert assumptions of required change.

- What are you good at? At school, at your job?
- What do you love doing?
- When you are at your best, how does that show?

Figure 20.4 The Client's Treasure Chest

- What are three positive things I should know about you?
- Looking back at last week, when did you shine? What did you notice about yourself?
- What have you found that is helpful in managing your situation?
- Considering all the problems you are facing, how on earth did you even manage to get out of bed this morning and make it to school?
- What keeps you going under such difficult circumstances?
- How do you explain how you have been able to get to school this week?
- How did you do that?
- How do you manage to cope with such a hard situation?

Clients are encouraged to fill their treasure chest. The entire line of questioning is focused on the clients' successes and achievements, giving the opportunity to unlock their resources. These resources create opportunities for personal growth. And that's what, from our point of view, Solution Focused therapy is all about: to highlight the clients' resources and to find out how they can be engaged to achieve the desired changes in daily life.

Significant others and their treasure chests

Whilst touching the square treasure chest right in front of the client's Lego® doll:
"Wow Mary, you already did a lot of good things that were helpful to you."
Mary smiles. *"Well yeah, actually . . . I mean . . . talking about it . . . I really do. Maybe I should make an new plan. . ."*
"That's a brilliant idea. And it's all yours! Wow."
"Hey, that plan of yours what does it look like?"

[. .].
By the way, there is something else I want to know."
(Touching the treasure chest of hope): "Who else may know about your best hopes and all the lovely things you want to achieve?"
"Everybody may know."
"Wow, can you tell me who for instance?"
"Well, my mom and dad of course, and my teach' at school."
Dolls representing dad and the teacher are put on the table.
"Who else may know?"
"Elise, she's my best friend since primary school."
"And who else?"
"John, he always helps me at the riding school."
(Smiling) *"And my horses may also know. I talk a lot to them. They never argue or contradict."*
(Pointing at the treasure chest of hope and summarising Mary's goals)
"And how about grandma and grandpa, are they allowed to know?"
"Of course they may! They show great interest. They often ask about it. I'm really grateful to them."

People often become happier and more resilient if they are able to enjoy warm social support by spending time with their family, friends, partners, children, colleagues, teachers and others. We are constantly searching for commitment and connection to others. But sometimes people hesitate to ask for help when the going gets tough. They don't want to be a burden to others or they feel ashamed of their failures. Feelings of isolation and the conviction that the problem is "only yours" often decrease the social support network. And yet, clients are much more determined to find solutions than often thought. Before taking the step to seek professional help, people "scan" their social support network, searching for help.

So we ask questions about the client's significant others and how they are helpful to the client moving towards the achievement of their goals.

- Who is aware that you are facing tough times?
- Who you can rely on?
- Who may know you are working on your best hopes?
- Who is concerned about you?
- Who do you trust to keep you safe?
- Is there someone you can turn to?
- How can he or she be helpful to you? When?
- How does that show?
- . . .

Whilst talking about the significant others in the client's social support network and how they help the client to move forward, a small round treasure chest, representing the way they are supportive, is put in front of the doll that represents the significant other. An additional option is inviting clients to describe their situation

Figure 20.5 The Treasure Chest of Significant Others

from the viewpoint of these significant others to highlight new ideas, new opportunities and perspectives.

- Suppose your mom, dad, best friend, teacher were here and I was to ask them what you did differently that helped so that things go better, what would they tell me? What else?
- When things are better, what will your parents notice you doing differently? What else?

A visual reminder

When clients find it hard to identify success in their lives or struggle to notice exceptions to the problem, we often suggest them taking a treasure chest home as a kind of visual reminder of the best things already happening in daily life.

"So, Mary I have a suggestion. Do you want to hear it? My suggestion is to take this treasure chest home. Every time you glance at it, remember all the good things that you experienced and how you made them happen. What did you do differently? What did others do differently? I'm really curious 'bout your findings next time we meet."

Or "Put it on your nightstand. Every night, before you go to bed, remember all the good things you experienced during the day. Think about what you did differently, how helpful that is to you."

Using the treasure chest as a kind of visual reminder has a surprisingly strong effect. People are invited to notice more consciously what already goes right in their lives.

Clients report what a joy it has been to work with creative tools seeking a way to tell their story, feelings and ideas. Back home, it helped them to recall the conversation they had in therapy.

From a client's view

Talking to a couple, a family or a team using creative tools is helpful to express and clarify interrelationships, mutual interests and goals, ideas and feelings.

"When you put the dolls on the table I remembered myself thinking, OK, give it a chance, it doesn't hurt to try. Honestly, at home I'm going to look for similar things so I can tell every little detail to my kids."

"All my life I was not that kind of a motormouth, but I'm astonished at how easy going this conversation was."

"Hey can I take a picture to show it to my mom and dad?"

"Therapy, from my point of view, seemed artificial, academic and theoretical. Using creative tools turned the conversation into something vivid and accessible. It's a very small step from the visualisation to real life. Looking at the dolls on the table and the treasure chest that represented our preferred future, we both knew and felt the same way. Of course, we would stay together! We are going to make that happen, c'mon, let's do this. Back home, it's sort of a visual reminder. The imaginary look at all that stuff on that table encouraged us to go on, to walk together and to grow little by little as a couple."

The importance of eye contact is often stressed and practiced in communication workshops. However, some clients feel uncomfortable and experience eye contact as unpleasant, even forced or artificial. When they are ashamed or shy, it's even more difficult. Visualisation, the use of the imagination and metaphors can stimulate an appreciative dialogue. In fact, imagination is part of everyday vocabulary. "I take it with a pinch of salt," "Once in a blue moon," "Beating about the bush," "I missed the boat," "It felt as if I had wings," "I went through hell," "Spring came into my life," "No man is an island," "The icing on the cake," "We'll cross that bridge."

Externalizing the client's situation by using creative material helps to create a safe environment. It helps clients to feel comfortable talking about their dreams, worries, doubts, strengths, hopes, joy . . . things that so often remain unspoken. Instead of looking down, staring at the wall or out of the window, clients concentrate on the treasure chests and dolls and stay focused on their authentic story.

Digging for gold, using the three treasure chests

Figuring Futures connects the technique of visualisation with the Solution Focused approach. It enables clients and practitioners to get insight into situations that the client wants to change. Adding creative tools to a Solution Focused conversation invites them to think out of the (problem) box and motivates them to generate new viewpoints.

It may sound unusual, but we don't explain the meaning of the material, nor do we talk about "dolls." We put the material on the table spontaneously during the talking, and it's obvious to the clients and makes sense to them. After all, the topic of the conversation is the client's preferred future, not the therapists' tools or metaphors.

Rather than digging into problems, Figuring Futures is directed towards developing and achieving the client's vision of solutions. The visualisation, using treasure chests and dolls, helps to clarify those solutions and the means of achieving them. If someone is already feeling down, we should not dig deeper. Figuring Futures also makes the switch from "visualisation to acting." By far, the major challenge in Solution Focused therapy is to find out what exactly works and to elicit in a very precise way how clients use their resources in moments when their best hopes are taking place. It puts clients back in the driver's seat and encourages them to make their own choices and to work towards a valuable perspective.

Treasure chests are fascinating, powerful, abundant and sparkling and stimulate creative thinking and encourage imagination.

Although visualisation is a very powerful tool, it's not an end in itself. Figuring Futures is no magical trick. It facilitates a careful Solution Focused conversation which recognises clients as the architects of their life. It's all about the questions we ask and the appreciation of the client's answers. Tools are only the vehicles for communication.

Imagination is one of the most powerful tools of the human mind. A picture speaks a thousand words. If you can picture it, you can understand it. Cognition and creative thinking go hand in hand and generate new insights and new ideas.

A fool with a tool is still a fool. Let's make it clear . . . it's the Solution Focused questioning and dialogue that does the job!

Reference

Gybels, E., & Prenen, R. (2015). *Van Klacht Naar Kracht (From Complaint to Strength)*. Tielt, Belgium: Lanoo Campus.

Chapter 21

Solution Focused work in high-risk child protection cases

How the Solution Focused mindset and creativity helped put the children in the centre of the work and create possibility for change

Michael Petersen and Rikke Ludvigsen

As social workers in the child protection field, we are working in problem focused settings, often with problem focused assessments and problem-solving actions plans as the basis for interventions. Because of the heavy bias towards problem talk and a problem focus, the Signs of Safety approach (Turnell & Edwards, 1999) was developed to make a balanced risk assessment (Turnell & Edwards, 1997) that focuses on both the risk and safety perspective in order to create enough safety for the child in the work with families and extended network. As most of our cases are high-risk cases with children's safety at stake, for years this method has been an integrated part of our work alongside the Resolution Approach (Turnell & Essex, 2006), Partnering for Safety (Parker, 2015b) and Solution Focused Brief Therapy (Ratner et al., 2012).

Our main task is to create safety for the children in a very anxious atmosphere with a lot of worried and problem focused professionals. In almost every case we work with, we struggle with a demand for certainty. In a high-risk field, we tend to seek safe certainty by, for example, making checklists and procedures to follow (Wheeler, 2015), and we also find that the solution to meet this demand for certainty is to remove the children from their parents. Often this happens without getting the children's perspective and without a plan for their safety in the long run, which means that many of the children stay in very insecure and unhealthy conditions, without knowing what their future placement might be.

A lot of children worry about things like: "Will I come back to live with my parents again? How long do I have to be in another family? What If I come back to my parents, will I be safe enough?"

Even though social workers try to involve and explain to the children what will happen, the demand for certainty, combined with a problem focused setting, means that many social workers are unable to create a picture of safety around the children and, therefore, despite the opposite intentions, leave them in unsafe, insecure and potentially traumatic conditions, where they might end up in a worse situation than before. This happens mostly because in a problem focused mindset, safety is equal to a lack of risks, and the work is centred around creating 100% safety by removing the risk factors. However, because you can never guarantee 100% safety, that is, certainty that the children who have been maltreated or sexually or violently abused will never experience it again, you will often fail. However, if you try to create safety by both strengthening the protective factors and reducing the risks factors, you will increase the chance of success, because it's much easier to create safety around a preferred future you are heading for than a past you are moving away from. Susie Essex, who has developed and done research on the Resolution approach, has shown that you can reduce the risk of re-abuse from between 20–40% in ordinary practice to 3–7% by using the safety planning developed by the Resolution Approach (Turnell & Essex, 2006).

Amongst other things, we have learnt from the aforementioned approaches that as professionals, if we are to become more successful in creating safety for children, we need to be in a state of safe uncertainty (Wheeler, 2015). This is where we don't seek the right answers, getting it right and understanding too quickly; instead we ask questions in order to be curious, understand, make people think and create safety in processes that are not a final product, but more an ongoing process of creating change, just like "a river we are always in flow" (Wheeler, 2015, p. 34).

Another of our clearest learning points in integrating the Solution Focused approach into the Danish Child Protection system over these years is that children are able to describe clear pictures of what safety looks like, if you ask them, and if you have the tools to start a conversation about a safe enough future. But tools are not worth much if you use them with a problem focused mindset. The Solution Focused approach and the mindset connected to it are often the most helpful route to having these conversations with children in very stressful situations.

Our purpose with this chapter is to demonstrate different examples of how we have used the Solution Focused mindset as a key to opening a conversation with children and young people. We have decided to show some of our examples from cases which seemed to be "stuck" and yet where we succeeded, in spite of the fact that the questions and tools we had planned to use turned out not to be of much use. We succeeded because of the Solution Focused mindset and creative thinking, which from our experience has the biggest impact on working with children. If you don't believe in and use the assumptions in the Solution Focused approach, you can easily end up being problem focused or solution forced, even in the presence of good tools. We fall into that trap now and then, and our examples in this chapter will show how the mindset was useful to us, when the conversations weren't working as smoothly as we had hoped for – despite good questions and good tools.

One of the main characteristics of the Solution Focused mindset is the belief that clients are experts on their own lives (De Jong & Berg, 2006) and, when it comes to children's safety and well-being, we always have in mind that the children are the experts and we take that expertise seriously. Another of the main points from the Solution Focused mindset that we have found very helpful in conversations with children is that we don't need to talk about the problems to build solutions (Ratner et al., 2012). With this in mind, we find it much more helpful to talk about safety and well-being and what it looks like in the child's preferred future, than investigating the past and interviewing them about the details of abuse, neglect and so on (Turnell & Essex, 2006). When doing this, most children will be able to tell us what they need from us for them to feel safe without putting themselves or their parents in difficult situations where they might find it hard to talk because of issues of loyalty, guilt, shame or fear of rejection and/or punishment from their parents. They know what safety for them looks like and if you ask, they will be able to describe it for you.

When we are creating safety by making a safety plan around the child's perspective, the most important step is putting the child in the centre of the conversation and having a conversation with him/her about safety – what will the child's life look like if this safety is created? What will the parents be doing instead of the harm and danger they are causing? To have these useful conversations with the children, we always bring a small suitcase of toys and Playmobil to use for conversations about safe adults and a safety network (Parker, 2015a) and crayons and papers to draw on using the 3 houses tool (Weld & Parker, 2015) or the safety house tool (Parker, 2009). But again, these are only tools to structure the conversations. Unless we are also bringing creativity and the Solution Focused mindset, we are in danger of having a problem focused or a solution forced conversation with the children, which often will lead to them not saying a word or saying what they think we would like to hear. In order for this not to happen, we must use whatever is available to meet the children on their terms.

Example 1: Chad, 8 years old

An example of this was Michael talking to an 8-year-old child, Chad, who according to other professionals around him was violent, difficult to reach and make contact with, and difficult to engage in useful conversations. Due to a traffic jam, Michael arrived at Chad's home around bedtime and was quite nervous that Chad would be tired and maybe have less concentration and be harder to talk to than usual. Chad knew Michael was coming, opened the door and introduced himself, and because Michael had never visited him before, he insisted on giving Michael a guided tour, showing him every single room in the house. Back in the living room, Michael complimented Chad on the tour and for being such a good host. Michael asked him whether he wanted to draw and showed him the 3 houses, and Chad was very open to that. After about 3 minutes, however, he was unable to concentrate on the process and Michael started to think about doing something different. He remembered that on the tour around the house, he had seen a pirate ship in Chad's room and instead of continuing the drawing Michael asked Chad whether he would to show him the ship once again. Chad agreed, and while he was showing Michael the ship, Michael asked questions about the pirate in the mast of the ship and how he was able to see things on the horizon that the pirates on the deck couldn't see. He could, so to speak, look into the future. Then, Michael asked, "If the pirate looked into Chad's future, what would he see?" Chad answered questions about the future, and when Michael noticed he was losing concentration, he asked about the people on the deck, with the idea that, if the mast was the future then the pirates on the deck had to be in the present. So, Michael continued asking questions about what the present pirates would say about the good things in Chad's life. Below deck, there was a prisoner's hole, where the pirates put prisoners and things they wouldn't be comfortable having on deck. This led to Michael asking Chad about what he would wish to put away under deck, so it wouldn't show. This meaningful conversation lasted about 40 minutes, and Michael complimented Chad for showing him the pirate ship and talking about all those things about his life.

As professionals, we are responsible for creating an atmosphere for change (O'Hanlon, 1987) and the outcome of it, so if the child won't talk or says "I don't know", we don't consider the child to be resistant or providing "wrong answers", as there are no wrong answers in the Solution Focused approach (Ratner et al., 2012). Instead we also understand the silence or "I don't know" answers as a form of communication, and we become curious about whether there is anything we can do differently to create a safe context, where change can occur (O'Hanlon, 1987). Then, we try harder to create that context, but we also follow up on the conversation anyway in a Solution Focused way to investigate whether any change has happened in between conversations. As Solution Focused practitioners, we believe that the change happens between sessions and even if the reply is "I don't know" in the conversation, it might have started a reflection process that can lead to change later, after the session.

Example 2: Paul, 15 years old

An example from Rikke's practice was a 15-year-old boy named Paul, who needed protection against emotional and mental abuse from his mom but was also experiencing school refusal. Concerning the school refusal, all he could say about his best hopes and preferred future was that he wanted to have an ordinary life and go to school like other young people his age. Otherwise, all the questions Rikke was asking to help him think about the change he hoped for and wanted to create were either answered with "I don't know" or "I don't know – if I knew it, I would do it". Asking about the incidences when he had succeeded in getting to school and what he had done to achieve that, he would answer "I just went" and "I did fine" or again "I don't know". Really struggling here, Rikke tried to ask all the different kinds of Solution Focused questions that she had been taught, with no change at all. So instead of asking more questions which he wouldn't answer, Rikke just acknowledged his struggle and focused on complimenting him for the one time he did succeed instead of the four times in a week he didn't. Afterwards, while he was listening, Rikke named to his father all the strengths, resources and social skills that the young man had, which she had seen in him just now and in her previous contact with him, and commented on how proud his father must be of him, which made his father acknowledge the same. The boy just listened and commented that he didn't realize all this about himself. He is still not yet able to answer much except "I don't know" in the conversations, but since the conversations started, he has continuously improved his attendance in school from no attendance to a stable 3 times a week in just a 2-month period. Who knows exactly why? But is seems that the continuous acknowledgment and compliments for his accomplishments helped him believe more in himself and make the struggle less of a struggle.

As you can see from this example, we also lean into the Solution Focused mindset of "If it doesn't work, do something else" (Ratner et al., 2012). So, if children don't want to talk with us or they answer "don't know", we might, as Rikke did, use our observations to acknowledge and give compliments to help engage the children in the conversation and/or to help them see their strengths, resources, skills and capabilities which they might have forgotten to notice. To be able to do this, we always pay close attention and listen with a constructive ear (Lipchik, 1986) and watch them with a constructive eye, so as to be able to compliment the children on something they say or do in conversation or even for being courageous enough to talk to us. Or if they don't want to talk about anything else, we shift to "problem free talk" (Ratner et al., 2012) about what they are good at and what they like to do, while we are watching out for strengths, resources, skills and capabilities of the child, believing that small steps can lead to big changes, for them and also in the way that we engage with children.

A very important assumption we make in working with families is that parents want to do the best for their children by having good relationships with them, giving them a good chance of success and a future better than their own (Berg & Steiner, 2009). Therefore, it is very powerful to bring the children's perspective of future safety into the center of the work with parents and the extended network to help create the safety plan, because the parents and the network will then take responsibility for the safety of the child, and we as social workers will play a supportive role in the process (Berg & Kelly, 2000). Sometimes we even find it helpful to have conversations with the children and their parents together, even though we aim to have conversations with the children alone and the Danish law also emphasizes that this is required. But again, there is no rule without exceptions, and we need to dare to do what is best and most helpful to the child, including when it comes to our presence in their life.

Example 3: Richard, 16 years old

One example of how this turned out to be helpful is the conversation with a 16-year-old boy called Richard. We were working with the family because the child protection agency was worried about domestic violence, drug abuse, maltreatment and neglect in the family. The child protection agency was worried that Richard and his two younger brothers, aged 8 and 10, were beaten by their father when he was drunk. We had this conversation at Richard's home with his 18-year-old brother and his mother at home, too, and we were trying to use the safety house tool, but the only answers we got from Richard were "I don´t know". Clearly, we were on the wrong track, and we struggled to come up with something different. Michael was asking himself how Chris Iveson would handle this situation, and the idea of lists (Ratner et al., 2012) came into mind, so he asked Richard whether he could mention the most important or valuable things he contributed to his family. Richard answered, "I don´t know". "What would your mother say?" we asked. "I don't know, why don´t you ask her?", he answered. So, we did, and she mentioned 3 things as a start. The big brother entered the room and said, "I can come up with a lot of things", and he continued the list and we kept asking him "What else?" until we got a very long list with at least 20 things. Towards the end of the conversation, we were able to share with them the worries of the child protection social workers and we asked them whether the child protection social workers were right to be worried. The answer was "Our father doesn't beat us but all the other things do happen in our family, so they are right about their worries, but we can handle them". Then we asked them how they handled these things, and they described to us how they created safety when risk was at stake for the children. This gave us a complete picture of the family´s own worries, similar to the child protection agency's worries, and a detailed description of the family's safety plan, involving extended family in a complete and safe plan that showed us that there was enough safety for the children. When we asked why they didn't tell the child protection agency about the plan, their answer was "They never asked in a way that gave us the opportunity to tell".

These are just a few illustrations of our work with children and adolescents in a Solution Focused way in a problem focused and high-risk context. By sharing our work in this way, we hope to have inspired people not to seek to always get it right but to be aware of the Solution Focused mindset and creativity, to be able to deal more adequately with all the difficulty and complexity that's in the child protection field, when engaging with the children and young people in changing their lives.

References

Berg, I. K., & Kelly, S. (2000). *Building Solutions in Child Protection Services*. New York: W. W. Norton.

Berg, I. K., & Steiner, T. (2009). *"Børn I terapi" Danish Edition of "Children's Solution Work"*, translated by Tom Bøgeskov. Denmark: Dansk Psykologisk Forlag.

De Jong, P., & Berg, I. K. (2006). *Løsningsfokuserede samtaler*. Danish edition of Interviewing for Solutions. København: Hans Reitzels Forlag.

Lipchik, E. (1986). The Purposeful Interview. *Journal of Strategic and Systemic Therapies*, 5(1), 88–99.

O'Hanlon, W. H. (1987). *Taproots: Underlying Principles of Milton Ericson's Therapy and Hypnosis*. New York: W. W. Norton.
Parker, S. (2009). *The Safety House Booklet*. Perth, Western Australia: SP Consultancy.
Parker, S. (2015a). *Circles of Safety and Support Booklet*. Perth, Western Australia: SP Consultancy.
Parker, S. (2015b). *Case Consultation Booklet*. Perth, Western Australia: SP Consultancy.
Ratner, H., George, E., & Iveson, C. (2012). *Solution Focused Brief Therapy: 100 Key Points and Techniques*. London: Routledge.
Turnell, A., & Edwards, S. (1997). Aspiring to partnership – the signs of safety approach to child protection. *Child Abuse Review*, 6, 179–190.
Turnell, A., & Edwards, S. (1999). *Signs of Safety – A Solution and Safety Oriented Approach to Child Protection Casework*. New York: W. W. Norton.
Turnell, A., & Essex, S. (2006). *Working with "Denied" Child Abuse, the Resolutions Approach*. Buckingham: Open University Press.
Weld, N., & Parker, S. (2015). *The Three Houses Booklet*. Perth, Western Australia: SP Consultancy.
Wheeler, J. (2015). Classic SF Paper: Introduction to Barry Mason (1993). *Towards Positions of Safe Uncertainty: Interaction*, 7(1), 24–43.

Chapter 22

Yes . . . and
Useful conversations around trauma

Pamela K. King

When a child breaks a vase and tells the truth about it, the vase is indeed broken, and a parent may say 'thank you for telling the truth.' Parent and child might then clean it up together. In this event, many things exist:

1 The vase is broken.
2 The child did something in the midst of the incident of which they can be proud.
3 The parent and child worked together.
4 The honesty might help build trust.
5 The child might learn something for the future about 'being careful.'

Breaking a vase is a simple infraction; building trust, learning something about oneself, or strengthening a relationship, we might agree are more important. The difficulties a teen or young adult face may have more far-reaching consequences than a shattered vase. In Solution Focused work, it is not the vase, trauma, conflict, or the problem that we necessarily need to learn more about (de Shazer et al., 2007). The agenda is set by our clients, what they want, how they coped, what they learned, or something completely unrelated to the problem: 'I need to get a job.'

The emphasis of this chapter is how to be Solution Focused when our agenda setting leads us to talking about the problem or conflict. Being Solution Focused does not mean being problem-phobic (Berg & Szabo, 2005). The following examples illustrate ways to notice Solution Focused opportunities in what might otherwise be considered problem talk.

When my twin daughters first started driving to school, parties, and high school activities, we told them repeatedly, if you ever need us, just call, no matter the reason, we will pick you up with no questions asked. A new driver might call and say: 'the traffic is too scary, I've been drinking, I'm too tired to drive, the car won't start,' or 'the party is getting out-of-hand.' The teen may have broken a rule and the parent is happy to be part of a safety plan.

Improvisation, as a theatre form, is informative here; it highlights the 'yes . . . and' aspect of conversation (Jackson, 2015), accepting what is there and building on it. In therapy, when my clients tell me about the difficult things happening in their lives, I always know there is more, there is an 'and.'

> ... and what do you want instead?
> ... and how did you make it through that?
> ... and what did you do that you are proud of?
> ... and what is already happening that is in the right direction?

While 'but' by contrast to 'and' negates or refutes what is said before, 'and' accepts and builds. This 'accept and build' is important in Solution Focused practices. We accept where a client is, accept their experience, and we carefully select what aspect of their narrative we will build on. De Jong and Berg (2013) call this co-constructive process 'listen, select, and build.'

1 Listen for hints of competence and Solution Focused possibilities.
2 Select those items to comment on and be curious about.
3 Respond in a way that 'invites the client to build in a solution-focused direction' (De Jong & Berg, 2013, p. 57).

I recently had a young adult client who had been involved in a fatal car accident. He was ordered to be in therapy, was on probation, was having a difficult time adjusting to college, and was struggling with nightmares. His best hopes from therapy were to 'get over' and 'get through' this ordeal. The young man was ticketed and judged responsible for the accident and therefore the fatality. He wanted to tell me about the accident and I said that was fine. I followed where he wanted to go and I led by asking questions to reveal competence. Rather than follow a line of questioning to hear the gruesome details of the accident and content of his nightmares, I asked him about what or who he was proud of in the midst of the accident. A much more interesting and helpful conversation followed. This intervention was inspired by a video out of the Solution Focused Institute of South Africa (von Cziffra-Bergs, 2015).

Here is part of our conversation:

Th: In the midst of this difficult situation, what happened that you are somehow proud of?
Cl: Umm ... right after we rolled over and landed, I turned around to see if Bo and Roland (buddies in the backseat) were okay.
Th: So, one of the first things you did was to see if Bo and Roland were okay. What else?
Cl: They were okay so we kinda huddled-up for a minute. (Therapist: Uh-huh.) Then I saw through my broken windshield the other car and I could sorta tell the passenger was, you know, gone, and I just prayed.
Th: You prayed.

Cl: Yeah, and I knew the other driver, a guy that goes to my school, and he was really freaking out, so I just reached my hand out and grabbed his wrist and said his name and we just sorta cried, and like, held onto each other.

Th: You were able to reach out to him and hold on to each other. What difference did that make?

Cl: Well, he sort of calmed down, at least was breathing, you know.

Th: Uh-huh.... What else happened that was helpful?

Cl: Bo and Roland had called their parents and they were there. They were hugging all of us, it was nice cause mine weren't there yet.

Th: So, in one of the most difficult situations imaginable, you were concerned about your friends and the other driver, you prayed and you reached out. The parents helped all the kids. It seems like there was a lot of kindness going around.

Cl: Yeah, and all the cops and firefighters were really cool too.

In this young man's recollections, he will have the reality of a fatal car accident, the legal challenges, <u>and</u> moments of competence and kindness. He could reflect on responding well to a challenging situation. When he came to his second appointment, he said when he had a flashback or woke up with a nightmare, he made himself think about this expanded narrative of his and others' kindness and competence, which helped him somewhat. He said, 'I know I caused a horrible accident <u>and</u> I'm trying to remember I am a good guy, I care about people.'

Like this young man, many people state they want to get their life back after a traumatic event but are troubled by frightening nightmares and intrusive memories. Firstly, I help them understand flashbacks are a normal part of our response system, a thought or memory about something that happened in the past. By expanding what we focus on from the event, it is possible to influence and even structure how we remember and what we flashback on.

John Henden, in *What It Takes to Thrive* (2018, pp. 24–25), describes a similar process of helping clients reflect on personal strengths and qualities during a crisis. He suggests people cut strips of white paper and strips of coloured paper, then in retelling the distressing event, lay down a white strip for a troubling fact and a coloured strip for a fact about a good thing they did in the moment. The resulting mixed stack of papers gives a visual representation of the event.

Yvonne Dolan has a four-step approach for overcoming the effects of flashbacks in *Resolving Sexual Abuse* (1991, p. 107) that I use with clients and have adapted to children (King, 2017, pp. 122–123).

1 Identify when you have felt this way before.
2 In what ways are your current situation and the past similar? Are there sights, sounds, or sensations that are similar to the past situation? Are there people who remind you of that past situation?

3   How is your current situation different from the time in the past when you felt similar feelings?
4   What action do you want to take?

After a few sessions, this young man stated he was having fewer nightmares and could manage the flashbacks. He said he was still dealing with the consequences of the accident but because he was sleeping better and able to focus at school, he felt like he had some of his life back. When clients come to an appointment in crisis or have experienced a recent crisis, our interventions can address client needs while directing them to small, useful achievements.

Details of a slightly less crappy day

A teen girl came in suicidal, shaky, and stating she was having a crappy day and a terrible panic attack. She made it clear that what would be most helpful would be to talk about her distressing week. I had the following thoughts:

- We could easily go into a problem-focused conversation.
- I wanted to solution-build and help her recognise competence.
- Imposing my solutions or ideas of what she 'should' do would have been solution-forced (Nylund & Corsiglia, 1994) and would shortchange her.
- A glib 'what is going well?' might have seemed problem-phobic (Berg & Szabo, 2005) and completely missed the mark.
- I needed to assess for safety.
- I wanted her to be able to identify something she could move towards.

I had a trusted relationship with this teen, as I had seen her several times. She was clearly distressed and I was concerned for her well-being. The following use of scaling was inspired by a conversation with Heather Fiske (2017).

Cl: I've had a really bad week and today is really crappy.
Th: Wow, sorry to hear that.
Cl: I thought about cutting or taking a bunch of pills or something.
Th: It must have been hard to get here.
Cl: Yeah, it's been really bad.

Th: OK, so you know how some days are really bad (outstretched arms, indicating a scale) and then others are . . . I don't know, something else. (Client nods) So I suppose some days are just kinda bad. (Cl: Uh-huh). Let's say on this scale (drawing on whiteboard) really bad is one and kinda bad is ten. Where are you today?

Cl: Four.
Th: A four? How is it that high on such a bad day?

Cl: I haven't hurt myself.
Th: You haven't hurt yourself! How have you managed that?
Cl: I just distract myself.
Th: With what?
Cl: Music.
Th: And that helps? (Client nods) What else helps?
Cl: I talked to my mom . . . and ate something. (Therapist nods, waits for more) I knew I was coming here.
Th: So, let me ask you this. . . . What is the lowest you have been in the last few months?
Cl: Two.
Th: Really, and today you are a four? When you were at a two, what helped you go up, even a little bit?

We talked for a few minutes about what helps her when she is feeling very low. She was able to identify five distinct behaviours that help her when she is as low as a two. I wanted to discover what other protective factors she had.

Th: Show me on the scale where suicide would be (She extended the line down to zero and wrote suicide). Okay, what is the lowest you have ever been? (She drew a line half a point up from zero) And it's been months since you have been *that* low (pointing to lowest ever mark).
Cl: Yeah.
Th: Okay, so, I imagine you have some warning signs or something that tell you to take action.
Cl: If I start to have a panic attack I need to get to a safe place.
Th: A safe place, like where?
Cl: Just not alone, be by somebody, like my mom.
Th: Good, what else?
Cl: When I feel like cutting.
Th: What do you do then?
Cl: (laughs) Simple, stay away from sharp stuff.
Th: (laughs) Good strategy! What else?
Cl: If I start feeling suicidal, I have to do something to distract myself.
Th: How do you do that?

We had five minutes of conversation about the ways she distracts herself and could change her actions and thinking to more hope-oriented. She was able to give details of what she is doing, who she is with, and what difference it makes.

Th: (Pointing to the mark for *now*) I am curious, after this conversation, if your number is the same or different.
Cl: Actually, it is maybe a six or seven. I feel better.

Th: Oh, Okay! How useful was this session, on a scale from (one) *waste of time* to (ten) *super helpful*?
Cl: (Drew a line above *super helpful* and made an X) like a twelve!

By the end of our session, we had talked about the difficult week and done it in a way to expose her many useful coping strategies. She hadn't cut herself, she talked to her mom, she listened to music, she came to her appointment . . . and on and on. We spent fifty minutes scaling on a big whiteboard. I was delighted by this young woman's insight and wisdom and pleased to see she went from highly distressed to solidly okay by the end of the session.

When clients are in crisis or have experienced a traumatic event, we can go where they need to go and stay firmly in Solution Focused conversations. People have more in their lives than the presenting difficult event. They may or may not find it useful to discuss the event. When they do, they are the experts on their lives and experiences. We can lead from one step behind and trust them to show us where to go. I hope this handful of interventions have prompted you to think about ways you can invite clients to think about a trauma or crisis in a broader way to expose new, valuable information to reflect on or flashback on.

References

Berg, I. K., & Szabo, P. (2005). *Brief Coaching for Lasting Solutions*. New York: W. W. Norton.

De Jong, P., & Berg, I. K. (2013). *Interviewing for Solutions*, 4th edition. Belmont, CA: Brooks, Cole.

de Shazer, S., Dolan, Y., Korman, H., Trepper, T., McCollum, E., & Berg, I. K. (2007). *More Than Miracles: The State of the Art of Solution Focused Brief Therapy*. New York: Routledge.

Dolan, Y. (1991). *Resolving Sexual Abuse: Solution-Focused Therapy and Ericksonian Hypnosis for Adult Survivors*. New York: W. W. Norton.

Fiske, H. (2017). Personal communication.

Henden, J. (2018). *What It Takes to Thrive: Techniques for Severe Trauma and Stress Recovery*. London: World Scientific.

Jackson, P. Z. (2015). *EASY: Your Lifepass to Creativity and Confidence*. London: The Solutions Focus.

King, P. K. (2017). *Tools for Effective Therapy with Children and Families: A Solution-Focused Approach*. New York: Routledge.

Nylund, D., & Corsiglia, V. (1994). Becoming Solution-Focused Forced in Brief Therapy: Remembering Something Important We Already Knew. *Journal of Systemic Therapies*, 13(1), 5–12.

von Cziffra-Bergs, J. (2015). *Solution Focused Trauma Therapy: Recreation of a Trauma Session* (DVD Download). www.solutionfocusedsa.com/shop/.SouthAfrica.

Chapter 23

Incorporating the Solution Focused approach in tackling selective mutism

Anita McKiernan

Selective mutism

Selective mutism (SM) is a debilitating anxiety disorder, whereby a person is unable to speak in certain everyday social situations, despite speaking normally in other situations where he or she feels comfortable. It is considered to be a specific phobia of speaking that can emerge in temperamentally-sensitive children, who are much more reactive to new situations than is usual (Gensthaler et al., 2016). The freeze (panic) response is triggered by the expectation to speak to certain people and this leaves the child unable to talk, even though he or she really wants to. This response is experienced as extremely distressing and the child soon learns to anticipate those situations that trigger the reaction and avoid them at all costs.

SM is usually triggered between 2 and 4 years of age and can also sometimes emerge in teenagerhood. It is common for individuals to present with other anxieties, particularly social anxiety, and some will also have additional difficulties or disorders. Each individual's pattern of speaking will be unique, but typically children can speak to close family members in familiar, comfortable situations and have most difficulty at school and other environments, where there are expectations for speaking.

The mute behaviour provides temporary relief for the child or young person, but over time it tends to maintain and strengthen the phobia. The phobia is also innocently reinforced by the behaviour of others, who may try to get the child to talk, speak for the child or avoid situations altogether. Any kind of pressure or avoidance tends to make things worse by strengthening the associations between speaking and anxiety (Johnson & Wintgens, 2016).

SM is best managed through a collaborative approach in which the parents, school staff and professionals involved all work closely together. Good outcomes are promoted when key people around the child have been educated on what SM is and know how to create the conditions conducive to social participation and communication across different environments (Shipon-Blum, 2007).

Johnson and Wintgens (2016) highlight the most effective ways of interacting with a person with a phobia of speaking. The first is through commentary-style talk, where the adult makes chatty comments about what is happening or something the individual is engaged in, leaving pauses so the individual experiences opportunity but no expectation to talk. When the individual is showing signs of comfort responding (relaxed nonverbal/verbal communication), the adult can then introduce some questions, following a graded process. This starts with simple yes/no questions and moves gradually to choice questions, such as, 'did you see X or Y?' Only when the individual is comfortable responding at this level does the adult move on to simple 'wh' questions that require one-word responses and, from here, moves gradually to more open-ended questions. In addition to these warm-up and graded questioning routines, parents and school staff will also need to practice a range of formal and informal 'talking-bridges' to help the child or young person achieve verbal communication with new people in small steps (Johnson & Wintgens, 2016). These behavioural approaches, including desensitisation and graded exposure, have the best evidence for effectiveness in tackling SM (Viana et al., 2009).

Introducing a Solution Focused perspective into the work

Although behavioural techniques are central in SM management, in my experience the work lends itself very well to incorporating the Solution Focused approach, and there are particular reasons why it is actually a good fit for many aspects of the work in SM.

Firstly, *exceptions* are one of the central pillars of the Solution Focused approach (de Shazer, 1985), and SM is a diagnosis that can only be made when there are exceptions to the problem behaviour. These exceptions can be deconstructed in order to find out what the child is doing and how those around them are interacting in these situations. This process often highlights hidden resources as well as the types of behaviours that support the child to communicate more comfortably and easily (solution patterns). In order to explore exceptions, a profile of the child or young person's talking habits will need to be gained in different situations from parents and school staff.

Mina, 6

Mina had SM from age 3 and, when first seen, was comfortable speaking with family, most relatives she saw frequently, and 2 of her classmates, provided they were in the playground. She did not speak to any other adults or children. During the initial meeting with school staff and her mum, I got curious about her ability to speak to 2 classmates in the playground. I asked staff what they thought might be happening there that was different to other situations. They reported that she could get absorbed in activities with her 2 classmates and could play in quieter areas outside. This led naturally to exploring whether these supportive factors might be available to her more often (doing more of what works). Her teacher and key worker came up with ideas such as putting the children together for learning tasks, engaging them in little errands and giving them time together in quieter areas of the classroom.

This exploratory process will often highlight *instances* or elements of preferred outcomes already happening (George et al., 1999). For example, Mina's mum mentioned that her daughter had only started speaking to one of the children (Zoe) within the last year. I asked how she had managed this, and she said that Mina talked a lot about this classmate, which led mum to set up some play-dates with her. Through this, Mina was able to get comfortable talking to Zoe in her most comfortable (home) environment, before speaking to her in the playground.

Beginning with a focus on *exceptions* and *instances* is very helpful in SM management, because it is not unusual for parents and school staff to feel incredibly stuck, particularly as any form of pressure or avoidance makes things worse. The Solution Focused approach orients people towards what is working by amplifying elements of the solution already up and running, which fosters a forward-looking and hopeful attitude.

Collaboration

Another aspect of SM management that sits well with the Solution Focused approach concerns the area of collaboration. Working collaboratively with the team around the child or young person is vital in ensuring that all parties create the right conditions to support participation and communication. A Solution Focused stance promotes collaboration naturally, by harnessing peoples' motivation (Ratner et al., 2012), valuing what is working already and affirming the strengths, skills and resources of all involved.

In the case of Mina, following the initial consultation and training of school staff and parents, a monitoring and review process was agreed, during which the Solution Focused approach was used extensively. Here is an excerpt from the first review meeting held at school, involving Mina's mum, her teacher, her key worker and myself.

Therapist: So, what's been better since we last spoke?
Teacher: Lots actually . . . for starters Mina is interacting more with children in the class and with the 2 kids she spoke to in the playground, and she now speaks to in class.
Therapist: That's great to hear. What did you do that helped bring that about?
Teacher: I had a chat with her and said that I understood that she finds it hard to speak sometimes and no one expects her to talk before she is ready. That made a big difference . . . I could see her body language in class was more relaxed and she was writing more stuff down.
Therapist: That's great. What else do you think you did that helped?

Teacher:	We gave her lots of time and little activities with the 2 children she was most comfortable with . . . you can see the friendships are really growing.
Therapist:	Wow, that's fantastic. What else has been different?
Key worker:	In our one-to-one sessions, she has gone from little phrases to using sentences at normal volume.
Therapist:	Wow great. How have you helped her use sentences at normal volume?
Key worker:	Well, mum mentioned that she loves craft activities, so I used lots of them . . . that helped her relax more and use louder sentences.
Therapist:	That's great . . . and how did you support this relaxation?
Key worker:	I think I was focusing on the props rather than on her, and I was using the commentary-style warm-up and graded questions as well.
Therapist:	That's great to hear. What difference is all this making?
Key worker:	Mina really responds to this low-key approach and when we let her choose a friend to join our session yesterday, she chose Zoe and continued talking in the session.
Therapist:	That's brilliant! What do you think you will notice as she continues to make progress?
Key worker:	Probably beginning to talk with new children. We will add in peers to her sessions, as this is working well so far.
Therapist:	That makes sense and builds on the great work you've all done. We can have a chat now about this next part of the work. (Note with this sentence I am stepping out of Solution Focused mode briefly and drawing on clinical expertise). Ethically this is important, because when a child with SM starts talking more, people can start expecting more than the child is ready for and things can quickly deteriorate. To keep the work safe, it needs to proceed systematically in small steps, so setting these parameters is vital. Once safe systems of working are in place, the Solution Focused approach can be used very fluidly, and its emphasis on small steps and going at the client's pace make it an excellent fit for the collaborative work needing to be done with the team around the child or young person.

Direct work with children and young people

Using the Solution Focused approach directly with children and young people who have a phobia of speaking certainly raises some important issues. Firstly, individuals with this need find open-ended questions that focus on personal topics the most difficult to manage. This is when they tend to have the greatest freeze reaction, often linked to the fear of making a mistake or saying the wrong thing (Johnson & Wintgens, 2016). Solution Focused questions are by nature open-ended, inviting description of what's wanted, the difference this will make and what the desired outcome will look like in terms of concrete observable behaviours (Ratner et al., 2012). Furthermore, the interactive dialogue at the heart of the solution-building process involves considerable communication and emotional demands, which can push the individual into a heightened anxiety state. Ethically, it is crucial to take steps to manage this, because a treating professional can inadvertently contribute to the individual's fear of speaking by failing to show understanding of the mutism. Many of the child-friendly adaptations of the Solution Focused approach such as those described by Berg and Steiner (2003) and Ratner and Yusuf (2015) are useful with this population, but in light of the child's phobia, additional steps are warranted.

My experience is that following a systematic rapport-building process, as outlined by Johnson and Wintgens (2016), gives the best chance of building trust and securing the child or young person's engagement. This includes:

- Openly acknowledging the difficulty speaking.
- Reassuring the individual that there is no pressure to speak, they can do so if they wish or if they prefer and they can communicate in other ways. Having other means of communication visible reinforces this message.
- Using a graded approach in interacting with the child/young person, beginning with commentary-style talk. When the individual is responding comfortably, graded questioning can be introduced, following the process described earlier.

During this sequence, I am actively learning the most helpful ways of interacting with the individual and will be making adjustments in my communication accordingly. With children, my preference is to join an activity the child enjoys, as he or she interacts with a comfortable talking partner, and ease into engaging directly with the child in small steps. Through this problem-free activity, often referred to as 'sliding-in', one is more likely to meet the child in a resourceful state. Problem-free talk, in contrast, involves general chat and is often too personal and unstructured for rapport-building when SM is part of the picture. With teens, I provide the necessary reassurances and key information, including how I work. I then engage them in nonverbal activities around their interests and communication habits in different situations, using simple tick-box questionnaires, so that again a communication-friendly environment is set up from the outset.

In establishing best hopes, I often use a process inspired by Johnson and Wintgens (2016) while using a tool called 'talking mats' (Murphy & Cameron, 2008), which is a visual means of enabling people with a range of communication needs to take part in conversations about their opinions, hopes and needs. It consists of a top-scale, a topic and set of options, all of which are visually represented. The items are displayed on the mat and the visual structure and gentle physical task supports engagement, as the person thinks through options at their own pace. Sitting alongside, I provide the child/young person with pictured or written options which represent common hopes individuals with SM often have, such as doing well in school, having friends and speaking more in class. The purpose of the activity is not to feed the individual ideas, but to provide a safe structure through which they can think about and express their hopes.

Zac, 13

Zac presented with longstanding SM and the improvised talking mats tool accommodated his early need for structure and safety. He sorted the cards and placed them on the mat along a scale, with 10 representing 'this is very important for me' and 1 representing 'not important at the moment'. I provided sticky notes, inviting him to write or draw in anything else he would like to achieve. With his permission, I gave his mum the option of doing the same. Zac then placed these additional hopes in the relevant positions on the mat, grouping similar items together. I then invited him to organise the items in the most important section so as to reflect his priorities and, as often happens at this point, he elevated his own best hopes above the pre-written ones, to provide a clear focus for the work.

Zac's best hopes were 'more independence', 'say more with peers', and 'more confidence speaking' and to help him build up a picture of what these would look like, visual supports were used. These included a mind map and 'wh' question prompts to help him describe the who, what and where of his desired outcomes, and he could draw, write or verbalise his ideas. At this point, Zac was using sentences with me during structured activities, but dropped back to single words and writing once tasks became less structured.

Zac wrote down one idea, 'speaking for myself', but quickly became inhibited during this process, as often happens when the task becomes more open and personal. I acknowledged the difficulty and said I'd like to think of a way to make it easier for him. Saying this helped him relax, and then I had the idea to build on an activity I'd used previously to support his comfort speaking with me. The activity involved one person selecting a picture from a pile of pictured objects and giving the other person some clues, as they tried to guess the hidden item, and then the roles were reversed. The familiar and safe structure of this enabled Zac to quickly reengage. As the game progressed, I said that I would be using different levels of confidence speaking on my turns and he might want to rate me on a 5-point scale, with 5 representing 'most confident'. Zac was very good at detecting how I came across and, with some initial scaffolding via choice options, he was able to say what he noticed that fitted with his ratings, for example for 3, he listed 'calm body language' and 'clear voice'. As the activity progressed, he became more confident in his ratings and observations as well as his verbal interaction with me. I asked him whether he would like me to rate his confidence on a subsequent turn, and he was happy to do this. This provided several opportunities to affirm his skills and deconstruct different confidence ratings. From this process, he highlighted 3 important aspects of confidence speaking for him, 'clear speech', 'looking at the person' and 'relaxed body language'.

Following this, Zac was in a more resourceful state and was able to use the mind map to flesh out further signs of independence and confidence speaking, including 'speaking more with Amir and Marcus', 'ordering my own food and drink' and 'speaking in shops', and his friends and family would notice he was 'smiling more'. He scaled himself at a 4 in terms of his desired outcome, and he was invited to think about reasons for this as a homework task and come up with 5 things that he would notice one point up.

Subsequent sessions began with games and activities to support Zac's confidence communicating with me, followed by use of scales, lists, and practical activities to explore the signs of change, strengths and next small steps. He really enjoyed card games and activities where he could manipulate props and act out elements of desired goals, so these were used extensively in sessions. Zac made steady progress over the next 6 months and began to notice an increasing number of changes consistent with his preferred outcomes, including using a louder voice and longer sentences with friends, talking to more classmates, texting his friends, going out more, ordering for himself in cafés and shops, speaking in French class, initiating conversations and using more eye contact.

Reflections on the work

The most challenging aspect of the Solution Focused approach when individuals have SM is in obtaining descriptive details of desired outcomes, progress, different perspectives and possible signs or steps. However, children and young people can often be supported to imagine the change taking place through different expressive modalities. These include writing, drawing, speaking through puppets or another person, acting things out, manipulating pictures or objects, using gestures, facial expression, body language or signs.

The principle of *utilisation*, championed by Milton Erikson (O'Hanlon & Beadle, 1994), is particularly useful in this regard in terms of seeing whatever the child or young person brings to the table as a potential resource. This allows the practitioner to value and include what might otherwise be overlooked and fosters a resourceful and improvisational attitude.

I make extensive use of games, resources and improvised activities to support the work with children and young people. Many structured card and board games and games involving elements of guessing and problem-solving are very useful, particularly those that involve short turn-taking. Resources will include paper, whiteboard and pens, toys, animals, puppets, everyday objects and malleable materials that can be moulded into desired shapes and forms. A variety of visual supports will also be accessible, including strengths cards, sticky notes, mind maps, rating scales, templates for various Solution Focused explorations and a talking mat. These provide opportunities to support the child or young person's confidence communicating and facilitate the expression of hopes, signs of change and exploratory next steps.

In my experience, activities and simple experiments that arise in the moment can often create a strong context for Solution Focused explorations, as happened with Zac. Such activities increase the level of structure and seem to act as a bridge between the known and familiar world of the speaking problem and the unfamiliar territory of a future without its influence. Often exceptions and instances of success will present themselves through activities, and these can be amplified to highlight important skills, resources and competencies that provide stepping stones to desired changes. It is vital that the communication demands of any activity are in line with the individual's current level of comfort communicating, so the child or young person can be in a resourceful state, while thinking about important topics.

With some children and young people, it makes sense to go for scaling once best hopes have been established and highlight what's happening already that provides a foundation for progress. Drawing on the observations of significant others during all this helps to build a sense of possibilities, strengths and small steps towards what's wanted. Sometimes it becomes clear that the child or young person needs to build key skills, either in a 1:1 or group situation, in which case the Solution Focused approach can be used with the individual and support team in facilitating the skill-building process. With some young people, the needs are such that options around medication or other interventions may also need to be explored with the multi-disciplinary team. With some individuals, it is possible to use a wide range of Solution Focused techniques and tools, while with others, relatively few are used, because the readiness is not yet there.

Whatever route I take in the work, I strive to maintain the Solution Focused stance, in terms of recognising the inherent resourcefulness and expertise of the child or young person, focusing on what they can do rather than on what they can't do, and being resolutely strengths-focused. Arising out of this attitude of openness and curiosity, what often happens is that novel opportunities present themselves and it becomes natural to extend the Solution Focused work, through various tools and techniques. As a speech and language therapist, I am positioned to assess and support children's speech, language and communication skills, so in reality, my Solution Focused explorations come out of the work I am doing in these areas. For me, these explorations are always in the context of ongoing collaborative work with the wider team, where I find the Solution Focused approach to be a very good fit.

What stands out for me the most from my experience of working in the area of Selective Mutism is the overarching need to acknowledge the child or young person's fear of speaking in certain situations. Many young people report that they have been misunderstood in the past and are fearful of being expected to say or do more than they can manage. It is vital, therefore, to demonstrate an understanding of this by ensuring that the necessary reassurances and safeguards are in place and by making adjustments in one's communication and expectations in response to the child or young person's needs. All this helps to build a supportive, communication-friendly environment, which provides the essential foundation for the child or young person to begin to explore new possibilities for themselves and their lives. Bill O'Hanlon's suggestion of having one foot in acknowledgement and one foot in possibility (Ratner et al., 2012) feels very apt for the kind, agile stance that is needed for this somewhat challenging work to go well.

References

Berg, I. K., & Steiner, T. (2003). *Children's Solution Work*. New York: W. W. Norton.

de Shazer, S. (1985). *Keys to Solutions in Brief Therapy*. New York: W. W. Norton.

Gensthaler, A., Khalaf, S., Ligges, M., Kaess, M., Freitag, C. M., & Schwenck, C. (2016). Selective Mutism and Temperament: The Silence and Behavioral Inhibition to the Unfamiliar. *European Child and Adolescent Psychiatry*, 25, 1113–1120.

George, E., Iveson, C., & Ratner, H. (1999). *Problem to Solution: Brief Therapy with Individuals and Families*, 2nd edition. London: BT Press.

Johnson, M., & Wintgens, A. (2016). *The Selective Mutism Resource Manual*, 2nd edition. London: Speechmark Publishing Limited.

Murphy, J., & Cameron, L. (2008). *Talking Mats: A Resource to Enhance Communication*. AAC Research Team, University of Stirling (online). www.talkingmats.com/projects/publications/. Accessed 1 May 2019.

O'Hanlon, W., & Beadle, S. (1994). *A Field Guide to Possibility Land: Possibility Therapy Methods*. London: BT Press.

Ratner, H., George, E., & Iveson, C. (2012). *Solution Focused Brief Therapy: 100 Key Points and Techniques*. London: Routledge.

Ratner, H., & Yusuf, D. (2015). *Brief Coaching with Children and Young People: A Solution Focused Approach:* London: Routledge.

Shipon-Blum, E. (2007). *When the Words Just Won't Come Out: Understanding Selective Mutism*. (online). www.selectivemutism.org/resources/library. Accessed 12 March 2019.

Viana, A. G., Beidel, D. C., & Rabian, B. (2009). Selective Mutism: A Review and Integration of the Last 15 Years. *Clinical Psychology Review*, 29(1), 57–67.

Chapter 24

A tiny little piece of hope
Accompanying parentally bereaved children and adolescents in their journey through parental terminal illness, grief and healing via a Solution Focused pathway

Xenia Anastassiou-Hadjicharalambous

Background

Any therapeutic work with bereaved individuals at any stage of their life necessitates a thorough appreciation of the bereavement process. Historically, the Victorian belief in the past that grief was a sign of a *broken heart* resulting from the loss of a loved one was followed by the psychodynamic view that grief was a painful experience resulting from the letting go of the attachment to the deceased (for review, see Archer, 2008). At a later stage, theories of grieving focused on the trajectory of the grieving process, with the more well-known Kubler-Ross (1969) model postulating that along the grieving process, the bereaved individuals progress through certain stages in order to reach some resolution or endpoint in the grieving process. It was proposed that the bereaved individuals would return to some pre-loss level of functioning after completion of their "grief work" (Gillies & Neimeyer, 2006).

From pathologising to shifting perspective towards resilience and reconstruction of meaning

While these traditional stage theories have provided substantial information to the field, much current research stems from a constructivist paradigm that emphasises the important role of meaning making throughout the grieving process (Niemeyer, 2001). For instance, in Stroebe and Schut's dual process model (Stroebe & Schut, 2001), a bereaved individual alternates between loss-oriented and restoration-oriented coping. Loss-oriented coping involves dealing with many of the intense emotions that follow the separation from the deceased attachment figure. Restoration-oriented coping refers to the ways in which bereaved individuals attempt to re-construct and re-engage in their life following loss. Restoration-oriented coping includes spiritual and symbolic identity changes that occur as the bereaved individuals attempt to re-define themselves and their attachment with the deceased. Meaning making is the task that drives these alternating forces in the dual process model (Gillies & Neimeyer, 2006). The Solution Focused model, which has its roots in social constructionism, fits quite well with restoration-oriented coping.

Understanding grief in the context of the developmental stages

Beyond the theoretical models, for a thorough appreciation of the bereavement process, it is necessary to consider developmental changes that occur during a particular life stage. Fleming and Adolph (1986) stressed that individuals' grief must be examined in the context of normative developmental challenges and tasks. These developmental challenges interact with grieving processes and could potentially have a substantial effect on therapeutic process and outcome that should not be neglected. Further, Solution Focused practices need to be examined within the framework of developmental processes, intertwined with family processes.

Understanding grief in the context of cultural processes

Cultural effects can potentially affect the journey of the bereaved child and young person through grief. Most cultures have grief-related rituals, yet these rituals differ. In certain eastern cultures that encourage the participation of children in these rituals in ways that facilitate grief to flow, it is much more likely for the children to advance through self-healing processes. In many, yet not all, families in our unique mixture of eastern and western practices in Cyprus, children, especially the younger ones, are often excluded from these rituals, in a sometimes enforced and not child-friendly way, for a diverse set of reasons. One of the main reasons, that has been repeatedly documented in our practice, is the unfounded protection of the child from extreme sadness, as if we have the magic ability to protect our children from sadness or as if by being excluded from the rituals they will not feel the deep pain resulting from their mother's or father's death deep inside their heart. Even relatives often try to keep as a secret the parental terminal illness or/and lie about issues concerning the parent's death. These issues complicate the natural flow of bereavement in the developing child and constitute an additional risk for his/her mental health. In our services, which will be described later, the affected child in a child-centreed perspective is facilitated to decide what is beneficial to him/her. We have been most impressed by the maturity children display in such adverse situations. We observe them growing up overnight, sometimes in a moment . . . some of them decide to join the rituals throughout the process, others choose the stance to decide as they go ahead. We choose to accompany them in the way they feel deep inside their heart.

The Solution Focused paradigm experience of our team at CARE

Our mental health and social support team of the non-profit foundation of CARE (**C**hild and **A**dolescent **R**esearch-**E**vidence-based practice) accompanies children and young people in their journey through parental terminal illness, death and bereavement in a goal-oriented, solution-building pathway. Empirical data support the claim that having a goal-oriented approach and focusing on resources rather than on losses can potentially boost individuals' capacity to cope with loss and bereavement. CARE aims to embrace the affected child and adolescent with a caring team that will help them to make sense of their parent's illness and subsequent death in a caring, supportive context. We aim to empower the young person to activate factors that are empirically documented to facilitate resilience. Most importantly, we aim to help each young person to construct their own unique possibility-oriented life pathway. Our team at CARE invites the young person to remember and focus on the resources they already possess in order to move forward in their lives.

Systematic group-based solution building path

Most of our work is done in a group-based format which, in a systematic way, extends the young person's social network of support. This is particularly important given the empirical data documenting that parentally bereaved children are more likely to undergo a change of home and school (Akerman & Statham, 2011), which limits their contact with their known support system. We aim to help the participating young people to construct their own unique solutions within the context of a group rather than in isolation. A group context enables the young person to go through grief within a systematic goal-directed framework of social support. Within the group, the members have the opportunity to work through issues of grief and share the challenges following the loss of a parent.

A pragmatic approach often needs to be generated; in other words, we work with what we have in front of us, meaning that we work with what we have (Gray et al., 1998). There is often a distance between how we need to do things and how, ideally, we would wish to do them. For instance, it is not indicated developmentally to form a group of young people with age differences of 8 years between them. Yet, we often need to do it. What is fundamental is that, within the framework of this mismatch, the power of the experience itself is so influential that it does not allow difficulties inherent in the heterogeneity of the samples to cause a huge problem in the therapeutic process.

A first step in the first session of the group work is the deliberate use of the "Best Hopes" rather than the sharing of any detailed experiences of the loss and the past, for example *"If you woke up tomorrow and your best hopes from coming here had been realised, what's the first thing you might notice yourself doing?"*,

"Who will be the first to notice?" (George et al., 1999). However, at this and every stage of the process, it is of paramount importance to exercise particular caution since the young people often need to share their stories and the worst thing that a clinician can do is to deal tactlessly with the pain of the bereaved youth. This pain is around, it will remain around, and it can be stimulated at any moment by conscious and non-conscious stimuli. As de Shazer nicely put it and later Cheung elaborated further on it, when the clients need to talk about problems, it is important that they feel that they are listened to (Cheung, 2001, 2005; de Shazer, 1985, 1988).

Then follows a series of future-oriented questions, again in a goal-directed way, aiming to channel the discussion into a pathway of possibilities and a detailed solution-building frame for the young people. Looking towards the future, the discussion is channelled towards a positive vision via a solution-constructing pathway. We hold a stance of respectful curiosity and we do our best to listen with a "constructive ear" (Lipchik, 1988); that is, instead of watching for clues about the problem, we carefully watch out for clues about resources.

Exception-finding questions constitute a major part of the process and they do help the young people to focus on moments in which things were slightly better, even very slightly better. While the clinician carefully listens for exceptions that will help the young people to see their resources which potentially have been unnoticed by them, the clinician also skilfully integrates into the process the empowering coping questions, for example *"I can see that things have been really hard for you, yet I noticed that despite the hard times you passed through, you still did really well at school?", "How did you manage all that?"* Authentic curiosity and genuine admiration help a great deal in the process of emphasising the resources of the young people without undermining their hard struggle.

Scaling questions are further utilised, aiming to help the participating young people identify their progress. For instance, *"On a scale of 1 to 10, with 1 being the hardest it's been and 10 being the decisive turning point in which you feel yourself moving on, where would you place yourself at this stage?", "What are you doing that is protecting you from getting worse?", "At that moment when you see yourself being one step forward, what will be the slightest sign that will tell you that you are there?", "What would that mean to you?", "Who will be the first to notice that things moved up one point on your scale?"* (George et al., 2014).

Towards the end of the first, as well as each subsequent, session we summarise the meeting highlights which are indicative of the resources that the participating young people have and that would enable them to focus on further progress.

From the second session onwards, we start by exploring what the participating young people did that has proven helpful to them, for example *"What's been better?", "What difference has that made?", "What have you been pleased to notice?"* (George et al., 2014). The "other person perspective" is also a frequently utilised tool (i.e. *who will be the least surprised by the progress you made?*).

Most of the sessions close with a request from the therapists: *"Do you mind looking for the slightest sign that you are taking your life in the direction that you want it to go?"*

It is important to bear in mind that there will be times when the participating young people find it really hard to cope. In such moments, it is of paramount importance to avoid pointing out positive things in a way that may be experienced by the young people as the therapist invalidating their pain. At a time like this, it is very important that the therapist does not try to change the young person's mind, but rather builds the discussion on authentic curiosity (i.e. "It *sounds like things have been overwhelming recently* [pause] . . . *what is it that gives you the strength to even get up in the morning? What has been helping you to survive? What have you been doing to stop things getting worse? What might your best friend admire about the way you have been struggling with this?*) (George et al., 2014).

To conclude, it is of paramount importance to stress that the whole conversation pattern of the group is by no means an exclusive function of skilful applications of techniques by the clinician; it is rather an alive collaborative process in the course of which the role of the clinician is to build as well as to catch every single given or skilfully constructed opportunity to stimulate the young people's thinking processes towards visualisations of as many as possible of their own unique resources. Upon the visualisations of their resources, the young people are invited to utilise them as a catalyst for envisioning a path of life in which suffering will still be around, but will not buffer their potential for a wounded, yet meaningful life.

At the level of reflective practice

For a reflective clinical practice, it is of vital importance to keep in mind that the journey through grief is a very private experience and as such it requires particular attention when dealing with it in adults, as well as in children and adolescents. Culture-specific processes affect substantially the young person's journey through grief for the death of his/her parent. Beyond cultural processes, in the developing child it gets even more complicated since this journey gets integrated with the developmental milestone across each individual's unique developmental pathway. While it is extremely important that the developing child/young person is allowed to move through this journey in his/her own unique way, it has been well documented that this journey can be facilitated by casting some light on the young people's ability to move through it and live a meaningful life.

Reflecting upon our services for parentally bereaved children, for us the casting of this light has been a challenge since, along the path of our services, we also had a paradigm shift from problem focused practice to (we hope, but we are not always sure the extent to which we achieve it) Solution Focused thinking and practice. A solution building paradigm necessitates a radical shift in thinking, and we sometimes find ourselves having huge difficulty in accomplishing this radical thinking. Possibly the many years of training and carrying the "baggage of a problem-focused training", intertwined with the personality characteristics of some of us, present an additional challenge for the Solution Focused, child-centred services we aim to offer to bereaved children and adolescents.

To us, while we do our best to shift the young people's, as well as our, attention to Solution Focused thinking, it is absolutely fundamental to remember that what these children go through is hard, really hard. There are moments, not rare ones, that your heart breaks along with theirs. . . . *"I miss you so much mummy . . . I miss your hug Mummy . . . the special way you used to read stories to me before going to bed, the way you used to make me laugh, the special way you would bath me, your special way of doing everything for me . . . I miss your food . . . the food has no taste any more . . . no smell is like yours . . . life is not the same without you mummy . . . .I miss you so much . . . I call you but you do not answer me like you used to . . ."*. Moments like this are our everyday experience at CARE. A lot of pauses during our sessions are a common practice in our work. The not-easily-achieved challenge for us is this: while still bearing in mind that what the children are going through is really hard, we continue to manage to help them to channel their energy towards the best outcome every single day, which will lead towards a path of a wounded yet meaningful life. It is equally important to remind ourselves that in the beginning the path will be difficult and we would not be helpful if we try to go too far too quickly. There might, or might not, be characteristic phases that the children potentially pass through in their journey through grief, but in any case, going too far too quickly could result in opposite results.

Further, our experience at CARE through the years of our practice revealed the paramount importance of empathic listening, sensitivity to and identification with the bereaved and an in-depth insight into the nature of grief. For some of us at CARE, these insights emerged from our own life path of a parentally bereaved childhood (CARE was born out of my need to build a meaningful life path following my own father's and subsequently mother's death), while for the whole team the years of engagement with the bereaved was catalytic for our insight into the nature of grief.

Conclusion

To conclude, loss and subsequent bereavement, no matter whether we like it or not, is an unavoidable part of life. Parental illness and anticipated death constitute one of the most traumatising experiences a developing child and adolescent can be faced with and has the power to change their life path. Living with the pain of parental terminal illness, anticipatory grief, loss and bereavement at a vulnerable age can potentially have devastating effects. For many of us, who have traditionally been trained in pathologising models of psychotherapy, it might look a little bit like a paradox to shift into Solution Focused models, especially for such a tragic life event as the death of a parent in childhood. Yet, despite the phenomenal paradox that resided solitarily in our pathologising-trained mind rather than being inherent in the Solution Focused model, it was the deep need for finding meaning in the suffering, embracing the loss, and moving forward to a purposeful life path that motivated our paradigm shift from problem-solving to solution-constructing services for parentally bereaved children and adolescents. This paradigm shift gives us almost – yet we need to admit not every single day – the tiny little piece of hope that we need to keep going, the deeply needed tiny little bit of hope in excess of what we had when we used to work with pathologising models. Since our paradigm shift, we further feel that we carry a lighter burden. To our eyes, the future of the Solution Focused paradigm lies within the therapeutic effect of its simplicity in description, rather than simplicity in its practice. In the end, what actually matters is being really helpful to the wounded soul of the young person traumatised by parental death. The intriguing question that naturally follows is: "*Are we?*" The answer lies deeply in the soul of our beloved young people who we serve . . . we hope that it is "*yes*".

References

Akerman, R., & Statham, J. (2011). *Childhood Bereavement: A Rapid Literature Review*. London: Child Wellbeing Research Centre.

Archer, J. (2008). Theories of Grief: Past, Present, and Future Perspectives. In M. S. Stroebe, R. O. Hansson, H. Schut, & W. Stroebe (Eds.), *Handbook of Bereavement Research and Practice: Advances in Theory and Intervention* (pp. 45–66). Washington, DC: American Psychological Association.

Cheung, S. (2001). Problem-Solving and Solution-Focused Therapy for Chinese: Recent Developments. *Asian Journal of Counselling*, 8(2), 111–128.

Cheung, S. (2005). Strategic and Solution-Focused Couples' Therapy. In M. Harway (Ed.), *Handbook of Couples Therapy* (pp. 194–210). New York: Wiley.

de Shazer, S. (1985). *Keys to Solution in Brief Therapy*. New York: W. W. Norton.

de Shazer, S. (1988). *Clues: Investigating Solutions in Brief Therapy*. New York: W. W. Norton.

Fleming, S. T., & Adolph, R. (1986). Helping Bereaved Adolescents: Needs and Responses. In C. A. Corr & J. N. McNeil (Eds.), *Adolescence and Death* (pp. 97–118). New York: Springer.

George, E., Iveson, C., & Ratner, H. (1999). *Problem to Solution: Brief Therapy with Individuals and Families*, 2nd edition. London: BT Press.

George, E., Iveson, C., & Ratner, H. (2014). *Briefer: A Solution Focused Manual*. London: Brief.

Gillies, J., & Neimeyer, R. A. (2006). Loss, Grief, and the Search for Significance: Toward a Model of Meaning Reconstruction in Bereavement. *Journal of Constructivist Psychology*, 19, 31–65.

Gray, S. W., Zide, M. R., & Wilker, H. (1998). *Using the Solution Focused Brief Therapy Model with Bereavement Groups in Rural Communities: Resiliency at Its Best*. Twentieth Annual Group Work Symposium, Miami, FL.

Kubler-Ross, E. (1969). *On Death and Dying*. New York: Macmillan.

Lipchik, E. (1988, Winter 3–7). *Interviewing with a Constructive Ear*. Dulwich Centre Newsletter.

Niemeyer, R. A. (2001). Reauthoring Life Narratives: Grief Therapy as Meaning Reconstruction. *Israel Journal of Psychiatry and Related Sciences*, 38, 171–183.

Stroebe, M. S., & Schut, H. (2001). Models of Coping with Bereavement: A Review. In M. S. Stroebe, R. O. Hansson, W. Stroebe, & H. Schut (Eds.), *Handbook of Bereavement Research: Consequences, Coping, and Care* (pp. 375–403). Washington, DC: American Psychological Association. http://dx.doi.org/10.1037/10436-016

Chapter 25

High-conflict divorce and parenting
How Solution Focused presence can help

Jeff Chang

High-conflict divorce harms children and adults and is wrenching for practitioners. Children of high-conflict divorces experience more mental health problems than either children from so-called intact families or children whose parents divorce without excessive conflict. They have poorer relationships with their parents and may feel obligated to choose one parent over another, with some even "solving" this problem by declining contact with one parent (Amato, 2010; Bacon & McKenzie, 2004; Carter, 2011; Deutsch, 2008; Strohschein, 2012). When parents are embroiled in litigation, they have less time and energy and fewer financial resources to devote to their children (Henry et al., 2009).

Services that reduce the intensity, frequency, or duration of high-conflict divorce can relieve suffering of children and adults and reduce public expenditures of court time. Although services such as parent education (Alberta Justice and Solicitor General, 2019; Eddy, 2013; Ontario Ministry of the Attorney General, 2019; Rauh et al., 2016), mediation (Emery, 2011; Folberg et al., 2004), and parenting coordination (Carter, 2014; Higuchi & Lally, 2014) are increasingly popular, some former couples' conflict requires skilful intervention and a perspective that permits the practitioner to avoid being drawn into the conflict or aligning with one parent over the other. Solution Focused (SF) practices are invaluable for this. In this chapter, I will describe the difficulties of working with high-conflict divorcing parents and how maintaining an SF presence and using SF practices can help therapists working with this difficult population.

High-conflict divorce: a primer

Litigation and its results

The British Commonwealth and the USA have common-law legal systems in which the parties to any court action are inherently defined as adversaries. Lawyers are trained, indeed ethically required, to be zealous advocates for their clients. In North America, approximately 40% of marriages end in divorce within 30 years (Centers for Disease Control and Prevention, 2017; O'Nions, 2018). Two-thirds to three-quarters of divorcing parents with children agree on parenting issues without litigation. Another 10% to 15% require one contested court application, leaving about 5% to 15% who engage in repeated litigation. These high-conflict co-parents seem entrenched in vicious cycles (Carter, 2011).

About 5% of divorcing couples require a bilateral custody evaluation, a highly intrusive form of psychological assessment in which both parents, the children, and the relationships between parent and children are assessed by a mental health practitioner. About 2% go to a trial regarding parenting issues, costing the parties tens, if not hundreds, of thousands of dollars (Carter & Hebert, 2012). While a court may eventually decide the parenting arrangements, this does not settle the conflict. Even amongst former couples who do not go to these lengths, conflict does not resolve over time. Maccoby et al. (1992) found that one-quarter of divorces were highly conflicted an average of 3.5 years after the separation, although almost all were divorced by then. Even after a trial that decides the proportion of parenting time, parents might still litigate issues like summer vacation, extracurricular activities, health care, and schooling.

Parents' interactions

Parents in high conflict interact in characteristic ways. Some practitioners find it important to ascertain who is responsible for high-conflict interactions. One prominent author suggests that some individuals display "high conflict personalities" (Eddy, 2013), some meeting the diagnostic criteria for a personality disorder. On the other hand, Eddy (personal communication, May 24, 2019) noted that once parental conflict is entrenched, it is difficult to tell who the "high-conflict person" is. Regardless of who is "more responsible," the conflictual patterns are evident and can be daunting for practitioners. Practitioners and researchers have noted these characteristics of high-conflict parents:

Blame toward, and one-dimensional characterisation of, the other parent

Parents embroiled in high-conflict divorces are prone to blame the other and to characterise them one-dimensional terms (Johnston, 1994; Lebow & Newcomb Rekart, 2007; Strohschein, 2012). For example, in a first session, Jose,[1] referring to his former partner Gabriella, said

> She does not see reality the way I see reality or probably you do. It always needs to fit her situation. She has a severe, and I mean severe, lying issue. You know, she lies when she's happy, she lies when she's sad, she lies when she's in trouble. It's really hard to see it sometimes. But some of her lies have been outrageous.

Conversely, later that week, Gabriella, referring to Jose, said

> I've always been really, really honest with [the children]. My son found a box of condoms in his dad's truck, and he said, "What the heck?" . . . And so,

I went off on Jose. I said, "How do you let your children see this? Why can't you just [be honest]?" Because his biggest excuse is, "I'm going to church." Well, I didn't know there was church between somebody's legs.

The divergent perspectives of the parents can be unsettling for practitioners.

Pathologizing/diagnosing the other parent

A father told me that his former spouse had borderline personality disorder, having concluded this from online research. Jen (a mother in a high-conflict separation) and I were discussing books she had found helpful to her high-conflict situation, she recalled reading *The Psychopath Next Door*,[2] but could not recall a second, recalling only that it was a "another psychopath book" (Department of Justice, Canada, 2015).

Active denigration of the other parent in the presence of the children

Some parents actively and directly denigrate the other parent. Some parents tell their children directly about the misdeeds or shortcomings of the other parent, sometimes with the rationale of "just being honest," or the child(ren) "needing to know the truth" about the other parent. Alternatively, some parents are less direct, solicitously explaining that the other parent is "ill," or "an addict," and professing care for them. Still others imply that the other parent is not safe to be around, for example, stating, "I just want you to be safe, so text me any time you want if you think Dad is out of control" (Johnston, 1994; Lebow & Newcomb Rekart, 2007; Strohschein, 2012).

Exaggerating parenting differences and slip-ups

Parents carried away by high-conflict situations are frequently highly vigilant with respect to the shortcomings of the other parent's parenting. Being a few minutes late picking up or dropping off a child is interpreted as gross neglect, and not sending along an item needed for a child's recreational activity invites a flurry of criticism. Often parents feel the need to record conversations and/or document their actions and the actions of their co-parent in case such evidence may be needed later in litigation (Johnston, 1994; Lebow & Newcomb Rekart, 2007; Strohschein, 2012).

Effects on children

The overall picture of children's adjustment in the face prolonged exposure to high-conflict parenting is bleak. Children of high-conflict divorces experience elevated incidence of alcohol and drug use, difficulties in school, behavioural problems, early sexual activity, antisocial behaviour, anxiety, and depression. They report poorer relationships with their parents, lower quality of life, and feelings of obligation to choose one parent over another. Lower academic achievement, poorer psychological well-being, and difficulty maintaining their own intimate relationships may follow some children to adulthood (Amato, 2010; Bacon & McKenzie, 2004; Carter, 2011; Deutsch, 2008; Strohschein, 2012). With parental time, energy, and resources being funneled into litigation, children typically pay the highest price in high-conflict divorce (Henry et al., 2009).

Professionals' responses

Professionals working with parents, children, and families embroiled in high-conflict separation and divorce may experience many conflicting feelings: tugs on our heartstrings to help the children and young people trapped in their parents' conflict; invitations to align with one parent or the other; and fear at the prospect of a complaint to our regulatory body or professional association. In fact, high-conflict divorce work leads to a disproportionate number of complaints to regulators (Bow et al., 2010; Kirkland & Kirkland, 2001).

Recently, I taught a workshop on therapy with high-conflict separating families in a large Canadian city. The director of a rural mental health clinic told me that she had offered two of her staff the opportunity to come to the workshop. She told me that they had declined, saying, "If we go to this training, you'll make us see these people." While there are a small number of specialists who routinely work with such families, most practitioners try to avoid these families if possible.

Service context

I have been fortunate to be able to apply SF ideas with high-conflict families in the supportive atmosphere of Calgary Family Therapy Centre (CFTC), a publicly funded clinic in Calgary, Alberta, Canada, serving families with a child or adolescent experiencing behavioural or emotional difficulties. In the last few years, I've generally seen families in which the parenting regime has been settled, but the parental conflict, which seems to contribute to their children's problems, persists. Notwithstanding a court order directing the parenting schedule, some parents continued to litigate over holiday plans, extracurricular activities, and changes of schedule. Some tended to use the children as messengers and engaged in many of the problematic behaviours described earlier.

In this context, I developed a flexible structure to engage with high-conflict families. Typically, I first meet with parents separately as much as necessary to gain their trust and perhaps interrupt their pattern of interaction with the other parent. Initially I present this as a chance to "get their side of the story." Then I alternate seeing the children with each parent. Eventually, I invite the parents to meet jointly. I prioritise work with parents as a pathway for alleviating children's suffering.

Solution Focused presence, Solution Focused practice

To manage the virulent conflict, many experts suggest that work with high-conflict parents should be highly structured. They urge practitioners to set firm boundaries and actively direct sessions (Lebow, 2018; Lebow & Newcomb Rekart, 2007). Additionally, some practitioners suggest that parents in high-conflict divorces require psychoeducation on how their conflict damages their children. This is quite different to how SF practitioners aspire to work. About the only apparent similarity to SF work is the emphasis on present and future. While I agree that boundaries and structure are important in working with high-conflict post-separation parents, SF presence and practice have much to offer these families. Earlier (Chang, 2013, p. 193), I formulated the term *solution-focused presence:*

> Solution-focused presence is an abiding belief that the [client] is already doing a great deal of what [they] would like to do, carefully noticing openings to ask about what [they are] doing that is consistent with [their] stated goal, and thinking about how one can invite [clients] to notice and do more of what works.

I operationalise this in several ways: *minimalism and pragmatism, disciplined listening for openings, focus on client preferences over prescriptions, making haste slowly,* and *relational positioning.*

Pragmatism and minimalism

"If something is working, do more of it" (Trepper et al., 2010). I propose the ideas in this chapter pragmatically and nonnormatively – *what has worked for me* – not as a prescription for how to work with high-conflict co-parents. This is simply is a description of how I have used SF ideas and practices with these clients.

Whom to see

In my work as a clinical supervisor, trainees will sometimes say something like, "I tried SF and it didn't work." This illustrates their belief that a model of counselling – SF or anything else – creates client change. In fact, counselling models are *performed* by counsellors with varying levels of skill. Working with high-conflict families requires a post-basic skill level. So, with high-conflict parents the first question I typically ask myself is, "In what circumstances, and with whom, can I sustain solution-focused presence?" When seen together without adequate preparation, high-conflict parents come in "loaded for bear." They are prone to defend themselves, blame the other parent, justify their position to the practitioner, and invite the practitioner to align with them. It is often useful to meet with parents separately at the start of therapy. This provides me with the chance to hear their story uninterrupted without having to work too hard to manage the interactions between them. Novice counsellors may not be able to stop overt conflict overwhelming their best efforts to conduct the session. I recommend having parents in the same room once you are reasonably certain you can manage their interactions. Until I ascertain that I can see that parents together successfully (or at least without facilitating more harm), I alternate having parents bring the child(ren) to deal with issues particular to that household.

Explanations for problems

Parents in high-conflict divorces often seek explanations for their former spouse's behaviour. Thinking minimalistically, it is not necessary to look for explanations of parents' pervasive conflict. All that is necessary is to listen carefully for what clients want and interview them skilfully to increase their noticing or doing what they want.

Preferences over prescriptions

In high-conflict divorces, parents are being told what to do a great deal by the other parent, judges, lawyers (giving legal advice based on precedent), parent educators, parenting coordinators, and others. When not being told directly what to do, they are often subject to a third party's efforts to convince them to do something they don't particularly want to do.

I have found it more useful to focus what clients want. Even when parents describe their preferences in terms of what the other parent would do, this can provide a pathway to solution development. As Steve de Shazer (personal communication, September 2004) stated, "There is only one question: *What does the client want?* All the other questions come out of this one."

What does the client want? If one listens carefully, one can usually hear parents' desires framed in this way.

- What's best for the kids
- Peace
- Reduced conflict (usually resulting from changes on the part of the other parent)
- The children to have a relationship with the other parent ("... as long as they are comfortable with it ...").

We should listen carefully and empathically, while eliciting detailed descriptions about what clients want without implying or nudging that they should change until we hear indications of their receptivity.

Focusing on description of sequences and patterns

As SF practitioners, we work with descriptions of behavioural sequences and relational patterns. This can give parents some relief from the relentless search for truth in affidavits, cross-examination, and "evidence." Asking about sequences can help deemphasise linear, typically blameful, descriptions of interactions between the parents and invite parents (individually or jointly) to see their conflict in terms of interpersonal patterns (Tomm et al., 2014). This can derail parents' invitations to us to align with them in affirming their correctness and the other parent's atrociousness.

Disciplined listening for openings

As part of solution-focused presence, I listen carefully for openings. I've distinguished five kinds of openings that might provide a pathway to invite conversations about preferred outcomes, hypothetical or real, with high-conflict parents:

Wishes, hopes, or dreams

Parents in high-conflict separations will plaintively express their desire for something to be different, often expressed in terms of the other parent's behaviour, for example, "I just wish he would be consistent" or "She needs to stop being so controlling." To this, an SF practitioner might reply, "What would *that* look like?"

Descriptions of difference

Sometimes parents will describe something that the other parent does that seems satisfactory, or at least closer to it. For example, a parent might remark, "He was not such an a – hole when I dropped the kids off." A question like, "You've told me what you think he's usually like. What was different this time?" might assist the client to construct a tentative, if rare, exception description. Scaling questions are useful to understand gradations in the problem and reduce the tendency of parents to see the other as "all one way."

Compliments from others

At times, a third party may praise a parent for their response to a high-conflict situation. For example, a client saying something like, "One of my buddies told me he thought I was pretty amazing for taking the high road" might provide an opening to ask, "Tell me what you're doing to keep going. What do you actually do to stay on the high road?"

Past successes

A parent may recall times when they used to get along better with their co-parent. Careful questioning about what was happening then, and what one or the other of them were doing and feeling differently, could open space for new observations.

Personal agency in the present

When parents describe something they have done to mitigate the conflict, or cope differently with it, it provides an opening to ask what the client has done.

These examples provide openings for useful lines of inquiry. When clients identify what the other parent does (even if it is infrequent), or hypothetically could do, it can assist them to crystalise what they would need to see to make a difference. Detailed descriptions can invite an embodied experience of possible differences and can create a context for noticing differences. Staying in the hypothetical realm can help pace with a client who initially, at least, comes to see you expressing blame toward the other parent and not asking for help to change their own behaviour.

Make haste slowly

In my private practice and at CFTC, I have the luxury of being able to see families as and when required, with little pressure to close files. I can take the time I need to nurture my relationship with each parent so that they experience me as an honest broker. Conducting myself with solution-focused presence, listening for openings, and moving only as fast as clients are prepared to go help develop the relationship with each parent. Inviting parents to focus on description only (*when things are better* or *what a [hypothetical] solution] would look like*) is useful to support clients to notice differences and diffuse the patterns of high conflict. There is no hurry to discuss *what you can do to make that [hypothetical solution] happen.*

This does not always work, however, and one must be prepared for how entrenched a parent's view of the other parent's shortcomings are. Consider the interaction I had with Jen, whom we met earlier.

Jeff: How do you do that . . . give him the benefit of the doubt? I imagine there must be some times when that's difficult.

Jen: I'm not a fighter. I don't like conflict. . . . I know that he wants what's best for the boys so based on that, I know that if he is intentionally damaging them he wouldn't want to do that. . . . He wants to damage me, but he doesn't want to damage his boys. And I think he could see that they were being hurt by him trying to hurt me.

Naturally, at the end of the session, I asked Jen to pay attention to anything that told her that her former spouse had the boys' best interests at heart in the hope that she would notice exceptions that we could amplify together. She sent me the following e-mail a few days later:

> I wanted to follow up with you on the question you asked me during our videotaped session. I said that Ken has the boys' best interests in mind. You asked

if that were true and then later to observe and reflect if that were just wishful thinking on my part. You were right – I was being PollyAnna. Thank you for your brilliant question to bring clarity to my situation.

This was clearly not my intent. As Walter and Peller (1992) note, "The meaning of the message is the response you receive" (p. 26). Alas.

Relational positioning

Early SF literature described *visiting*, *complainant*, and *customer* relationships (de Shazer, 1988), cautioning these are descriptions of relationships, not classifications of persons or ascriptions of inherent motivation. By contrast, for every visiting relationship there is a host, for every complainant there is a listener, and for every customer there is a service provider. This provides a useful heuristic to assist me to position myself in relation to clients.

Gabriella, Jose, and Monica

We met Gabriella and Jose briefly earlier in this chapter. When I saw them, they had been separated for 2 years and had settled into a week on/week off parenting schedule, although neither thought the other capable of handling this much parenting time. Jose thought that Gabriella was too preoccupied with her new relationship, was not present for the children and, as noted earlier, was a chronic liar. Gabriella viewed Jose as irresponsible and thought he had been spending time indiscriminately with a number of women, setting a poor example for the children, Jose, Jr. (17) and Monica (12).

While the parents agreed that Jose, Jr. was coping well, Monica was suffering. She was exhibiting depression and had been self-harming by cutting and scratching her wrists. She had a brief hospitalisation and was referred to CFTC, as she told her psychiatrist, "I can't stand how my parents fight and always put each other down."

Initially, I chose to see the parents separately. I presented this as a time to get their respective views of the situation. However, when I do this, I typically end up doing solution-building.

Gabriella, Part 1

Here, I start with coping questions (De Jong & Berg, 2013) to have Gabriella describe how she manages what she sees as Jose's irresponsible behaviour.

Jeff: I think I mentioned on the phone that I mostly see families going through difficult separations, so I do hear many stories like yours, and I always wonder how people manage. So right now, I'm just curious. What do you actually do to keep your cool?

Gabriella:	You know what, sometimes I write. . . . So, I write as if I was writing to him. . .
Jeff:	Mm hmmm. . .
Gabriella:	And I just remember to write my thoughts on a little piece of paper.
Jeff:	What a good idea.
Gabriella:	Sometimes I write it on a text. I just never send it. Right? I just let it go and then I just let it be. Well, sometimes I do hit the send button. . .
Jeff:	There's times I've pressed "send" by accident too. So sometimes it's better to do it on paper.
Gabriella:	eah, it's better to scribble.
Jeff:	And then put it in the shredder. I am curious about this . . . when you write, maybe you write some things that are not so nice, which is understandable, but how does that actually help you kind of calm down?
Gabriella:	It almost makes me feel like a balloon. Right? Like I hear these things from my kids and my head goes "fffff" (sound of a balloon inflating, moving her hands apart), and then I'm writing and I'm writing, and I feel like it's coming down, coming down (moving her hands together), and I can actually feel the color in my face and the heat from my head to start to go down. . .
Jeff:	So, you actually feel the physical change.
Gabriella:	I do, I do. I totally do, because I can feel it when it starts, and I can feel it when it goes down. I must change colors. . .

Coping questions helped Gabriella to describe her skills at managing her reactions to Jose. Later in the session, as we see below, this invited her to notice when she considers Jose more reasonable.

Again, I started with coping questions, and later Jose is able to describe how he resists invitations to engage in conflict.

Jose

Jeff:	So, with all this, and also the frustration that you experience with Gabriella, like how are you maintaining an even keel?
Jose:	Well I try . . . I am stretched to the limit some days, but you know what? I just got make sure that [the children] are OK. . . . So, the other day, [Monica] went downstairs, and I said, you know, "What is going on?" She's like, "Nobody knows me," and she cried and cried. And I said, "I know you." She said, "I know that," and she got annoyed at me so, I backed off. So anyway . . .
Jeff:	So, you have a sense of when to acknowledge and when to pull back.
Jose:	I learned that. . .
Jeff:	How did you learn that?
Jose:	Just by watching her reactions.
Jeff:	That's the trickiest thing with teenagers isn't it? Knowing when to pull back and when to support. Tell me about a time when you got the right balance.

Jose:	You know sometimes I sit beside her, and she'll lean over, and I'll put my arm around her. And sometimes she'll respond. . . . We ended up having a really good talk about what's been going on. She said that she was kind of mad at her mom, and I wanted to jump in and agree with her, but I knew that would be not helpful to her.
Jeff:	It must have taken a lot to hold yourself back.
Jose:	Not really. I'm used to doing it now.
Jeff:	So, it was easy? How did you work yourself up to the point that it's no big deal?
Jose:	Well, you know, I just started to say to myself, "It's not worth it. I can't change her." I just have to support my kids whatever they are going through. Believe me, it took practice.
Jeff:	Tell me about how you practiced.
Jose:	You know, sometimes I was so pissed off at her. I had to just take a deep breath and think to myself "Stay calm, man. I need to do this for the kids. I can't change her." Also, my friend told me that their relationship with her was their relationship with her. I can't tell them what to think of her. They will make up their own mind about her.
Jeff:	What difference does that make?
Jose:	Well, now I have kind of a routine for when I hear about something she has done. Believe me, I've had to repeat this many, many times, because there have been many, many times she has done something that's just wrong. But it's getting easier.

Gabriella, Part 2

Here Gabriella is able to identify exceptions in Jose's behaviour.

Jeff:	I'm curious. Are there any times when you see, like, little glimpses of not being alone and maybe being more of a team as parents?
Gabriella:	There is a few times. There is a few times. But they are very, very, very rare. Like he seems more soft, more open, and like he'll . . . even if it's through text. We've had a couple conversations. . .
Jeff:	Really?
Gabriella:	Where he's like, "What are you doing? This (an idea she suggested) works for me." So, I've seen it. It's something visible. It's something that could happen, and I don't know if it's because he's been with somebody and he got his frustrations under control, or if he actually makes an effort to say, "OK, I'm going to listen to this woman for once." I don't know whether it's out of stubbornness sometimes. . .
Jeff:	It's interesting, right, because you know, either way it's a shift that you notice. . . . It's almost wanting to assume that he's doing it for the right reasons. You want to hope. . .

Gabriella: Exactly.
Jeff: What's actually different about him when that happens?
Gabriella: I don't know.
Jeff: So softer, more open.
Gabriella More open. Like he'll answer texts right away. Or I'll call and he'll answer, and his tone is not agitated. His tone is not finger pointing, and his tone is very cool, calm, and collected per se.
Jeff: Ha! Interesting.
Gabriella: Yeah, so I don't know if it's the way his day is going, I have no idea why, but it shifts. And sometimes it's nice to feel that. Because I feel a weight off my shoulders which I don't have to put into my relationship with somebody else (referring to her new partner) because really, it's not [his] children.
Jeff: So, let me get this straight. These are rare. I understand these are rare, right? So sometimes he's more open, softer, so that gives you the idea that, OK, this could happen maybe in our future or consistently, right? And he might respond right away whether it's a text or a phone call, he doesn't see the call display and go, "Forget it. I don't want to talk to her." And more calm, cool, and collected. Anything else that you notice about how he's different?
Gabriella: He's more mellow.
Jeff: OK, describe mellow to me.
Gabriella: It's just the tone, like he's, like he's fully aware of what we're talking about, and that it is about the children, and maybe it's something about my tone of voice. I don't know.
Jeff: About your tone of voice?
Gabriella: Maybe.
Jeff: Let me come back to that, because I'm going to finish up what you notice about him. And he seems like he's. . .
Gabriella: . . . processing everything that I'm telling him a little bit slower than usual.
Jeff: Do you mind if I tell him that?
Gabriella: No, not at all.

I later asked Gabriella about what it was about the tone of her voice that perhaps shaped Jose's response to her, and she identified a number of things she might have done. In our next session, I did in fact tell Jose about how Gabriella had noticed and appreciated his different approach. He and I further amplified what he does to diminish the conflict with her. In turn he could identify what she did in response. We did some parallel sessions with Monica and each of her parents, in which we dealt quite straightforwardly with her depression – feelings of disconnection more than sadness – and self-harm. During these sessions, I fed each parent compliments from the other and kept interviewing them separately to highlight patterns of interaction they, individually, preferred.

I eventually asked them whether they felt comfortable meeting together to discuss some decisions they needed to make. Their best hopes for the meeting were that they would be able to make clear decisions, which they did. Monica's improvement continued and seemed to accelerate as her parents communicated more effectively.

Conclusion

High-conflict separation, divorce, and parenting harm children and youth. Professionals avoid these cases because they are draining, require a great deal of energy to manage, and invite a much greater-than-average proportion of complaints.

I have found that SF presence can prepare a practitioner to be pragmatic and minimalist, focus on preferences as opposed to prescriptions, emphasise description of sequences and patterns, listen in a disciplined way for openings, make haste slowly, and position oneself relationally. SF practice enables practitioners to have more manoeuvrability, invites parents to focus on what they want, rather than problems, and can help parents to create a co-parenting relationship that supports their children to thrive.

Notes

1 All client names used in this chapter are pseudonyms. Direct quotes are actual client statements.
2 I could not find such a book, although I did find one entitled *The Sociopath Next Door* (Stout, 2006).

References

Alberta Justice and Solicitor General. (2019, January 26). *Parenting After Separation (PAS) Course*. www.alberta.ca/pas.aspx/.
Amato, P. R. (2010). Research on Divorce: Continuing Trends and New Developments. *Journal of Marriage and Family*, 72(3), 650–666. http://dx.doi.org/10.1111/j.1741-3737.2010.00723.x.
Bacon, B. L., & McKenzie, B. (2004). Parent Education After Separation/Divorce. *Family Court Review*, 42(1), 85–98. http://dx.doi.org/10.1111/j.174-1617.2004.tb00635.x.
Bow, J. N., Gottleib, M. C., Siegel, J. C., & Noble, G. S. (2010). Licensing Board Complaints in Child Custody Practice. *Journal of Forensic Psychology Practice*, 10(5), 403–418. http://dx.doi.org/10.1080/15228932.2010.489851.
Carter, S. (2011). *Family Restructuring Therapy: Interventions with High Conflict Separations and Divorces*. Scottsdale, AZ: High Conflict Institute Press.
Carter, S. (2014). *Parenting Coordination: A Practical Guide for Family Law Professionals*. New York: Springer Publishing.
Carter, S., & Hebert, P. (2012). Working with Children of Separation and Divorce: Pitfalls, Misconceptions and Best Practices. *CAP Monitor*, 41, 5–7. www.cap.ab.ca/pdfs/capmonitor41.pdf.

Centers for Disease Control and Prevention. (2017). *Key Statistics from the National Survey of Family Growth.* www.cdc.gov/nchs/nsfg/key_statistics.htm. Accessed 2 August 2019.

Chang, J. (2013). On Being Solution-Focused in Adversarial Places: Supervising Parenting Evaluations in Family Court. In F. N. Thomas (Ed.), *Solution-Focused Supervision: A Resource-Oriented Approach to Developing Clinical Expertise* (pp. 187–196). New York: Springer Science and Business.

De Jong, P., & Berg, I. K. (2013). *Interviewing for Solutions*, 4th edition. Belmont, CA: Brooks, Cole.

Department of Justice Canada. (2015). *Patterns of High Conflict in Divorce.* www.justice.gc.ca/eng/rp-pr/fl-lf/divorce/2001_7/pat2-mod2.html. Accessed 3 August 2019.

De Shazer, S. (1988). *Clues: Investigating Solutions in Brief Therapy.* New York: W. W. Norton.

Deutsch, R. M. (2008). Divorce in the 21st Century: Multidisciplinary Family Interventions. *Journal of Psychiatry & Law*, 36(1), 41–66. https://journals.sagepub.com/home/plx.

Eddy, B. (2013). *High Conflict People in Legal Disputes*, 2nd edition. Scottsdale, AZ: High Conflict Institute Press.

Eddy, B. (2013). *New Ways for Families: Professional Guidebook*, 2nd edition. Scottsdale, AZ: High Conflict Institute Press.

Emery, R. E. (2011). *Renegotiating Family Relationships*, 2nd edition. New York: The Guilford Press.

Folberg, J., Milne, A. L., & Salem, P. (Eds.). (2004). *Divorce and Family Mediation: Models, Techniques, and Applications.* New York: The Guilford Press.

Henry, W. J., Fieldstone, L., & Bohac, K. (2009). Parenting Coordination and Court Relitigation: A Case Study. *Family Court Review*, 47, 682–697. http://dx.doi.org/10.1111/j.1744-1617.2009.01281.x.

Higuchi, S. A., & Lally, S. (Eds.). (2014). *Parenting Coordination in Postseparation Disputes: A Comprehensive Guide for Practitioners.* Washington, DC: American Psychological Association.

Johnston, J. R. (1994). High-Conflict Divorce. *The Future of Children*, 165–182. ww.ncbi.nlm.nih.gov/pubmed/7922278.

Kirkland, K., & Kirkland, K. L. (2001). Frequency of Child Custody Evaluation Complaints and Related Disciplinary Action: A Survey of the Association of State and Provincial Psychology Boards. *Professional Psychology: Research and Practice*, 32(2), 171–174. http://dx.doi.org/10.1037//0735-7028.32.2.171.

Lebow, J. (2018). *Treating the Difficult Divorce: A Practical Guide for Psychotherapists.* Washington, DC: American Psychological Association.

Lebow, J., & Newcomb Rekart, K. (2007). Integrative Family Therapy for High-Conflict Divorce with Disputes Over Child Custody and Visitation. *Family Process*, 46(1), 79–91. doi:10.1111/j.1545-5300.2006.00193.x.

Maccoby, E. E., Mnookin, R. H., Depner, C. E., & Peters, H. E. (1992). *Dividing the Child: Social and Legal Dilemmas of Custody.* Cambridge, MA: Harvard University Press.

O'Nions, M.-J. (2018). *Divorce Rates in Canada.* https://ecwww.mjonions.com/divorce-rates-in-canada/. Accessed 2 August 2019.

Ontario Ministry of the Attorney General. (2019, January 26). *Mandatory Information Programs (MIPs).* www.attorneygeneral.jus.gov.on.ca/english/family/family_justice_services.php]).

Rauh, S., Irwin, P., & Vath, N. (2016). Giving Children Hope: A Treatment Model for High-Conflict Separation Families. *Canadian Journal of Counselling and Psychotherapy*, 50(3S), S93–S108.

Stout, M. (2006). *The Sociopath Next Door*. New York: Broadway Books.

Strohschein, L. (2012). Parental Divorce and Child Mental Health: Accounting for Predisruption Differences. *Journal of Divorce & Remarriage*, 53(6), 489–502. doi:10.1080/1 0502556.2012.682903.

Tomm, K., St. George, S., Wulff, D., & Strong, T. (Eds.). (2014). *Patterns in Interpersonal Interactions: Inviting Relational Understandings for Therapeutic Change*. New York: Routledge.

Trepper, T. R., McCollum, E. E., De Jong, P, Korman, H., Gingerich, W., & Franklin, C. (2010). *Solution Focused Therapy Treatment Manual for Working with Individuals*. Santa Fe, NM: Solution Focused Brief Therapy Association.

Walter, J., & Peller, J. (1992). *Becoming Solution-Focused in Brief Therapy*. New York: Brunner, Mazel.

Chapter 26

Spreading kindness
The alchemy of translation

Denise Yusuf

The Solution Focused (SF) approach is used in different ways in multiple professional contexts to help children and young people. Some people use elements and techniques of SF as part of their own unique approach, and some use a wholly SF approach, although even then each practitioner's interpretation and practice of SF will never be exactly the same as that of their SF colleague and will change over time. In this chapter I want to describe a school-based intervention which started as a project using an SF approach and ended with the SF approach becoming the hidden lining of something different. It is the story of a project developing its own energy and direction, with a model migrating alongside.

Background

Some years ago, I began to work in a primary school offering a programme called Coaching 4 Fives. The head teacher at the time wanted extra support provided for all the Year 5 children aged around 10 years old. In Year 6, the final year in primary school, these children faced national assessment tests, applications and interviews for secondary schools, and then of course the transition to these bigger schools. I have worked with a number of secondary-aged children for whom this transition proved to be difficult and sometimes became associated with more challenges for the child. The head teacher hoped that this project, alongside other school provision and initiatives, would contribute towards helping the Year 5 children to increase their confidence and resilience, so that they would be better prepared to deal with the demands of Year 6 and the transition to their secondary schools.

The Coaching 4 Fives programme

The programme included some initial whole class sessions explaining the project, with each child in the class (30 children) offered 2 individual coaching sessions per term (6 a year for each child). In the individual coaching sessions, the children were invited to talk about what they were proud of in themselves, the things they were good at or enjoyed learning or doing, and whatever they wanted to improve.

The children spoke about the many different things which were important to them, including academic subjects, sports activities in and out of school, recent achievements such as travelling to school alone, looking after pets and cooking, and skills such as being able to make friends, feel more confident, be more independent and keep calm. Subsequent sessions focused on signs of progress and how they would recognise more signs of success in the future, which the children enjoyed describing, drawing, and acting out with me. Solution Focused coaching tools and techniques were used, such as scales, lists, coaching cards and strength cards (Ratner and Yusuf, 2015). Children noticed their skill fluidity, being able to transfer skills, to develop skills and to learn new skills, and they were encouraged to notice their talents and particularly their efforts.

During these SF sessions, the idea of the children showing kindness, towards themselves and towards others, began to emerge as a theme in many of the conversations, and seemed to be an important idea for the children. Talking about it and noticing it also appeared to have some unexpected effects. For example, talking about being kind to themselves seemed to help the children to feel more connected to each other, something which Dr Kristin Neff, a pioneering researcher of self-compassion, has identified. (Neff, 2011). She notes that self-compassionate people can separate themselves from their failures and see themselves as interconnected, rather than emphasising their own uniqueness, whereas self-esteem works in the opposite way, relying more on comparative self-evaluation.

In addition, talking about being kind to others seemed to have a positive effect on the children's own mood, an effect highlighted by the work of the charity Action for Happiness. The latest research from positive psychology and related fields was used by Action for Happiness to develop their 'Ten Keys to Happier Living.' The first key is 'Giving: Doing Things for Others,' which they show is associated with both psychological and physical levels of health and well-being. They also point out the virtuous circles in this process: *'There's a virtuous circle between happiness and giving – happier people give more, and giving to others can make us happier. Kindness can be catching too – seeing other people helping makes us more likely to help others too'* (King, 2016).

Ideas about kindness were beginning to resonate within the Coaching 4 Fives programme.

Individual referrals

The coaching programme began to receive referrals from the school staff about individual children from other year groups. It seemed easier for these children, who were referred for particular issues, to come to coaching sessions since the Year 5 children had spread positive messages about coaching throughout the school! A similar SF structure was used and it was an opportunity to move away from problem focused to Solution Focused referrals, to invite teachers and parents to talk about their best hopes too, although the child's own best hopes, if different, were the starting point as much as possible in the conversations. Ideas about being kind continued to be part of these conversations and to be useful and helpful, and so, spread further in the school.

An example of an individual referral: Abdi

Abdi wanted to change his behaviour so he could get into a good secondary school. At times he could get very angry, especially if he perceived that he, or indeed another child, was being unfairly treated. However, often this resulted in him getting into arguments with his teachers and with other children. He knew that he needed a good report to give him a chance of getting a place in the secondary school he wanted. His parents knew this too and they had talked about rewarding him if his behaviour improved. Abdi also wanted to enjoy nicer times with his classmates.

We started to talk about what he wanted and as Abdi enjoyed drawing, he drew a cartoon strip of how he wanted things to be. As the sessions continued, he began to notice small changes in his behaviour as well as little successes that had been there before. He liked to draw these successes and changes and make me guess what they were, and the combination of his artwork and my guesswork only gave us more opportunities for delight, wonder and appreciation of his talents and skills. There were pictures of him avoiding 'silly' people; other people arguing but Abdi whistling instead of getting involved; Abdi thinking before he acted, about whether in fact something might be fair, or about any consequences to his actions; and Abdi ignoring provocation. The idea of being kind was useful to him too. He started to look at himself in a kinder way as he noticed other children faced similar challenges to him, and this made him feel more connected. He acted with more kindness towards other children and found that he felt good when he was helping them with their work, for example, rather than taking sides in arguments. Abdi did not lose his strong sense of justice but found that he could manage it in a calmer way. He also noticed the many ways he could be happy with his friends and classmates. It was not easy to do all of this, and he gave himself a lot of coaching cards and stickers along the way, to highlight all his efforts and his progress. He wrote himself a certificate when he felt he deserved it, but his best reward (a holiday) came from his parents who were very pleased firstly with his behaviour, and later, with the letter from the secondary school offering their child a place.

Feedback from children on their coaching sessions

I am not so annoyed and angry and it helped me with my art and my hobbies.

> Before coaching I got sent inside (from the playground) and now I don't because I don't get into trouble.
> It was really fun but it was also helpful, it showed me how ignoring is actually a good thing to do!
> It helped me to be more focused and now I've been awarded for this.
> It made me feel different about my shyness and I put my hand up a lot more in class.
> It really helped me and if it wasn't for coaching my confidence still wouldn't be there.
> It helped me in talking more to people and being nicer and kinder to them.
> Coaching wasn't scary and I became braver.
> It was really fun to have coaching I really really liked it, it helped me a lot with behaviour and confidence and this made me realise how sensible I could have been before!
> I got happier.

Whole-class coaching

Following the Coaching 4 Fives and Individual Referrals programmes, other whole classes were referred for coaching sessions, and ideas about kindness emerged here too. For example a Year 4 class (8- to 9-year-olds) were referred for difficult relationships within the class, which were causing problems in the playground and difficulties in the class getting down to work. The class and their teacher talked about this and thought that they would like to try to be a kinder class and talked with me about what this would look like for them.

Some children described this in words, some children made drawings and paintings of it and some children made little plays about it and acted them out. There were lots of ideas which we recorded on a very large coaching card. These included things such as sharing, being honest, agreeing to what others wanted to do sometimes, letting people into games, forgiving and forgetting, talking to people if you felt upset, talking nicely to yourself and to others, helping people who are sad, making sure everyone understands the teacher, asking for help, helping people who ask for help, offering help even if people don't ask for help and lots more. Descriptions of kindness seemed to naturally include kindness to others and kindness to oneself. The children made a human scale to explore what they were already doing and what might be the next signs of progress. It was a bit chaotic at times, as the children changed positions to demonstrate their different ideas on this, but the chaos helpfully demonstrated the change possibilities rather than the fixed nature of things! I gave the class a supply of coaching cards which they could to give to themselves and to their classmates for kind acts noticed. I met with the class and their teacher at regular times and we talked about what they had noticed, they nominated the kindest act for a big thank you card and they scaled their progress in the ever-changing human scale. The teacher made a kindness tree on the wall of the classroom for them to write all their kind acts on. The class playground behaviour improved as did their concentration on their work.

The Year 6 project

Kindness was now firmly on the map and part of the territory for self and school improvement. The top class in the school, the Year 6 class, asked whether they could do something to improve relationships and well-being. They liked the coaching cards and asked whether they could use them to encourage more kindness around the school. They began to give out thank you cards to whomever they noticed was being kind towards them or anyone else. Of course, there were already many effective strategies that the school employed to recognise, discuss, reward, celebrate and develop positive actions and special achievements, and so this project ran alongside these strategies. The Year 6 children were noticing and celebrating often very, very small acts of kindness that sometimes might have run under the radar but whose signals got picked up by these children, often before the actions were even completed:

I smiled at someone who looked sad and thought about going to talk to her.

Children treating themselves in a kind way:

I made a mistake, but everyone makes mistakes.

also received a card. There appeared to be fewer incidents around the school where children needed to be asked to stop doing something and many more situations where they were being encouraged to do more of something. Being kind could be a small action, but it seemed to have a transformative effect.

SF parents' evenings

Parents' evenings at the school were an opportunity for parents to discuss their child's progress with their teachers; to find out about curriculum topics, school development and other education matters; and for social and fundraising purposes. Parents also expressed an interest in talking about parenting topics such as managing children's behaviour, helping children with stress, how to support homework and building resilience. I offered to support these evenings with short presentations and plenty of time for small and large group discussions. Some potentially useful SF ideas were introduced to the parents such as:

1. If it's not broken don't try to fix it.
2. If it's working do more of it.

3   If it's not working do something different.
4   Focus on what you want (not what you don't want).
5   There are always exceptions and instances if you keep looking for them.

The parents spent time in small groups discussing parenting topics and used these ideas to come up with creative ways forward. I gave parents some homework, and ideas about kindness spread into this too.

Example homework sheet: Choose one activity a week

1   *Do one thing a day you know you will enjoy.*
2   *Say something different to your child that you haven't said before.*
3   *Pay yourself a compliment every day.*
4   *Ask your child to teach you a skill.*
5   *Make a list of what you are grateful for.*
6   *Notice acts of kindness in your life, by you and by others.*

The final activity, acts of kindness, was the most popular amongst parents.

The happiness project

The school was teaching a number of key values over this period, one of which was happiness. As we have seen, in the seams of many conversations over the preceding months throughout the different parts of the SF coaching project were ideas about kindness, to oneself and to others, and a connection between kind acts and happiness. The idea of a happiness project was born, with a particular focus on the active role of kindness in making self and others happy. Children began work in classes, in assemblies and across the curriculum on what made them and others happy, what actions they could take to promote happiness and the role of kindness in this. They began to give thank you cards for the kind acts of children, teachers and parents which had made them or others happy, and they were encouraged to be specific and detailed. For example, *'helping me to be brave'* or *'telling me it will be OK even when I say it won't be'*. A large wire-constructed heart found its way into the staffroom, where teachers posted stick it notes thanking each other for kindnesses shown. In the school foyer a happiness book took up residence, where children, staff and parents could write about someone in the school community who had made them happy by showing kindness and doing kind acts. Children, parents and staff could often be found writing in this book and reading about the active and varied examples of kindness in their community. This seemed to multiply the uplifting and contagious effects of each action.

> **Examples of children's contributions in the happiness book**
>
> A (a child) makes me happy because he always passes the ball to me when I am upset.
> S (the premises officer) made me happy because he brought spacehoppers for us to play with.
> G (a child) makes me happy because when I hurt myself and when I have no one to play with she comes to help me.

> **Examples of teachers' contributions in the happiness book**
>
> A (a child) made me happy because he told someone not to playfight.
> M and A (children) made me happy because they sold apples before school and used the money to buy David Walliams' new book for the class.
> S made me happy because when he saw me coming with a big box of bean bags he was holding the door for me so I could go through.'

The children began to think about people in the local community and how they could spread these ideas of happiness and kindness, especially to people who were not connected to the school community and might not have heard about these ideas. They visited a local coffee shop, near the local train station, and explained what they had been learning about happiness and kindness. The owner was very kind too, and they decided together that the children would write kind and happy messages on labels which the owner put on the coffee cups for his customers. After a while the school began to receive emails from these customers who had bought a coffee and been pleased and happy to read their message. The children put these email messages in to the happiness book so that everyone could read them and see what a difference kind words could make, even to strangers.

Examples of messages from the community

Thank you so much for my beautiful sticker. You brightened up my day and I shared my happiness with my colleagues when I got to work. Well done to everyone involved! From a very happy coffee drinker.

Thank you very much for the lovely and unexpected little work of art that I found on my coffee cup this morning. Grown ups can be preoccupied with their working lives, commuting to work and rushing around trying to do all their grown-up things. And so it's very nice to be reminded to 'Enjoy Your Day' as my coffee cup advised this morning. Thank you for spreading happiness. We all need as much happiness as we can create for each other!

Dear children, thank you so much for decorating my coffee cup so nicely with the stickers you have made. It really brightened up my day when I popped into the coffee shop for my breakfast this morning. I have been meaning to do some volunteering for a while and reading your message 'If You Want To See Good Do Good' has been a good reminder. Because of your kindness and the brilliant project you are doing I have just sent an email to a charity offering my time to help others in need. I have also shared the news of your project with some friends who all think it's such a great idea. Maybe they'll be inspired to do good too or set up a similar project to keep spreading happiness. Thank you very much indeed.

Conclusion

Many of us who work with children and young people use a Solution Focused approach because we find it to be a child-centred, collaborative, hopeful, respectful, empowering and effective approach, harnessing children's resources and centralising children's wishes and feelings. It is an approach which glides smoothly between the present, past and future life of the child, finding in the weave of the child's past the threads of a desired future, and in the future, glittering fibres that can be seen to loop back into the child's present. Along the way, it can help to build children's emotional well-being and resilience, as they begin to experience themselves as resourceful, capable, and able to change.

The SF approach can also migrate, or perhaps, like the characters in *A Midsummer Night's Dream*, translate into something else. In this piece of work, what started as SF conversations with children grew into a project focusing on children developing kindness skills and creating happiness for themselves, their school community and the wider community. The threads of the Solution Focused approach can still be recognised, but something different was created. Sometimes, instead of looking back we can look forward, letting go of rigour and allowing in its place the alchemy of translation.

References

King, V. (2016). *10 Keys to Happier Living*. London: Headline.
Neff, K. (2011). *Self Compassion*. New York: Harper Collins.
Ratner, H., & Yusuf, D. (2015). *Brief Coaching with Children and Young People: A Solution Focused Approach*. London: Routledge.

Index

Note: page numbers in *italic* indicate a figure and page numbers in **bold** indicate a table on the corresponding page.

Academy of Experience 130
adolescents 55–60, 126–129; Roma 130–139
Ajmal, Yasmin 58
Ambassadors 100
appreciation 137–138; *see also* celebration
assessment 61, 118, 124, 149, 169; psychoeducational 62
assumptions 56, 109, 133–134, 138

bags of confidence 14
behavior, clinical 66–67
bereavement *see* parentally bereaved children and adolescents
best hopes 4, 74, 88–90, 96, 99, 126–127; the butterfly effect 52–53; co-operation and engagement with adolescents 56–57; play therapy 19–20; selective mutism 166–167
BRIEF 35, 43, 79–80, 110
Brief Therapy *see* Solution Focused Brief Therapy (SFBT)
Britain *see* United Kingdom
Brunel University London 95–96, 100–101
Buddies 100
butterfly effect 50–54

Calgary Family Therapy Centre (CFTC) 182, 186–187
care, duty of 95–96, 100; edge of 123–129
CARE (*Child and Adolescent Research-Evidence-based practice*) 173
case study 22–27, 90–94, 97–99, 151–154, 163–164, 167–168, 187–191

celebration 32, **105**, 137–138
CFTC *see* Calgary Family Therapy Centre
Child and Adolescent Research-Evidence-based practice see CARE
child protection cases 149–154
children, vulnerable 22–27
choice 22–27
circles 8–10, 195
client's treasure chest *141*, 142–143, *143–144*, 143–144; from a client's view 147; of significant others 144–146, *146*; using the three treasure chests 147–148; as a visual reminder 146
clinical behavior 66–67
clinical description 66–67; clinical choice 56
coaching 103–107; whole-class 197–198
Coaching 4 Fives 194–195, 197
co-creation 137
collaboration 164–165; collaborative approach 67; collaborative effort 175; collaborative perspective 73; live collaborative process 175
community: messages from 201; school community education 46–47
compliments 185
confidence: bags of confidence 14; staff confidence 101
conflict: case studies 187–191; high-conflict divorce 179–182, 191; service context 182; Solution Focused presence, Solution Focused practice 183–187
consultation 69
conversations 11, 15, 22; *see also* peer conversations; team conversation
co-operation 55–60

counseling referral system 44–45
creativity 149–154; creative tools 141–142, *141*
cultural divides 43–49
cultural processes 172; socio-cultural filters 139

descriptions 36–37, 127, 186; clinical 66–67; of difference 185; of sequences and patterns 184–185
developmental stages 172
diagnosing 181
differences 181; descriptions of 185
direct work 165–167
diversity 109–110
divorce, high-conflict 179–182, 191; case studies 187–191; service context 182; Solution Focused presence, Solution Focused practice 183–187
duty of care 95–96, 100

education: school community education 46–47; *see also* educators; international schools; schools; universities
educators 72–78
engagement 55–60
exceptions 64–65, 74–75, 90, 109, 118, 163, 174; exception findings 75
expertise 15, 61, 109, 133–135, 150

family meetings 45–46
feedback 69, 196–197
Figuring Futures 6, 140–148
Flashbacks 158
follow-up 33–34, 37, 53, 127
formulation 68–69
"From Us to You" 131; and the Solution Focused approach 133–135; the structure of 131–133
fun xviii–xix
future focused xviii, 105
futures *see* Figuring Futures; future focused

goals 74, 88–89; goal formulation **105**
good things 35–36
grief 171–177; and cultural processes 172; and developmental stages 172
group-based solution building path 173–174
group sessions 48–49

happiness book 199–200
happiness project 199–200
healing 171–177

health: SF in 110–111; SF language in 111; *see also* pediatric settings
helping others 134
history 63–66
homework 199
hope 74, 171–177, 185; *see also* best hopes; client's treasure chest
Hungary 130–139

I-Coach programme **105**
imaginary supporter 32
implementation 47–48; areas of 43–44
individual sessions 48–49
informal learning *see under* learning
institutional setting: coaching for youth offenders in 103–107
interaction patterns 38–39
interactive element 48–49
international schools 43–49
interviews 106–107
Iveson, Chris 4, 55, 154

Kids' Skills 28–36; case example 30; how it came about 29; step by step 29–30
kindness 194–201

language: in health 111; positive 88; Solution Focused 90
learning: benefits of learning skills 31–32; informal and non-formal ways of 137–138; Learning Ambassadors 40–41; learning problems 61–70; learning process 130–139
Learning Ambassadors 40–41
listening 10, 12, 60, 65, 185–186
Lists 5
litigation 179–180
local realty 135

MDT *see* multidisciplinary team
meaning, reconstruction of 171–172
medical context 111–114; *see also* pediatric settings
meetings: consultation and feedback 69; family and staff 45–46
Metcalf, Linda 43, 48
mindset 87–88, 149–154
minimalism 183–184
Miracle question 118
multidisciplinary team (MDT) 109–110, 114

naming 35–36
New Zealand Police 116–122

next steps 20
non-formal learning *see under* learning
noticing 35–36

observations 105–106
offenders 103–107
one-dimensional characterisation 180–181
openings 185–186

parentally bereaved children and adolescents 171–177
parenting 179–182, 191; parents' interactions 180–181; *see also* divorce, high-conflict
parenting coordinators 184
parents' evenings 198–199
pathologising 69, 171–172, 176–177, 181
patterns 184–185
pediatric settings 108–114
peer conversations 39–40
performance, peak **105**
personal agency 186
perspective taking **105**; shifting perspective 171–172
play: as a therapeutic tool 16; play scaling 16–18; *see also* play therapy
play therapy 15–16
police *see* New Zealand Police
positioning 187
positive differences 135
possibility 109; for change 149–154
pragmatism xviii, 183–184
preferences 184
Preferred Future 4, 118, 127
prescriptions 184
problems 109; explanations for 184; problem focused 45–46; problem free talk 3; as symptoms 28
process 72–73; learning process 130–139
progress 20, 136; signs of 135, 137–138
protective factors 160
psychoeducational assessment 62; the report 66–69; Solution Focused practices in 62–69

questions 12, 51, 64 *see under* referral; scaling

Ratner, Harvey 55, 166
recommendations 69
reconstruction of meaning 171–172
referral: individual 195–196; reason for 66; referral questions 63; referral system 44–45

reflections 105–106, 168–170; reflected after the session 81; *see also* reflective practice
reflective practice 175–176
reframing 140–148
relational positioning 187
resilience 171–172; in action 37
resources 109, 131
responses: of professionals 182
responsibility 134–135
results 67–68
risk: high risk field 149; risk factors 150
Roma adolescents 130–139

Safety 125, 128
safeguarding 149–151, 153
scaling 159; 5 point scale 167; current progress and next steps 20; interactive scale 49; play scaling 16–18; scale questions 79–86; scale rating 5, 45; scaling questions 169, 174; in school 82–86; for success **105**
School of Merit 87–88, 90–94
schools: scales in 82–86; school community education 46–47; school refusal 76; school settings 72; *see also* international schools; universities
selective mutism (SM) 162–170
Sensory path 49
sequences 184–185
service context 182
sessions: adding visual and interactive elements to 48–49; I-Coach **105**; reflections and observations of 105–106; session summary 20–21; testing sessions 65–66, 96
setbacks 33
SF *see* Solution Focused (SF) approach
SFBT *see* Solution Focused Brief Therapy
shifting perspective 171–172
significant others 144–146, *146*
skills: benefits of learning skills 31–32; finding skills for children to learn 30–31; *see also* Kids'Skills
slip-ups 181
SM *see* selective mutism
Solution Focused Brief Therapy (SFBT) 2–3, 55–61, 65
solutions *see* group-based solution building path; Solution Focused (SF) approach
South Africa 87–94

sparkles 36
sparkling moments 36
staff: staff meetings 45–46; staff training 100–102
story: stories of being brave 2; stories of magic 68, 117
strategies 75
strengths 89, 109, 120, 135, *141*, 169; assessment of learning problems 65; children and young people on the edge of care 128–129; play therapy 16
success 73–74; past successes 185; scaling for **105**
suicide: suicidal thoughts 101, 128
supporters 32; imaginary 32
summarising 62, 73, 75, 145, 174
systemic approaches 78

targets 4, 19–21
team conversation 72–78
technology 97
teenagers *see* adolescents
terminal illness *see* parentally bereaved children and adolescents
testing sessions 65–66
therapeutic process xviii

training 100–101
translation 194–201
trauma 156–161
treasure chest *see* client's treasure chest
trust 123–129

United Kingdom (UK) 95–102
universities 95–102
usefulness: signs of 135–138

visual element 48–49
visualisation 4–5, 140–141, *140*, 147–148, 175
visual reminder 146–147
voice 22–27; of the child 10–12
volunteering project 130–139
vulnerable children 22–27

Watson, Merritt 88–90
whole-class coaching 197–198
wishes 185
WOWW model 35–36

Year 6 project 198
Yes . . . and 156–161
Yusuf, Denise xix, 166